HOW TO DO BUSINESS
WITH RUSSIANS

HOW TO DO BUSINESS
WITH RUSSIANS

*A Handbook and Guide
for Western World Business People*

MISHA G. KNIGHT

Foreword by Tom Sealy

Q

QUORUM BOOKS
New York • Westport, Connecticut • London

Library of Congress Cataloging-in-Publication Data

Knight, Misha G.
  How to do business with Russians.

  Bibliography: p.
  Includes index.
    1. Soviet Union—Foreign economic relations—
United States. 2. United States—Foreign economic
relations—Soviet Union. 3. East-West trade
(1945-). 4. Soviet Union—Economic conditions—
1976- . I. Title.
HF1558.5.U6K56 1987   658.8'48'0947   86-30396
ISBN 0-89930-211-4 (lib. bdg. : alk. paper)

Library of Congress Catalog Card Number: 86-30396
ISBN: 0-89930-211-4

First published in 1987 by Quorum Books

Greenwood Press, Inc.
88 Post Road West, Westport, Connecticut 06881

Printed in the United States of America

The paper used in this book complies with the
Permanent Paper Standard issued by the National
Information Standards Organization (Z39.48-1984).

10 9 8 7 6 5 4 3 2

Copyright Acknowledgments

The author gratefully acknowledges permission to use
portions of the following copyrighted material.

"Advertising in Eastern Europe: A Corporate Checklist" is
reprinted from the November 7, 1980, issue of *Business
Eastern Europe*, with the permission of the publisher, Business
International Corporation, Geneva, Switzerland.

"The Russian Bear Turns Bullish on Trade" is reprinted with
permission from *Business Marketing*, Vol. 72, No. 4 (April
1987). Copyright © 1987 by Crain Communications, Inc.

To Dr. Armand Hammer—
Pioneer, architect, statesman, and peacemaker
for the past, present, and future generations
of the American and Russian people

CONTENTS

PART TWO
The Structure of Soviet Foreign Trade Operations and Orders of a Business Transaction

FIGURES AND TABLES

FIGURES

TABLES

FOREWORD

ANY book on any country should be welcomed if for no other reason than that it helps to dispel our ignorance of our neighbors. On that basis this particular book is to be doubly welcomed for it deals with the world's second superpower and with the ways and means of trading with it. Business people are any country's first diplomats, and trade is one important means of reducing ignorance and misunderstanding between nations. The importance of the Soviet Union in the superpower balance and our general ignorance of it, therefore, make Misha Knight's contribution to our greater understanding particularly important.

But it does more than that. The potential for trade between East and West is perhaps greater now than it has ever been. The arrival of Soviet leader Mikhail Gorbachev on the world stage has changed all the parameters. For the first time since the establishment of Soviet might on the shattered remains of Eastern Europe after the Second World War, there is the chance of a new relationship between East and West. Internally, Mikhail Gorbachev's twin policies of *glasnost* (openness) and *perestroika* (reconstruction) have already shaken up the USSR's monolithic economic management.

Of course it is much too early to declare either the new external or internal Soviet policies a success. But one thing is beyond doubt: The USSR stands today at a crossroads, and the direction it takes will affect every one of us, no matter what country we live in or language we speak. It is therefore in all our interests that we encourage any movement in the USSR towards more responsible, tension-easing policies at home and abroad.

The role of trade and business in such an effort is vital. Mutual trade brings mutual respect and mutual dependence. It is, at its most basic, a nonthreatening and indirect means of deepening understanding and influencing opinion—a fundamental human exchange from which we can only benefit.

But this political role in trade, if it is to have any validity, must always be secondary to its fundamental role—the production of an economic benefit for both buyer and seller. And that depends on the opportunities for trade, the real opportunities for that fundamental role. So, what are the opportunities for trade with the USSR?

Ever since Dr. Armand Hammer helped the first national Soviet establish itself after the Russian revolution, democratic western entrepreneurs have found profitable and ethical business opportunities in Communist Russia. Trade with the USSR is not new, and many major western companies count the USSR in as a valued trading partner. But the USSR has always been a notoriously difficult market to penetrate, with high access costs and a frequently slow return. It has, in short, been a market for the trader with the long-view.

That, in its general terms, is still true. But there is a difference now, and that difference is Mikhail Gorbachev and his recognition of the sickness of the Soviet economy. With *perestroika* as the watchword, Soviet industry and commerce are being prodded out of a decades-long lethargy. The first phase of that process, ridding industry and business of incompetent and corrupt managers and bosses, is already underway. The second phase, re-equipping Soviet industry with modern tools, equipment, and techniques, is about to begin. That is the difference and that is the new opportunity.

The USSR has always needed trade with the West, but that need has been traditionally kept at an artifical minimum for ideological reasons. As a result the USSR is saddled with a culture of making do with second-best, and a widening gap between its proud claims and its shabby reality—a first-world power with a third-world economy. Mikhail Gorbachev has made it plain that he believes in first-best and that the USSR is not realizing its potential with its excessive, all-pervading, talent-sapping military industrial complex, inefficient agriculture, wasteful energy consumption, and poorly equipped and managed industry.

But if the USSR is to obtain first-best and to overcome its long list of deficiencies, it needs us, the developed West, to provide the technologies it lacks.

Simply recognizing the need, however, is not enough for the potential trader. True the USSR is a vast potential marketplace—after all, it covers one-sixth of the world's land surface and contains some 275 million people—but it also employs a language of which far too many of us are ignorant and a centrally planned trading system which few of us in the West understand. Here again, however, Misha Knight makes a unique contribution. Misha, a former citizen of the USSR, was himself a Soviet foreign trade official before coming to the West. Now living in the U.S., he has become a western entrepreneur in his own right. His inside knowledge of the way in which the Soviet Foreign Trade Ministry and other purchasing ministries work is invaluable. It is here in this book for you to acquire.

But of course there is a broader political dimension to all of this. We have lived for decades under what we have perceived as the threat of Communism. It is a fair question to ask whether we should help the USSR to grow even stronger than it is, to fatten up the USSR and hope that it will not use its increased strength against us. This is a real concern, but, to paraphrase Shakespeare, "let me have men about me that are fat, lean men are dangerous." In other words, I think we have more to fear from a USSR which is thin, poor, and envious than a USSR which is fat, successful, and happy.

Also, I think that no one can doubt the credentials of British Prime Minister Margaret Thatcher as a defender of democracy. Yet, after her first meeting with Mikhail Gorbachev, she said he was a man that she could do business with. If you want to do business with Gorbachev's Russia, this book is your essential guide.

Tom Sealy
Financial Times Business Information
London

ACKNOWLEDGMENTS

THIS book owes much to the assistance and encouragement of many people from the U.S. Department of Commerce and the Ministry of Foreign Trade of the USSR. But especially, I wish to express my appreciation to those who helped: To William Hayes, Walter N. Frank & Co.; to Daniel O'Flaherty, Vice President International, National Foreign Trade Council; and to John Reuther, Director, Commission on U.S.-Soviet Relations of the International Center for Development Policy, I am indebted for their inspiration and encouragement, and for continually reminding me that it could be done.

I also wish to thank James Ciften, President of the U.S.-USSR Trade and Economic Council, whose special seminar "U.S.-USSR Trade and Economic Relations" at the Columbia University Graduate School of Business taught me about the importance of working toward the improvement of Soviet-American trade and economic relations.

Finally, I offer my thanks to Armand Hammer, Chairman of the Board, Occidental Petroleum Corporation, for his more than 60 years of devotion to the cause of building better and lasting relations between the United States and the Soviet Union. Without his efforts, this book might never have been written.

INTRODUCTION: THE RUSSIAN BEAR TURNS BULLISH ON TRADE

THERE's a new optimism among Soviet foreign traders, and new opportunities for Western exporters patient enough to wait for reforms to blossom.

The personal side of the new Soviet attitude was particularly striking last July at "Vienna III: New Horizons in East-West Trade," a conference attended by American, Soviet and Eastern and Western European trade experts. Soviet officials were at ease, freely exchanging opinions about the problems in the Soviet foreign trade system and domestic economy in ways that one normally sees only in the West.

Their leader, Mikhail S. Gorbachev, general secretary of the Communist Party of the Soviet Union, has brought a new foreign trade strategy to the Soviet Union. As part of the economic shake-up he is attempting, Mr. Gorbachev's trade program of reform and joint-venture opportunities aims to take Russia into the age of modern technology and hard-currency security.

But directives from the top don't necessarily lead to immediate reforms in the rank and file, particularly in the bureaucracy of a vast, centrally-planned superpower economy. Friction between reformers and the Soviet old guard, and the relative trade inexperience of many Soviet officials thrust into a new trade role, aren't making reform easy. As one Soviet official at Vienna III acknowledged privately, "Reforms in our country, in a socialist society, are very different and therefore, very difficult to accomplish in a short time—not like in the West. But we have great hope."

As of January 1, 1987, more than twenty Soviet industrial ministries and 70 of the nation's largest industrial enterprises received the authority to deal directly with Western firms. Mr. Gorbachev decentralized importing authority in order to end the stultifying monopoly control over trade held by the Foreign Trade Ministry. His program also has begun to create a format for joint business ventures between industrial ministries and Western firms. It is the biggest change undertaken in the structure of Soviet trade since the 1920s.

Until now, Soviet doctrine emphasized trade with socialist countries. The new emphasis makes room for relations with market economies and indicates that Western business people—even those who've never before considered Soviet trade—can expect expanded, long-term trade relations with Russia and the other USSR republics.

But the process of bringing trade decision-making down to the level of industrial users and manufacturers will be a slow one and, in the near term, a more expensive one for foreigners. Westerners familiar with established patterns of selling to socialist planners will have to experiment with new approaches. And they will have to deal with many more contacts throughout the Soviet bureaucracy.

CURRENCY OF CONCERN

The reforms do not affect the entire foreign and domestic trade system. The Ministry of Foreign Trade still controls exports and imports of fuels and raw materials, for example. It also manages major resource commitments, such as the importation of manufacturing plants from the West.

Instead, reform focuses on the right of industrial enterprises to directly negotiate compensation deals, and to keep 90% of earned foreign currency. Specifically, the central government grants those rights to the State Foreign Economic Commission of the Council of Ministries of the USSR (SFECCM), which includes 21 ministries. The hard currency must be spent on imports needed for industrial capacity expansion. The state takes 10% of hard currency receipts as taxes.

Manufacturers producing export goods previously did not have hard currency benefits, which limited their ability to improve product quality. Enterprises had to receive authorization from the Foreign Trade Bank of the USSR (Vneshtorgbank), which had a powerful influence over which enterprises could spend hard currency on imports, and how they could spend it.

Last November, that ostensibly changed with publication of a list of ministries, organizations, state committees, production enterprises, and trusts which obtained direct foreign trade rights in January. Under the reforms, the government will allocate hard currency according to a new five-year plan, and Soviet enterprises will be expected to earn their own convertible funds from export sales.

Pressed for details, Soviet foreign trade officials stick to the story that a manufacturing enterprise will keep 85% to 90% of its foreign currency fund; the money won't be funneled to a superior ministry. Enterprises will have all rights to spend those funds, and even borrow from Vneshtorgbank, to pay for technology needed to modernize and re-equip production lines.

Were it not for outdated technology, quite a few Soviet manufacturing enterprises could export to the West. Vneshtorgbank's role is to help those with the greatest chance to become exporters and re-pay the bank within four years.

CONFUSION STILL

Vladimir Kamentsev, a high-ranking official as deputy chairman of the Council of Ministers, was appointed chairman of the SFECCM. In that role, he will oversee the Foreign Trade Ministry, the Foreign Trade Bank, the State Committee for Foreign Economic Relations, and the 21 ministries which received foreign trade rights. High-ranking officials from the most important trade-oriented ministries were selected to join Mr. Kamentsev on the economic commission.

However, there is still some confusion about how foreign trade rights will be allocated. Not all of the 21 ministries received equivalent rights; and there is still confusion in personnel as well. Many but not all ministers were appointed by Mr. Gorbachev or his predecessor, Yuri Andropov. (Most of the Andropov appointees stay in their jobs.) Some are old Brezhnevists, who soon will be replaced.

Many Western business executives have received word that their old foreign trade contacts will leave their positions this year. Meanwhile, end-user officials are telling Westerners that they should ignore the Ministry of Foreign Trade in Moscow, because the end users now make import and export decisions.

In addition, the 1986-1990 five-year plan indicates that Mr. Gorbachev wants more economic decision-making power in the hands of the fifteen Soviet republics, and less in the central bureaucracy. That means Western companies will have to deal with the two levels of Soviet bureaucracy: central planners setting overall goals and policies, and republic and enterprise officials outside Moscow. The plan allows first-hand contact with end users, albeit with difficulties and complications.

The question for the future is whether established patterns of superiority within the Soviet hierarchy can survive. Reform already is fomenting competition among Soviet officials over who will be the first to successfully negotiate new contracts with the West. It all leaves Western companies in a delicate position. They must skillfully balance their relationships in the labyrinth of Soviet reform.

GRASS ROOTS CONTROL

The Gorbachev reforms emphasize decentralized initiative. Soviet manufacturers have to decide how to modernize their plants and improve productivity, quality and planning. The resources on which they draw are to be totally dependent on economic achievement. The ministries and other agencies that constantly interfered with manufacturing management will be playing a limited role, according to the plan.

On the incentive side, hard currency bonuses will be awarded to any Soviet enterprise that exceeds foreign currency earnings from exports specified for it by the plan. The reward will be used to improve products, social services and export competitiveness. According to the new law, ministries won't be able to confiscate or restrict foreign currency allocations to enterprises that earn them from exports.

Grass roots rewards theoretically have existed since 1978. In reality, they never worked that way. Most enterprises had never received bonuses in foreign currency. But with Gorbachev installing his own team, it may work now.

The central ministries' role will be to develop long-term plans for their respective sectors. Overall coordination of the Soviet economy will be in the hands of Gosplan (State Planning Committee) and Gossnab (State Committee for Material and Technical Provision). Both agencies now are headed by Gorbachev appointees. Gosplan will be playing a greater role as the key economic coordinator.

LIMITS TO REFORM

Gorbachev intends to preserve the centrally planned system, and at the same time eliminate unnecessary bureaucracy, rationalize planning, boost incentives, and speed decision making. He will not, however, establish free-market mechanisms or give a greater role to private enterprises, particularly in the key sector of agriculture. His goal is to strengthen the role of planners at the top, increase and expand the decision-making influence of enterprise directors at the bottom, and effectively eliminate ministry bureaucrats, planners, and other unnecessary mid-level managers.

Last year's reorganization of the Soviet agroindustrial complex into the State Agroindustrial Committee, or Gosagroprom, illustrates the Gorbachev plan and the confusion it can generate. As of January 1986, five ministries and other related organizations merged to form Gosagroprom: the all-union Ministries of Agriculture, Food, Fruit and Vegetables, Meat and Dairy, and Rural Construction as well as the State Committee for Technical Supply to Agriculture.

Other ministries also were incorporated under Gosagroprom's jurisdiction. One of them is the Ministry of Procurement, which is responsible for purchasing and checking the quality of agricultural and food products. Another is the Ministry of Light Industry, which is responsible for processing cotton, flax and wool.

But, the management and planning of land reclamation was removed totally from the Ministry of Reclamation and water resources and attached to Gosagroprom.

As new Soviet officials settle into their jobs, Western traders face uncertainty, confusion and indecision. There are attempts to help, however. Foreign relations departments established within the ministries of production include central protocol departments, which coordinate activities among the Ministry of Foreign Trade. Soviet foreign trade organizations (FTOs), and Western firms.

For example, the new administrations for the tobacco, soft drink, and meat processing industries retain an office to deal with Western business executives. That unit usually arranges meetings with industry experts, helps in translation, and coordinates activities with FTOs.

The role and function of FTOs, which execute import-export contracts, are to remain largely the same as before. As of now, Western representatives who negotiate sales with Soviet counterparts will do so the same way as they did before. Soviet technical discussions include specialists from enterprises and other related organizations. Prices, financing and all other aspects of a commercial transaction are in the hands of the relevant FTO. Most ministries of production are not qualified and lack the motivation, contract knowledge and basic market information needed to buy and sell on world markets.

POWERFUL REPUBLIC VOICES

As part of the reforms, the fifteen republics of the Soviet Union received a powerful voice in deciding their own needs. They have had the same structure of production ministries, trusts and enterprises as central institutions in Moscow. But before reform, none could make their own decisions about imports from the West. Now the republics have an equal say with Moscow.

Western companies will need to understand the specific cultural and national traditions of individual republics. It is very important to recognize that ways of thinking, language and customs are quite different between the Russians, Ukrainians, Georgians and other nationalities of the vast Soviet nation. If, before reform, Western representatives had to contact only FTOs, foreign trade ministries, research institutes, and production ministries only in Moscow, now they also must individually contact the same entities in Kiev (Ukrainian Republic), Tbilisi (Georgian Republic), and other republic capitals.

For example, the Austrian subsidiary of the Swedish construction company ABV (Amerad Betong Vagforbattringar) is building a ski and tourism center in Soviet Georgia. The $30 million project includes a 300-bed hotel, tourist village, and ski lifts.

ABV began negotiations with strong competition from other Western suppliers. Two different sets of negotiations were conducted. One was with the Foreign Trade Ministry, relevant FTO and other authorities in Moscow. The other talks were with Georgian republic authorities in Tbilisi.

But in allowing republics to have more trading power, experts from FTOs and centralized trade ministries will have to be transferred to republic organizations. Few local officials have had experience in dealing with foreign business people and markets.

A Western firm negotiating in Erivan, capital of the Armenian Republic, encountered this problem when it was offered fruit juice concentrate in countertrade. The price quoted by the Armenian ministry was five times higher than the world market. Local officials often don't know the way world prices operate.

COUNTERTRADE COUNTERFORCE

Direct business with Soviet Republics can be very successful, but Western firms must prepare to take countertrade. To achieve their export goals, Soviet enterprises must press for countertrade in order to sell Soviet-made goods to the West.

However, because of product quality and other factors, many Soviet industrial products are difficult to market in the West. The USSR earns about 85% of its convertible foreign exchange from fuels and raw materials.

Ministry of Foreign Trade instructions to negotiators stipulate that Soviets must examine two or three offers from Western countries. Western competitors must skillfully evaluate every possible opportunity that could help them to win a contract.

In the case of the Swedish construction firm ABV, Soviet negotiators were impressed by the firm's willingness to take 70% of its compensation in countertrade. ABV's trading house selected carefully among products offered by the Georgians. The tea and tea concentrates it chose were sold at a profit in the United States.

But in another instance, a Western company negotiating in Tbilisi wanted to take Georgian oranges in countertrade. The central import-export authority in Moscow said that, if Georgian oranges were to be exported, then the Western company must bring back oranges from the West. The whole transaction was not easy.

CAN IT WORK?

One important question will remain unanswered for some time: Will the reforms work?

It is already known that Moscow officials—in the Ministry of Foreign Trade, FTOs, and Gosplan's foreign trade department—have resisted the idea that enterprise directors independently make foreign exchange spending decisions. The Muscovites argue for established trade priorities of, say, grain or machinery, and insist that decisions must be made by experienced traders. And they fear for the privileged positions they worked so hard to earn. The small elite of foreign trade officials who carefully guard their turf want to remain in charge of the overall trade decision process.

Frictions are beginning to show. According to an article in *Pravda*, the Communist Party Central Committee newspaper, a dispute erupted between directors at the VAZ (Volgsky Automotive Factory) in Tolgatti and the State Planning Committee (Gosplan). The enterprise "experienced difficulties in convincing Gosplan to recognize VAZ's foreign currency entitlement."

VAZ produces Lada cars in Tolgatti, a high-profile Soviet export. The factory's economic and planning department director complained that the new system isn't working. He said that when VAZ wanted to use its hard currency fund to import needed production technology, it encountered many obstacles from too many ministries that had to give approval. Enterprises may have new trade rights, but exercising them still isn't easy.

Despite the problems, Mr. Gorbachev and his ministers insist that the plan will continue. Tremendous pressure is on him to succeed with his reforms, in trade and other aspects of Soviet society.

Meanwhile, Western business executives need patience to solve new problems, such as getting visas for the many new locations their representatives must visit. Old trading contacts established for decades may vanish, with foreigners left to deal with unfamiliar new organizations and a society testing the limits of a new openness.

A few organizations, such as the Ministry of the Maritime Fleet or the

Central Union of Consumers Cooperatives, have had foreign trade rights for a long period. Managers in those bodies will have little problem adjusting to the new environment.

Ministries and enterprises in other parts of the Soviet trade bureaucracy are just beginning to learn how to use their hard currency power and exposure to the West. That definitely causes frustrations on both sides.

But Western traders, particularly those from the United States, cannot afford to ignore the opportunities in one of the world's largest marketplaces, with the richest natural resources in the world. New doors have opened.

ORGANIZATION OF THIS BOOK

To help the Western business person understand the environment in which Soviet trade takes place, I begin with an outline of economic and political conditions existing in the USSR today, with particular emphasis on how Russians do business at home and abroad. Among the topics considered in Part I are the organization of foreign trade, the general business outlook and prospects in specific export areas, industrial cooperation, trade fairs and exhibitions, the process of setting up an office in the USSR, U.S. trade regulations, and Soviet customs regulations.

Part II gives detailed guidance on the procedures, protocols, strategies, and cultural nuances that the Western business person will encounter in commercial negotiations and transactions with the Soviets. Elements of the negotiation process, such as making enquiries, accepting or declining offers, revising prices and terms, and negotiating contracts, are discussed. Other areas covered are commercial letters, orders and their execution, sale of goods through agents, and arbitration of complaints and claims.

PART ONE

Trading with the Soviet Union: The Way It Operates

1

THE UNION OF SOVIET SOCIALIST REPUBLICS: AN OVERVIEW

GOVERNMENT

THE Union of Soviet Socialist Republics (USSR) is a federation of fifteen republics: the Soviet Federative Socialist Republic of Russia and the Soviet Socialist Republics of Ukraine, Kazakstan, Uzbekistan, Belorussia, Georgia, Azerbaijan, Moldavia, Lithuania, Kirgizia, Tadzkikistan, Latvia, Armenia, Turkmenistan, and Estonia. The Supreme Soviet is the highest legislative organ of the USSR. It consists of two chambers with equal legislative rights, the Union Soviet and the National Soviet. Each has 750 members elected for five-year terms by universal and secret suffrage. The Union Soviet represents the country's general interests, its members being elected by the citizens of the USSR on the basis of constituencies with similar populations and approximately one deputy for 300,000 inhabitants. The members of the National Soviet are elected as well by the citizens of the USSR on the basis of national territorial areas: 32 from each union republic, eleven from each autonomous republic, and one from each autonomous district. The Supreme Soviet holds twice-a-year sessions lasting two to three days at a time. Each chamber elects seventeen standing commissions. The Council of Ministers is elected by the Supreme Soviet at a joint session of both chambers.

The coordination of current government affairs is delegated to the Council of Ministers, the USSR's highest executive and administrative organ. It has more than 100 members, including a chairman, first vice-chairman, vice-chairmen, federal ministers, ministers of the union republics, and the heads of other bodies and organizations of the USSR. (See Figure 1.1.) Sessions take place approximately once a week. The council is responsible to the Supreme Soviet and, between sessions, to the Presidium of the Supreme Soviet. (Figure 1.2 shows the organizational structure of a typical ministry.)

The Presidium of the Supreme Soviet is elected among the deputies of the Supreme Soviet at a joint session of both chambers. It consists of a chairman, a first vice-chairman, fifteen vice-chairmen (one for each union republic), twenty-one members, and a secretary. It coordinates the work of standing commissions, interprets the law of the USSR, ratifies and denounces international treaties, and so on. It exercises the functions of a collegiate state leadership, acting on a standing basis as the highest state authority on behalf of the Supreme Soviet. (See Figure 1.3 for a more detailed breakdown of the functions of the Council of Ministers and the Presidium.)

However, the highest authority of the USSR is the Communist Party. Its supreme organ is the Politburo, which is headed by the party's general secre-

Figure 1.1
Composition of the Soviet Council of Ministers

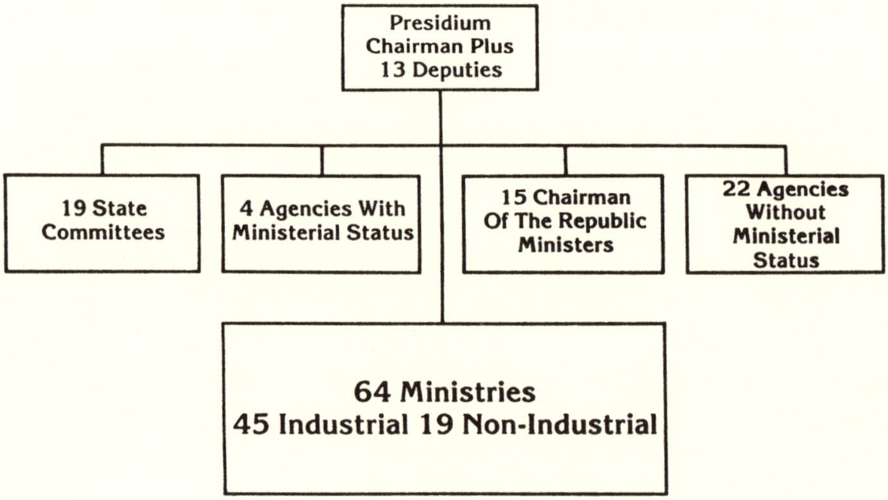

Source: USSR Ministry of Foreign Trade, Moscow, 1985.

Figure 1.2
Conceptual Organizational Structure of a Typical Ministry

Source: USSR Ministry of Foreign Trade, Moscow, 1985.

Figure 1.3
Functions of the Soviet Presidium and the Council of Ministers

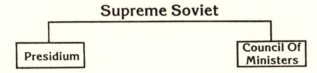

Functions

1. Convening sessions of supreme soviet
2. Giving interpretations of laws in operation
3. Annulling decisions & orders of council of minister
4. Releasing & appointing ministers
5. Ratifying & renouncing international treaties

Functions

1. Coordinates & directs work of all-union & union republic ministers
2. Adopts measures to implement national economic plan and state budget
3. Adopts measures for maintenance of public order
4. Exercises general guidance in foreign trade
5. Fixes annual military draft
6. Sets up committees for economic & cultural affairs & defense

Source: USSR Ministry of Foreign Trade, Moscow, 1985.

tary, and consists of twelve members and six candidates. It is assisted by the Central Committee Secretariat, which presently consists of ten secretaries. The Central Committee, which is in theory a subcommittee of the Politburo, presently has 280 members.

The actual powers of the president of the Supreme Soviet and general secretary of the Politburo are vested in the same person.

FEATURES OF THE ECONOMY

With a population totaling about 274.66 million inhabitants at the beginning of 1984 and an area of 22.4 million square kilometers, the USSR is one of the world's most powerful countries. Its national product represents approximately one-tenth of the world total. (See Table 1.1.)

Nevertheless, the population's standard of living is still much lower than that achieved by other countries with a similar level of economic wealth. Despite the efforts made in recent years (the consumption level per inhabitant has tripled in the past 30 years), consumption levels are still low. This situation mainly results from the scarce supply of consumer goods; thus, although in the second half of the 1970s salaries increased on average at an annual rate of 3%, the scarce supply of consumer goods has divested most of the available income toward saving deposits, which increased by 11.5% in this period. During the past few years, steps were taken to solve this problem and promote the production of consumer goods, with agriculture and light industries selected as priority investment targets. The limited existing prospects regarding an improvement in the availability of supplies along with the rigid government-controlled wages and salaries, established to promote the production of consumer goods regardless of demand and supply considerations, have had a negative impact on labor productivity. The USSR's labor productivity is markedly lower than the Organization for Economic Cooperation and Development (OECD) average, creating, above all, the lack of individual incentives. Furthermore, the centralized management of the economy in a country as huge and complex as the USSR has caused a lack of coordination between central bodies and production units.

The twofold problem of low productivity and inefficient management,

Table 1.1
The Soviet Union: Demographic Data

Population (millions), 1981	268.84
Annual growth rate (%), 1976–80	0.8
Birth rate (per thousand), 1981	18.5
Death rate (per thousand), 1982	10.1
Infant mortality rate (per thousand), 1982	27.7
Life expectancy (years), 1981	72
Demographic density (inh/sq. km.), 1981	12.00
Urban population (%), 1981	63.87
Area (thousands of sq. km.)	22,402

Source: United Nations, *Demographic Yearbook, 1982* (New York, 1984); World Bank, *Informe sobre el desarrolla mundial, 1983* (Washington, D.C., 1983); United Nations, *Statistical Abstract, 1981* (New York, 1983); Vienna Institute for Comparative Economic Studies, *Comecon Data, 1983* (Southampton, Eng., 1984).

which has restrained the economic development in the past few years, has brought about changes in the Soviet political leadership itself. There has been movement favorable to far-reaching reform, oriented toward a greater decentralization and higher productivity incentives, with prices and salaries more closely linked to production levels.

Improved productivity is also necessary to maintain a steady economic growth rate, since, considering the decrease in demographic growth rates, the number of workers being incorporated into the productive process is lower every year.

Another factor that has impeded an increase in the population's standard of living is the high volume of national income assigned to the defense budget. The USSR allocates about 16% of its national product to defense expenditures, more than twice the share assigned to this purpose by the United States. Despite this fact, between 1976 and 1982, military expenses increased by only 2.5% compared with nearly 5% in the preceding ten years.

Although natural resources are abundant, their exploitation is increasingly more expensive. Available resources have decreased in the western part of the country, where their exploitation is easier because of the existing infrastructure and climatic conditions. The exploitation costs of the immense reserves located in Western Siberia are very high, and there are problems related to the transportation of raw materials to production plants in the European part of the country.

But industrial production is not the Soviet authorities' major concern, since the share of the secondary sector in national production has increased. The decrease in the share corresponding to the primary sector is more worrisome, since it has been caused by successive years of poor crops, which in turn have had a negative impact on livestock production. Soviet food production, particularly that of cereals, is insufficient to meet domestic requirements, and it is thus necessary to resort to costly imports, representing a heavy share of the total volume of purchases abroad.

Adverse climatic conditions have had negative effects on the production levels of the primary sector in recent years and have led to an increase in imports. However, the Soviet trade balance has shown a surplus due to the high level and distribution pattern of the exports.

About 60% of Soviet external earnings come from the sale of crude petroleum and by-products. Allowing for the oil price increases of the 1970s, export earnings have increased at a satisfactory rate. Although a downward trend of oil prices has been recorded in the present decade, it is gradually being offset by an increase in sales of natural gas. To improve gas distribution, a pipeline has been built to link the production plants of Siberia to European countries, the main customers of Siberian gas.

ECONOMIC PRODUCTION AND BASIC MAGNITUDES

The economic growth rate of the Soviet net material product dropped markedly from the mid-1970s. One must take into account that the net material product (NMP) does not correspond exactly to the concept of the gross domestic product (GDP) used in Western countries, since most services are excluded.

Nevertheless, a marked economic recovery took place in 1983 as the NMP increased by 3% while the per capita income increased by 2%, industrial production by 4%, and productivity by 3.5%. The production of the primary sector showed an improvement as well. The results, however, are still below the levels forecast.

According to preliminary estimates, although domestic production in 1984 was to reach a similar or even higher level than that of the previous year, a downward revision of these figures was necessary. Because of poor farm crops, domestic production decreased to a level close to that registered in 1982, the worst year recorded since the end of World War II. However, it is estimated that industrial production might have increased by 4.2% in 1983, four one-hundredths over the official target. The productivity should have increased by approximately half a percentage point, compared to 1983, according to forecasts. Consumption absorbed 72.3% of the NMP investment and the external balance representing, respectively, 25.6% and 21.1% of the NMP. Regarding the sectoral origin of the NMP, 15.3% of it corresponds to the primary sector, 60.9% to the secondary sector (51.0% to mining and manufacturing and 9.9% to construction), and the remaining 23.7% to the tertiary sector.

In 1982, 10.8% of the economically active population was employed in the primary sector. (See Table 1.2.) The contribution of agricultural production to the national product corresponded to approximately 15% of the national product. As in other countries in recent years, in the USSR the contribution of the primary sector to the national product has followed a downward trend due to a decrease in the production of this sector in recent years. The decrease in the economically active population was not as noteworthy due to the rigidity of the Soviet labor market.

Collective farms (*kolkozes*) have been the major agricultural production units. They are organized on a cooperative basis and enjoy a certain independence as far as their management is concerned. The land is state owned and ceded to individuals for production purposes in exchange for a quota, set in advance and paid for at government-fixed prices. The farm workers' remunerations are calculated according to the revenue surplus over non-labor costs. Each family is also entitled to a small private plot (of about 0.5 hectares, depending on the region) and a small number of livestock. The

Table 1.2

Distribution by Sectors of the Economically Active Population

(In percentage)

	1965	1975	1982
Agriculture and forestry	12.1	10.7	10.8
Industry	35.7	33.3	32.6
Construction	9.5	10.4	9.8
Trade	7.8	8.7	8.6
Transport and communication	10.7	10.5	10.7
Housing and Local Administration	3.1	3.7	4.0
Science and Research	3.1	3.7	3.9
Art and Education	8.6	9.0	9.4
Health and Welfare	5.6	5.6	5.6
Government Administration, Justice and Finance	2.3	2.6	2.8
Total (in thousands)	76,900	102.160	115,200

Source: Vienna Institute for Comparative Economic Studies, *Comecon Data, 1983* (Southampton, Eng., 1984).

products thus obtained are mainly destined for self-consumption or sold directly in local markets. The government mainly purchases grain crops, but the remainder of the farm output may be freely sold by the growers at market prices. The significance of private farms is shown by the fact that although they represent only 3% of the total arable acreage, they produce nearly a fourth of the country's agricultural output, playing a particularly significant role in regard to deliveries of fresh vegetables, meat, and milk. Other agricultural production units are the state farms (*sovkozes*), which are mainly located on the virgin land area.

The main products of the primary sector are grains, raw cotton, sugar beets, potatoes, meat, milk, and eggs (see Table 1.3). The gross production of this sector decreased in three successive years, between 1979 and 1981, although at a lower rate in the third year. This continuous decrease was induced by the low production of the agricultural sector, since livestock figures, after having decreased in 1978 and 1979, remained at nearly the same level in 1980 and increased about 1% the following year. In 1982 a recovery of the primary production was recorded as it rose by 4.2%, farm crops having increased by 8.1%. Although the gross production of the primary sector increased again by 3.6% in 1983, it was still below the forecasted levels.

The total area under production decreased between 1978 and 1982 to 214.3 million hectares. The area devoted to the cultivation of grains decreased by 4.3% in the period under review, representing 57.4% of the total area under production in 1982. Agricultural production has suffered since 1979 from successive poor crops, which were insufficient to meet domestic requirements, particularly of grains.

Table 1.3

Main Farm Crops of the Soviet Union

(By 1,000 Tons for 1,000 Hectares of Sown Area)

	1978	1979	1980	1982 (1)
Grains, total harvest	229.638	174.833	182.730	173.300
Wheat, harvest	120.936	90.207	98.182	84.000
Sown area	62.898	57.682	61.475	n. a.
Rye, harvest	13.612	8.117	10.210	10.000
Sown area	7.719	6.476	8.645	n. a.
Barley, harvest	62.118	47.954	43.450	48.000
Sown area	32.690	37.005	31.583	n. a.
Oats, harvest	18.578	15.173	15.544	n. a.
Maize, harvest	8.898	8.373	9.454	11.000
Sown area	2.535	2.667	2.977	n. a.
Potatoes, harvest	86.124	90.956	67.023	78.047
Sown area	7.042	6.966	6.936	n. a.
Sugar beets, harvest	93.488	76.212	80.987	71.300
Sown area	3.763	3.739	3.710	n. a.

(1) Provisional data.
n. a. Non available.

Source: Vienna Institute for Comparative Economic Studies, *Comecon Data, 1983* (Southampton, Eng., 1984).

Soviet food imports, nearly half of which are grain purchases, represent about 40% of the total imports. In 1983, 28% of the grain purchases abroad came from the United States, 26% from Argentina, and 21% from Australia. After the disastrous crops of the preceding years, grain imports reached the record figure of 46 million tons in the 1981-82 period. In the following period, 1983-84, they decreased to under 30 million tons after the recovery of the agricultural output in 1982 and 1983. In 1984 grain imports increased again, up to 43 million tons.

After the excellent grain harvest of 1978, which reached 229.6 million tons, the output fluctuated, recording slight ups and downs from one year to another. Thus in 1982, although an increase was recorded, the production reached only 173.3 million tons. It increased again to 190 million tons in 1983, decreasing to 175 million tons in 1983, 64 million tons less than forecast. Among the total production of grains, harvests of wheat, rye, barley, oats, and maize were particularly noteworthy.

Wheat production, after having reached the record figure of 120.9 million tons in 1978, followed a downward trend, except in 1980, when a slight recovery was observed. The 1982 crop, 84 million tons, was markedly lower than the levels reached in the five preceding years.

The harvest of rye was exceptionally good in 1974, reaching 15.2 million tons. Up and down swings were recorded in following years. In 1982, 10 million tons were produced, a level similar to that recorded in 1973.

After a harvest of 15.2 million tons in 1976, a downward trend was recorded by the production of barley, except in 1978. In 1982 only 48 million tons were produced.

After three successive years of good crops, which reached more than 18 million tons, oats crops declined in 1979 and only a slight recovery was recorded in 1980, when they reached 15.5 million tons.

The production of maize, after reaching 13.2 million tons in 1973, diminished gradually, except in 1976 and 1977. It reached 11 million tons in 1982, the highest figure in the past six years.

Potato crops—108.2 million tons in 1973—declined in the first three years of the present decade to levels markedly lower than those achieved in the previous decade. Nevertheless, a slight recovery was recorded in 1983, up to 83 million tons, a level similar to that reached in 1977.

The production of sugar beets also featured a recovery in 1983, reaching 82 million tons, a figure much lower, however, than that of nearly 100 million tons in 1976.

It is estimated that the crop of raw cotton reached 9.2 million tons, after having decreased in three successive years (1981-893). In 1984 the livestock consisted of 119.9 million heads of cattle, 78.5 million heads of pigs, and 151.4 million heads of sheep and goats; 80% were reared in state and collective farms, which also had 755 million fowl.

Although in the first three years of the present decade, only insignificant increases in livestock were recorded, when numbers did not decrease, an increase was registered in the past two years, due to the recovery of the grain production in 1982 and 1983. (Soviet farm animals are highly dependent on grains.) It is estimated that meat production represented 16 million tons in 1983, thus showing only a small variation over preceding years, although a slight upward tendency has been observed since 1980. A limited increase in livestock production is forecast for 1985, due to the insignificant agricultural growth that was recorded in 1984.

Milk production increased for three successive years beginning in 1981, reaching 96.4 million tons in 1983. The production of eggs increased without interruption beginning in 1975 to 74.7 million tons in 1983.

In 1982, 32.6% of the population was engaged in industry, a proportion that has shown a downward tendency since the end of the 1970s. The extent of Soviet industrial power is obvious from the fact that it represents approximately one-fifth of the world's industrial output. Nearly three-fourths of it is produced in the European part of the USSR. Since the second half of the 1970s, industrial labor productivity has shown lower growth rates—2.5% on average at the end of that decade. Although it increased by only 2% in 1982, it showed a marked improvement in 1983, increasing beyond the rates forecasted. Nevertheless, Soviet industrial labor productivity is still equivalent to half of that reached by U.S. industry. The low industrial productivity is partially due to the low level of automation, 40% of the work being done manually. A large part of the equipment has become obsolete, and present production patterns are inadequate.

There are about 45,000 enterprises, 4,000 of which are production associations that contributed 50% of the overall industrial output at the end of 1982. About 40 industrial branch ministries control the production of the different sectors. Since 1973 industrial associations have been self-financing rather than funded through budget allocations, as had been the case previously.

A total of 60% of the workers carry out their duties on a team basis, although their self-management capacity is minimal. Teams are small groups of fifteen to twenty workers to which a specific task is assigned and which are given the means necessary to carry out their work. They receive an overall remuneration, which is to be distributed among the team components according to respective contributions. This system, which was established recently, is meant to promote industrial production through greater incentives.

Overall, the growth rate of Soviet industrial production has decreased since the second half of the 1970s. Nevertheless, an acceleration of industrial output was observed again in 1982, a trend that continued in 1983, when it increased by 4%, compared with 2.8% in the previous year (the lowest rate in 35 years). However, initial data for 1984 reflect that the rate of recovery was not maintained, the growth rate having dropped by 3.5%.

In the present decade, the increase in the production of consumer goods has been particularly noteworthy. They increased by 4.1% in 1983, while capital goods increased by 3.9%. The output of high technological products (industrial robots, digital machine tools, computers, and so on) increased as well, fostered by efforts to modernize and automate the industry as a whole.

Soviet industry has to cope with several structural problems such as inefficient scientific and technical policies, obsolete productive equipment, an inadequate transport infrastructure, and worsening of the problems of coordination induced by centralized planning. The priority given to the armament industry also has a negative impact. In 1981, 8.4% of the industrial workers were engaged in the food industry. In 1982 the production of this sector represented 14.7% of the total industrial output, compared with 21.7% in 1960. This decrease in its contribution was due to a decline in production growth rates, especially since 1978. In 1982 a recovery was recorded with a rate similar to that of 1977.

In 1981, 14.1% of the industrial workers were engaged in light industry, where the rate of expansion has followed a downward trend since the second half of the 1970s, although a slight recovery was recorded in 1980 and 1982, a 4% growth rate being recorded in the latter year. As a result, the contribution of light industry to the total industrial output decreased from 14.8% in 1965 to 12.4% in 1982.

In recent times, a more satisfactory evolution has been that shown by the chemical and engineering industries. Their respective growth rates were higher than 10.0% between the mid-1960s and the mid-1970s; although the rates decreased afterwards, they still are—particularly as far as engineering is concerned—the most dynamic branches of the whole industry. (See Table 1.4.) Their share of the overall industrial output increased to 8.4% and 46.1%, respectively, in 1982 (compared with 4.4% and 21.3% in 1960). The chemical industry employs 5.1% of the industrial workers, and the engineering industry employs 41%.

The metallurgical industry's relative significance in the industrial output as a whole has decreased, especially since the second half of the 1970s, since it represented only 3.8% of the overall industrial output in 1982 (compared with 5.8% in 1975). In 1979 and 1981 it was almost sluggish, with a growth rate lower than 1% recorded in 1980. Nevertheless, a marked recovery was observed in 1982, with a growth rate of 8.3%. This industrial branch employed 3.8% of the industrial workers in 1981.

The USSR is a leader in the production of steel, since it represents 21% of the world's total (compared with 15.2% for the United States and 14.3% for Japan). The electric-power industry represented 3.9% of the total industrial output, employing 2.1% of the industrial workers in 1981. Production, which showed particularly high growth rates in the 1970s, remained steady in the following decade, despite slight ups and downs until 1981, when it increased by only 2.2%. However, its growth rate was almost 4% in the following year.

Table 1.4
Gross Production of the Major Industrial Sectors
(Average Annual Growth Rate in Percentages)

	1965 % s/total	1966/70	1971/75	1976/80	1981	1982	1982 % s/total
Food products	20.9	5.9	5.4	1.5	2.1	4.6	14.7
Light industry	14.8	8.6	4.6	3.4	2.7	4.0	12.4
Chemical industry	5.5	12.2	10.5	5.7	5.5	5.4	8.4
Engineering	25.8	11.8	11.6	8.2	5.9	7.3	46.1
Metallurgy	5.8	5.7	5.1	2.0	0.0	8.3	3.8
Electricity	2.7	9.0	7.1	5.0	2.2	3.9	2.8
Total	100	8.6	7.4	4.5	3.4	2.8	100

Source: Vienna Institute for Comparative Economic Studies, *Comecon Data, 1983* (Southampton, Eng., 1984).

PRIMARY ENERGY SOURCES

Huge fields of the three main primary energy sources (oil, natural gas, and coal) have converted the USSR into a net energy exporting country. Oil and natural gas are mainly obtained in Western Siberia; plans are to extract 62% of the oil and more than 54% of the natural gas from that region. In 1982, 16% of Soviet energy production was exported, with 94% of it in oil, natural gas, and coal.

The domestic consumption of energy has increased at a lower rate in the present decade, and it dropped by 2% per year on average between 1981 and 1983. Thus although the overall output of the three basic fuels increased, respectively, by only 2%, 3%, and 2.3% in the above-mentioned years, it was significant enough to meet domestic requirements and provide an exportable surplus.

Nearly half of the Soviet oil production is extracted from the region of Tyumen in Western Siberia. About half of these exports are channeled toward Eastern Europe. Since the mid-1970s, the crude-petroleum production has lagged behind targets, representing 609 million tons in 1981. Nevertheless, it reached 616 million tons in 1983 (0.6% more than in the previous year but 3 million tons less than forecast; see Table 1.5), which is equivalent to an increase of 7.7% over the level recorded in 1978. Thus in the 1978-83 period, the oil and condensed gas production rose on average at an annual rate of 1.5%. In the first nine years of 1984, the production totaled 461 million tons, which represents a 0.4% decrease, compared to the same period of 1983. The production quota set for 1985 is 628 million tons.

Oil production has increased in recent years only in proportion to the increase in domestic consumption, which has affected exports. Thus in the

Table 1.5
Evolution of the Production of the Main Basic Fuels
and of the Electricity Output

	1978	Variation rate (%)					1983
		1979/78	1980/79	1981/80	1982/81	1983/82	
Oil and condensated gas (in million m. T.)	572	2.4	2.9	1.0	0.6	0.5	616
Natural gas (in billion cubic meters)	372	9.4	6.9	6.9	7.7	6.9	536
Coal (in million m. T.)	724	− 0.7	0.4	− 1.1	1.4	− 0.3	716
Electricity (in billion kWh.)	1,202	3.0	4.5	2.5	3.0	3.7	1,416

Source: Narodnoe Khozyaistvo SSR, *National Economy of the USSR* (Pravda, January 29, 1984).

1980s, oil exports and by-products showed lower growth rates. Consequently, in the first three years of the present decade, crude-petroleum exports to Western countries increased from 57 million tons in 1980 to 77 million in 1983, which represents an overall growth of 35%. In 1983 56.5% of these exports were crude petroleum and the remainder by-products.

The production of natural gas is replacing that of oil as the USSR's main energy source. In 1983 the USSR became the world's first producer and consumer of natural gas, with 536 billion cubic meters being extracted, which corresponds to an increase of 7% over that of the previous year and 44% over 1978 figures. The annual average growth rate was thus 7.6% between 1978 and 1983.

Natural gas should become the USSR's major energy and foreign currency source. Likewise, Soviet authorities plan to increase the use of natural gas by domestic industry and to convert petroleum-power stations into gas-consuming plants. At present natural gas represents 30% of the country's energy balance. Gas exports are channeled toward eleven countries, five of which are Western nations. To make exports easier, two gas pipelines were built, one to supply Western Europe and the other, which reaches the Soviet border, to supply Eastern Europe. The first one, known as the Euro-Siberian gas pipeline, linking Urengai wells to customer countries, is 4,451 kilometers long and is the world's major pipeline.

Coal production has suffered from even more adverse geological exploitation conditions. Thus in 1983, 716 million tons were produced, a level similar to that reached in 1980 and 1.1% lower than that recorded in 1978. Between 1978 and 1983 production decreased at an average annual rate of 0.2%.

Although in the 1950s the USSR was the first country to start operations at a nuclear plant to produce electricity, the development of nuclear power afterwards followed a slower course than it did in other countries. In 1984, fifteen nuclear plants, representing a fixed capacity of 21 megawatts, were operative. Their 40 reactors produced 6.5% of the Soviet electricity. A project is being developed to increase nuclear-power production, and eighteen new plants are under construction. The electricity output of 1983 reached 1 trillion, 416 billion kilowatt hours, which represents 4% more than that in the previous year. It is estimated that an even higher increase was recorded in the previous year.

ECONOMIC POLICY

Considering that the USSR is a planned centralized economy, economic policies are designed to meet different requirements than those in capitalist countries. They are essentially meant to act upon certain priority economic sectors. Economic policy is thus a sectoral policy, since the application of fiscal and monetary measures such as those used in non-government-centralized countries would be meaningless. The economy's planning is entrusted to the State Planning Commission (Gosplan). The economic targets set by this body have been established within the framework of successive plans. The fifth five-year plan, for the 1986-90 period, is being applied at present. Instead of fostering an extensive development of the economy, which occurred in the 1960s, a more intensive growth pattern is favored at present.

The deceleration of economic growth since the second half of the previous decade is mainly attributable to inefficient management, which, moreover, had to cope with structural problems. The present plan thus aims to solve these problems. Planning and management methods were altered for this purpose, and production units were granted more decision-making capacity while the Soviet authorities also fostered faster innovation processes, a more effective allocation of investments, and rational use of resources, as well as greater labor incentives.

During the so-called Andropov era, a program was drawn up to improve the procurement of food products, thus reducing food-import requirements. A long-term food program is being followed by the agricultural sector to augment the land exploitation and yields. It might be achieved by expanding the drained and irrigated area. An increase in investments in the farming sector, up to 50 billion roubles, is planned for the 1986-90 period. It would represent a 12% increase over the investments contemplated in the previous five-year plan. The farming sector would thus absorb about 7% of the investment in the economy as a whole. Special incentives will also be granted to private farms, which will benefit by easier access to energy resources and fertilizers.

To foster the production of state and collective farms, it has been stipulated that when collective-farm production exceeds the targets set by 40%, the surplus obtained may be used freely by farm workers. Their remunerations may also increase if the production quota set is exceeded. The sole requirement will be the achievement of planned production quotas, with greater independence granted for the selection of crops and the organization of production. Nevertheless, acknowledging the present dependence on imported food products, Soviet authorities have tried at least to diversify procurement sources, particularly in relation to grains. In fact, the USSR has signed a contract with the United States, effective since October 1, 1983, for five years, which implies the purchase of at least 9 million tons of grain per year (consisting of similar amounts of wheat and maize).

To improve the population procurement standards, special attention has been paid since 1982 to the industry of consumer goods, the capacity of which has been increased and was given the highest priority for the allocation of raw materials and equipment.

As far as the energy policy is concerned, one can note the support granted to the production of gas with the construction of the Euro-Siberian gas pipeline and the intensification of domestic gas consumption by converting petroleum use into gas- and electric-power plants. Special emphasis also has been given to the development of nuclear power, and a nuclear program was started in 1973.

Another major concern of Soviet economic authorities is how to increase labor-productivity figures. Andropov, and then Gorbachev, personally launched a campaign to increase discipline at work and fight corruption and bureaucracy. Labor incentives are to be increased, with salaries directly linked to output. The new economic philosophy, entirely focused toward the improvement of management and productivity, is inspired from the so-called Novosibirsk papers issued in April 1983. They presented the views of certain political circles, close to the government, concerning the need to carry out structural changes in accordance with the country's economic situation and to abandon old planning patterns that had become obsolete. Consequently, a two-year program was undertaken, at the end of 1983, that was in principle limited to only five sectors and consisted of the creation of workers' squads effecting their respective tasks on a self-organization basis in all production units. The salaries and bonuses obtained by these squads were to be distributed according to the results achieved. At the end of 1984, this experience was extended to other sectors. Nevertheless, the future success of its generalization is uncertain, since initial achievements were partially attributable to the priority given to the sectors selected for this purpose.

The price policy has basically consisted in government subsidies to essential products. The prices of other items are fixed by the government, a rise having been recorded recently by those that had showed an improvement in their quality standards. The prices of certain current consumer goods were reduced throughout 1983, which implied a significant reduction—of nearly 3 billion roubles—in government receipts.

FOREIGN TRADE

Between 1978 and 1984 Soviet exports increased at an interannual average rate of 13.8% while imports increased by 11.5%. With this favorable trade balance, the coverage rate increased by 10.8% in the period under review, reaching nearly 114% in 1984.

In the first half of 1984, exports grew by 9%, compared to the same period in 1983. Imports, however, increased by only 4.5%, and a significant trade surplus was thus achieved. One may observe that a trend toward the expansion of trade with industrialized Western countries has subsided. Although trade with these countries had grown rapidly in the first half of the 1970s, a deceleration was recorded in a later stage. Commercial relations with developing countries have shown a rapid expansion but are concentrated in a few countries. (See Table 1.6.)

Exports to socialist countries in 1984 represented 55.6% of the total while imports accounted for 56.5% (in 1978, their respective contributions were 59.5% and 60%). Exports to these countries between 1978 and 1984 increased on average at an interannual rate of 12.2% while imports increased by 10.2%, and the trade surplus recorded with this interchange increased in this period from 472 million to 4,023 million roubles. The coverage rate reached 112% in 1984. Among these socialist countries, the COMECON members accounted for 91.3% of the exports to other socialist countries in 1984 (compared with 93% in 1978) and 91.4% of the imports (compared with 93% in 1978), with a coverage rate of 112%. Exports to industrialized capitalist countries in 1984 accounted for 28.9% of the total exports while imports from them amounted to 31.4% of the total purchases abroad (compared with 24.4% and 31.8%, respectively). Between 1978 and 1984 exports to these capitalist countries increased at an interannual average rate of 17.7% and imports by 11.3%, which converted a deficit of 2,280 million roubles into a surplus of 930 million roubles in 1984. Although a slight surplus had been achieved in 1980, a deficit was recorded again in the following two years. The coverage rate reached 105% in 1984. (See Figures 1.4 and 1.5 and Table 1.7.)

Soviet trade with developing countries has been continuously favorable, increasing from 2,895 million roubles in 1978 to 3,349 million in 1984, when the coverage rate reached 147%. Between 1978 and 1984, exports increased at an interannual average rate of 12.9%, and imports increased by 20.4%.

Table 1.6
Soviet Volume of Trade, 1984
(139.7 Billion Roubles; $172.5 Billion)

Soviet Trade Partners by Groups of Countries

	Percent
Developed Countries	29
Developing Countries	13
Socialist Countries	58

Source: USSR Ministry of Foreign Trade, Moscow, 1985.

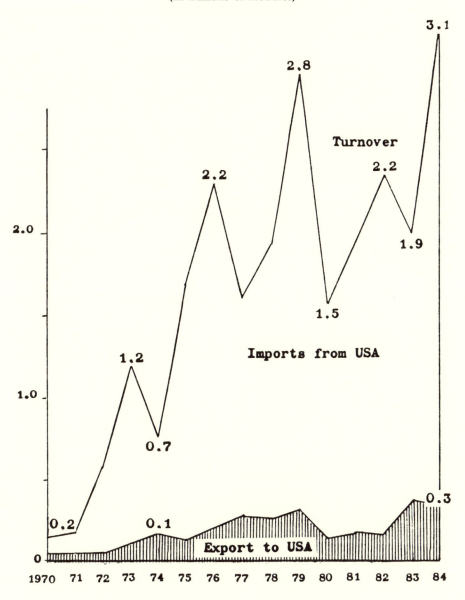

Figure 1.4
Soviet Trade with the United States
(In Billions of Roubles)

Source: USSR Ministry of Foreign Trade, Moscow, 1985.

Table 1.7
Soviet Imports of Machinery and Equipment from the United States:
Share of the United States Soviet Imports of Machinery and Equipment
by Main Groups of Products
(In Millions of Roubles and in Percentages)

Schedule Number	Group of Products		1972	1973	1974	1975	1976	1977	1978	1979	1980	1981	1982	1983	1984
10-19	Machinery, Equipment, and Means of Transport	value	47.6	168.6	188.8	454.3	621.0	350.8	273.5	342.2	311.5	300.7	186.2	143.9	137.2
		percent	1.0	3.2	3.1	5.0	6.0	3.1	1.9	2.4	2.1	1.2	1.0	0.6	0.6
100-103	Metal Cutting and Metal Forming Machine Tools*	value	16.0	11.9	9.3	9.5	8.7	1.3	7.8	4.9	3.3	15.5	2.4	1.9	3.3
		percent	9.6	4.7	4.4	3.8	1.9	0.2	1.2	0.7	0.4	1.8	0.2	0.1	0.2
104	Automatic Metalworking Lines	value	3.3	23.2	20.1	47.0	29.8	15.8	3.2	2.6	5.8	0.9	2.2	0.04	--
		percent	8.5	39.7	57.6	31.8	30.7	18.0	6.4	4.7	8.1	1.2	2.9	0	--
10514	Machinery for Car Plants	value	1.2	16.4	26.0	34.8	32.6	17.1	6.5	4.0	3.4	2.2	3.8	5.6	1.5
		percent	2.1	12.7	7.7	12.1	14.5	8.8	5.5	2.8	2.5	1.7	3.3	2.6	1.1
110	Electrical Power Machinery	value	--	--	--	--	--	--	0.4	20.3	2.5	0.8	4.3	3.1	2.1
		percent	--	--	--	--	--	--	0.2	5.8	0.7	0.2	1.0	0.6	0.3
111	Electrical Equipment	value	--	--	8.2	18.0	13.6	13.5	5.5	--	--	12.2	0.7	0.8	0.8
		percent	--	--	3.9	6.3	3.9	3.2	1.2	--	--	2.2	0.2	0.1	0.1
120	Mining Equipment	value	0.4	0.4	0.4	7.9	7.3	0.7	2.8	10.0	6.5	12.5	16.3	21.9	22.3
		percent	4.6	3.1	1.6	13.5	14.6	1.9	3.1	13.5	6.6	8.8	9.3	7.0	5.7
121	Crushing, Grinding, and Pulverizing Equipment	value	--	--	0.004	17.3	24.7	19.3	4.1	0.4	1.6	0.3	0.5	0.8	0.7
		percent	--	--	0.04	44.2	41.6	21.6	3.4	0.3	1.4	0.4	0.8	1.0	0.7
12303	Rolling Equipment	value	--	1.9	--	1.4	1.0	0.2	0.5	0.04	--	--	--	--	--
		percent	--	2.6	--	0.9	1.0	0	0.2	0.02	--	--	--	--	--
12305	Foundry Equipment	value	1.5	3.9	16.5	52.0	48.2	21.8	4.9	1.0	2.9	2.5	2.2	2.2	2.0
		percent	5.7	8.2	24.9	43.0	43.7	27.0	9.1	2.6	8.0	5.5	2.9	3.6	3.2
128	Drilling Equipment	value	3.8	3.2	0.4	35.6	30.1	21.2	37.9	21.9	37.3	5.5	19.5	4.8	5.5
		percent	10.4	10.1	1.2	26.7	15.2	16.8	15.1	16.1	15.0	2.8	3.0	0.4	0.5

20

Schedule	Description		1	2	3	4	5	6	7	8	9	10	11	12	13
13309	Loading Machinery (excluding Underground Loading Machinery)	value	1.4	0.3	2.0	7.5	0.2	0.7	3.9	5.0	6.3	0.7	9.2	7.8	0.4
		percent	3.1	0.8	4.3	35.8	0.6	0.9	5.4	6.7	7.1	1.0	8.8	0.6	2.9
140	Food Processing Machinery	value	--	--	2.7	5.8	8.8	4.7	2.7	14.6	8.8	3.5	0.9	0.1	2.8
		percent	--	--	1.4	2.5	3.8	2.0	1.0	4.4	1.9	0.8	0.2	0.01	0.3
144	Textile Machinery	value	0.3	0.04	5.0	3.5	15.3	4.5	0.4	0.1	0.2	0.2	0.2	0.6	1.1
		percent	0.3	0.03	3.1	1.3	5.0	1.5	0.1	0.03	0.04	0.06	0.03	0.08	0.2
150	Chemical Machinery	value	5.3	7.4	8.1	29.8	143.8	112.8	42.7	12.2	5.2	3.1	3.0	6.3	4.6
		percent	1.4	1.7	1.7	4.7	12.7	6.6	2.5	0.7	0.4	0.4	0.4	0.6	0.4
153	Construction Materials Equipment	value	--	--	--	--	--	--	1.5	3.0	0.3	0.5	7.3	1.1	6.3
		percent	--	--	--	--	--	--	1.7	3.1	0.3	0.5	5.6	0.6	2.8
154	Road and Road Construction Machinery and Equipment	value	1.6	66.9	20.3	91.6	148.3	30.7	52.9	71.3	72.4	77.7	65.0	50.0	45.4
		percent	...	...	54.6	19.6	...	20.6	28.5	31.1	25.6	16.6	8.2	9.5	10.6
15501	Pumps**	value	--	--	--	15.2	26.2	17.0	7.0	17.9	1.3	--	--	--	--
		percent	--	--	--	19.6	30.0	18.4	7.3	19.6	1.7	--	--	--	--
15931, 15932, 15941	Computers***	value	1.3	0.5	3.0	8.5	15.5	8.4	24.8	30.6	4.7	7.0	0.8	0.07	1.4
		percent	6.4	1.7	4.5	7.0	13.0	10.9	20.6	20.6	3.6	3.8	0.3	0.08	1.1
170, 171, 178, 179	Instruments and Laboratory Equipment	value	3.0	4.4	5.0	12.8	5.5	8.2	8.1	10.7	10.7	12.0	11.2	12.6	7.0
		percent	2.0	3.2	3.3	6.7	2.5	3.2	3.1	3.4	3.2	3.0	2.2	2.3	1.2
172	Medical Equipment and Instruments (excluding equipment for pharmaceutical industry)	value	0.3	10.7	0.9	1.5	2.2	2.4	2.3	2.6	4.5	5.1	3.3	4.1	5.2
		percent	0.5	1.1	1.4	1.8	2.2	2.0	1.7	1.7	2.5	2.3	1.3	1.5	1.7
181	Agricultural Machinery and Equipment	value	0.2	3.3	0.6	3.5	1.4	3.2	8.2	5.7	9.1	7.2	4.0	1.0	0.9
		percent	0.1	1.1	0.2	1.0	0.3	0.6	1.3	0.7	1.2	0.9	0.5	0.1	0.1

* 1972-1975 data on Schedule Number 100, "Metal Cutting Machine Tools" only.
** 1973, 1974 data on Schedule Number 15501, "Pumps," and 15503, "Turbocompressors."
*** 1972-1974 data on Schedule Number 15941 "Computers."
... Absence of comparable data.

Source: USSR Ministry of Foreign Trade, Moscow, 1985.

21

Figure 1.5
Soviet Imports of Machinery and Equipment
(In Billions of Roubles)

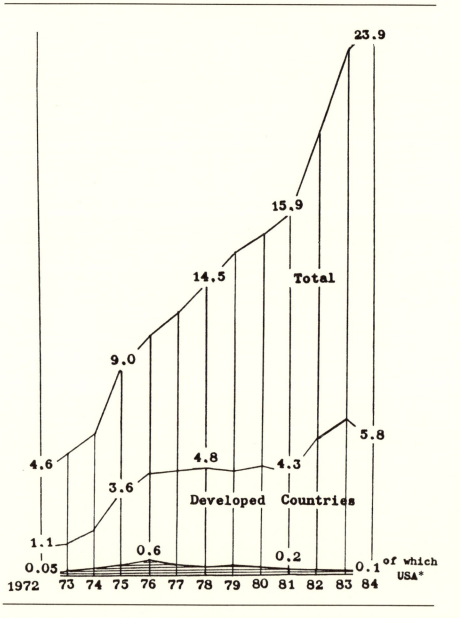

Source: USSR Ministry of Foreign Trade, Moscow, 1985.
*Represents Soviet import of machines and equipment from the United States.

Among COMECON countries, the German Democratic Republic accounted for 19.7% of the exports and 21.4% of the imports in 1984; Czechoslovakia, 17% and 17.6%; Poland, 15.3% and 15.5%; Bulgaria, 16% and 16.3%; Hungary, 11.8% and 13%; Rumania, 4.8% and 5.4%; Cuba, 9.9% and 8.7%; and Yugoslavia, 7.8% and 7.5%.

Among industrialized Western countries, Finland absorbed 12.6% of the exports and 14.4% of the imports in 1984; the United Kingdom, 6% and 3.4%; the Federal Republic of Germany, 19.2% and 17.4%; Italy, 15.3% and 7.7%; France, 12.3% and 9.2%; Canada, 0.1% and 6.8%; Japan, 4.2% and 11.6%; and the United States, 1.7% and 8.4%.

Regarding less developed countries, Soviet trade with India represents 12.1% of the exports to these nations and 14.6% of the imports, accounting in turn for 1.9% of the total sales and 1.8% of the total purchases abroad.

Regarding the distribution of Soviet foreign trade by products, its concentration on a few products is particularly noteworthy. The USSR mainly imports food products (specially grains) and industrial machinery and equipment. It exports oil and gas, its sales of armaments being important as well, especially to developing countries.

2

ORGANIZATION OF SOVIET FOREIGN TRADE

THE entire foreign trade of the USSR is a state monopoly, vested in the Ministry of Foreign Trade. It is in practice carried out by a number of specialized foreign trade organizations whose head offices are located in Moscow.

These foreign trade organizations are the only bodies in the USSR authorized to conduct trading operations with foreign firms or individuals and to conclude contracts for such transactions. Their activities are carried out under the general control of the Ministry of Foreign Trade (see Figure 2.1). They are independent trading and legal entities, having their own capital and operating on much the same lines as British limited-liability companies. At the same time, although the state assumes no responsibility for their operations or negotiations, they can place orders only abroad—and pay for them—by virtue of import licenses and foreign exchange allocations granted by the Soviet authorities. If they conclude contracts, it means that they have the necessary licenses and foreign currency.

Each foreign trade organization (Vsesoyusnoye Obyedinyeniye [V/O]) specializes in particular classes of commodities—or in the goods required for the needs of, or produced by, particular branches of the Soviet economy.

Complete lists of the Soviet foreign trade organizations with addresses and telephone and telex numbers are circulated by the Chamber of Commerce and

Industry; any changes in the meantime are reported in its Information Bulletin. (See also Chapter 23.)

The Ministry of Foreign Trade administers Soviet foreign trade. It oversees the fulfillment of export and import plans and trade agreements with foreign countries, and it controls the activities of the foreign trade organizations. The ministry develops commercial relations with foreign nations, negotiates bilateral trade agreements, and directs the work of Soviet trade representatives and commercial counselors abroad. Main administrations of the ministry regulate foreign trade and payments and administer the customs system, and a Market Research Institute studies developments in world markets.

The functions of the Ministry of Foreign Trade include:

—Elaboration and implementation of measures aimed at the development of the Soviet Union's commerce with foreign states

—Developments of draft commercial treaties, agreements, and conventions of foreign trade

—Contact of corresponding negotiations with foreign countries

—Signing, with the authorization of the Soviet government, treaties and agreements and exercising control over their execution

—Planning, regulating, and supervising the implementation of plans adopted for foreign trade

—Controlling the quality of exported and imported goods and equipment

—Directing the activity of all-Union foreign trade organizations, trade missions of the USSR abroad, and commercial counselors in embassies and missions of the USSR and other ministerial organizations

—Authorizing exports and imports

—Elaboration and implementation of monetary measures in the realm of foreign trade and regulation of payment for foreign goods through Soviet territory

—Supervision over the transportation and storage of foreign consignments and the order of transit of foreign goods through Soviet territory

—Supervision of customs policy and guidance of customs work on Soviet territory

—Ensuring that the laws, regulations, and rules pertaining to foreign trade are observed

The Ministry of Foreign Trade is headed by a minister appointed by the Presidium of the Supreme Soviet of the USSR on the recommendation of the chairman of the Council of Ministers of the USSR. The minister has a number of deputies who direct individual areas of work (see Figure 2.2). As an advisory organ, a collegium is formed under the minister; deputy ministers and some department heads are members of this collegium.

Figure 2.1
Conceptual Overview of the Soviet Ministry of Foreign Trade

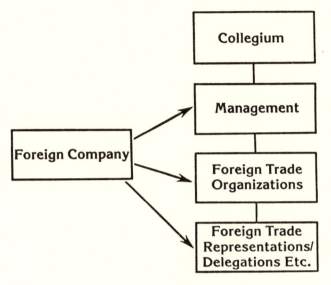

Source: USSR Ministry of Foreign Trade, Moscow, 1985.

Figure 2.2
Management of the Soviet Ministry of Foreign Trade

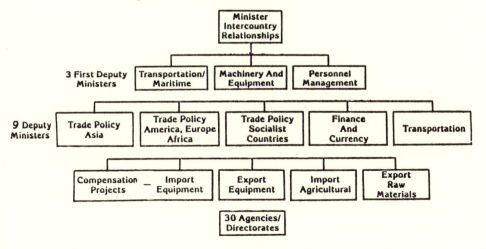

Source: USSR Ministry of Foreign Trade, Moscow, 1985.

The basic structural unit of the ministry is the department. Departments are grouped, according to their activity, as follows: commercial-political (regional), sectoral (commodities), and functional departments and sections.

The commercial-political apparatus includes a number of departments concerned with trade with different groups of countries. These departments include the Department for Cooperation with the CMEA (Committee of Mutual Economic Assistance) Member-Countries; Department for Commerce with the Socialist Countries of Europe; Eastern Department; Department of Commerce with Western Countries; Department of Commerce with South-East Asia and the Middle East; Department of Commerce with the Countries of Africa; Department of Commerce with the Countries of America; and Department for International Economic Organizations. These departments are to coordinate the work of foreign trade organizations in their dealings with foreign countries, to develop measures for expanding the Soviet Union's economic contacts, and to prepare and conduct commercial negotiations.

The sectoral apparatus includes a number of general departments on the export and import of goods from different groups of countries. They include the General Department on the Export of Transport, Road-building and Agricultural Machines; General Department for the Export of Industrial Equipment; General Department for the Export of Raw Materials; General Department for the Export of Finished Products and Consumer Goods; General Department for the Import of Machines and Equipment from Socialist Countries; General Department for the Import of Machines and Equipment from Capitalist Countries; and General Department for the Import of Industrial Raw Material, Food and Finished Products.

The functions of the general export and import departments include control over the fulfillment of plans by the all-Union foreign trade organizations (V/O) and the coordination of their activities.

The functional apparatus includes a number of departments: The Economic Planning Department is concerned with developing export-import plans and maintaining current and statistical account of the fulfillment of plans and commercial agreements. The Legal Department drafts commercial treaties, agreements, and other legal documents. The General Currency Department draws up and coordinates with the Gosplan and the Finance Ministry the currency plans, supervises their execution, gives authorization to V/Os on payments, and studies and supervises prices on deals made by V/Os. The Finance Department draws up the finance plan for the ministry (income and expenditure balance) and supervises the financial work of foreign trade organizations. The Transport Department ensures the timely shipment of foreign trade consignments. The General Customs Department supervises local customs offices, draws up customs policy, and drafts tariff schedules. The State Inspectorate on the Quality of Exported Goods checks the quality of exported goods.

The ministry has authorized representatives in some of the union republics and in the country's economic regions.

FOREIGN TRADE ORGANIZATION
PROFILE: STANKOIMPORT

The Soviet Union is one of the world's largest manufacturers of metalworking machine tools, pressing and forging machinery, tools, and bearings.

In the international market V/O Stankoimport represents the interests of all factories and works of the machine-tool and bearing industry of the USSR. (Figure 2.3 illustrates the organization of a typical foreign trade firm.) This industry manufactures about 1,750 models and standard sizes of all-purpose metalworking machine tools, 525 models and standard sizes of multipurpose pressing and forging machines, and more than 400 models of woodworking machines.

V/O Stankoimport maintains business ties with engineering enterprises and firms in nearly 90 nations, with an annual trade turnover amounting to 2 billion roubles. Trade is conducted through a network of agents who sell Soviet-made machinery, as well as provide service, maintenance, and spare and replacement parts and units. As an importer, V/O Stankoimport cooperates closely with nearly every major machine-tool engineering company in the world.

Figure 2.3
Conceptual Overview of a Typical Foreign Trade Organization

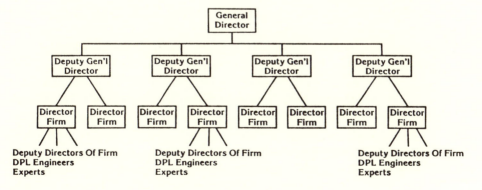

Source: USSR Ministry of Foreign Trade, Moscow, 1985.

As recently as ten to fifteen years ago, most firms bought all-purpose equipment from V/O Stankoimport. Recently, however, there has been a clearly observed tendency toward varying the structure of sales, as more and more demand arises for large, unique machines, numerically controlled (NC) machine tools, and machining centers.

Thus V/O Stankoimport can deliver heavy-duty lathes from its Kramatorsk Factory, which handles work weighing from 16 to 250 tons and with diameters from 1,250mm to 4,000mm, with a 6.3m to 20m distance between centers.

Approximately 30% of the machine tools produced at the Leningrad Machine Tool Engineering Production Amalgamation are delivered to clients abroad; they are currently operating in more than 50 countries. There are horizontal boring machines with spindle diameters from 90mm to 200mm; jug-boring machines with 1,000mm × 1,600mm and 1,400mm × 2,240mm worktables; NC horizontal knee-type routing machines; and special-purpose and specialized machine tools for working large housing and body parts of turbines, diesel engines, diesel and electric locomotives, and ships and marine equipment.

A number of shipbuilding companies in Britain, Norway, Sweden, and Japan have acquired heavy-duty horizontal machines (with a boring spindle of 150mm diameter) from the Leningrad Amalgamation through V/O Stanko-import. The machines feature a stationary plate or bed, a built-in faceplate with radially movable carriage, and a removable rotary worktable. The end-support design permits boring throughgoing openings in the machine.

Among other Soviet factories whose products can be of definite interest to companies in the United States, Canada, and other countries are the S. V. Kosior Works in Kharkov, fabricating circular-grinding and roll-grinding machines for working shafts and rolls as long as 12m and of diameters to 2m; and factories in Ulyanovsk, Minsk, and Novosibirsk, which specialize in the production of heavy-duty milling, milling-and-boring, planing, and combination longitudinal working machines.

Numerous international manufacturers of NC systems, electric drives, hydraulic systems, and other devices and apparatus used in metalworking machines have engaged in extensive cooperation wth Soviet machine-tool makers. These manufacturers include Bosch, Siemens, Fanuk, and Olivetti. Machines produced through such collaboration are sold in countries worldwide and are used by numerous engineering enterprises within the Soviet Union.

Recently, V/O Stankoimport began active cooperation abroad in the joint development, manufacture, marketing, and servicing of machinery delivered to users. This cooperation is now taking place with a number of companies in Austria, France, the Federal Republic of Germany, Switzerland, and several other countries.

The Soviet Union is one of the top producers of pressing and forging machines. They are manufactured serially, and in great demand in the international market are items such as precision-cutting crank shears for rolled stock, with cutting force up to 1,000 tons; sheet-cutting crank shears for cutting sheets and plate up to 32mm thick; plate-stamping presses with pressing force to 4,000 tons; hot-stamping crankpresses with force to 6,300 tons; trimming presses with force to 1,600 tons; hydraulic presses with force to 24,000 tons, and horizontal forging machines with force to 3,150 tons.

V/O Stankoimport is particularly concerned with ensuring proper service and maintenance, and specific service facilities have been created at numerous technical centers, agent companies, and joint-stock corporations, which employ some 350 Soviet and foreign professionals skilled in mechanics, electrical operations, and electronics. In addition, Soviet manufacturers send abroad 350 to 400 specialists every year to assist users of Soviet machines, as well as to train customers' and national personnel.

Noteworthy is the active role played by V/O Stankoimport's representative in Canada—Stan-Canada, Inc. This firm operates its own well-supplied warehouse and is fully capable not only of selling, quickly delivering, and servicing a variety of Soviet-made metalworking but also of conducting professional training both in Canada and the United States.

Purchased from American companies were sets of production equipment, automatic machining lines, and other special-purpose machinery now in operation at machine-building enterprises of the Soviet Union.

This activity is further proof that there are goods and equipment both in the USSR and the United States that are of interest to partners on each side.

FOREIGN TRADE POLICY

Foreign trade policy is determined primarily through the following state bodies:

1. *The Council of Ministers* is the highest government organ, responsible for determining overall national economic policy. The council approves national economic development plans, which include sections covering the redevelopment of foreign trade.

2. *The State Planning Committee* (Gosplan), which reports to the Council of Ministers, draws up the annual, five-year, and long-range national economic-development plans, of which foreign trade is an integral part (see Figure 2.4). In consultation with other organizations, Gosplan plans the patterns and levels of foreign trade, the balance of payments, and imports by country of origin and Soviet end-user organization. In regard to imports from Western countries, the decision about where to buy is usually left to the Ministry of Foreign

Trade and the foreign trade organizations (FTOs). The general foreign trade plans, which are subject to constant modification, are given to the Ministry of Foreign Trade for development and execution. Occasionally, Gosplan takes part in discussions with Western firms when particularly large deals are under consideration.

Through counterparts in each of the fifteen Soviet republics (e.g., Gosplan Uzbekistan, Gosplan Ukraine), it supervises and coordinates all planning activity in the country. Although Gosplan has no operating authority, its word is law where national economic development priorities and allocation of resources are concerned.

Gosplan is a unique body of highly competent professional and technical experts presided over by Nikolai V. Talyzin. He is assisted by some fifteen deputy chairmen, including four first deputies.

The basic structure of Gosplan consists of functional sections corresponding to the countrywide or all-Union ministries. There are, for example, sections for foreign trade, light industry, oil and gas, geology and mineral resources, and transport. These sections are complemented by others with planning functions on a general economic or industrial level, such as the sections for mathematical methods and computer technology, for introduction of new technology, for norms and standards, for introduction of new planning methods, for economic stimulation, and for planning of living standards.

Under Gosplan there are also several research institutes—one for planning and norms, the Scientific Research Economic Institute, and one for complex fuel and energy problems—which enjoy an autonomous status in the committee.

The institute for fuel and energy problems, organized in 1974, is headed by Sergei Yatroc, a noted authority in the oil and gas field. To date the range of activities in this institute is not entirely clear, although in the development of new energy sources, long-range assessments of the country's fossil-fuel resources will be important.

A highly important organization within the State Planning Committee is the Main Computer Center, which has a key role in the implementation of plans to computerize the whole economy. The center, headed by Gosplan Deputy Chairman Nikolai P. Lebedinski, has already been in operation for a number of years. It is a major component of the so-called State Network of Computer Centers, with overall supervision of centers in the planning committees and other agencies in the republics. The work of the latter is in turn tied in with operational computer installations for processing data in large industrial associations and enterprises. The entire system is in the process of being installed, using hardware largely of domestic origin, although equipment and perhaps some software and peripherals may be provided by Western firms.

Figure 2.4
Conceptual Overview of the State Planning Process and Foreign Trade

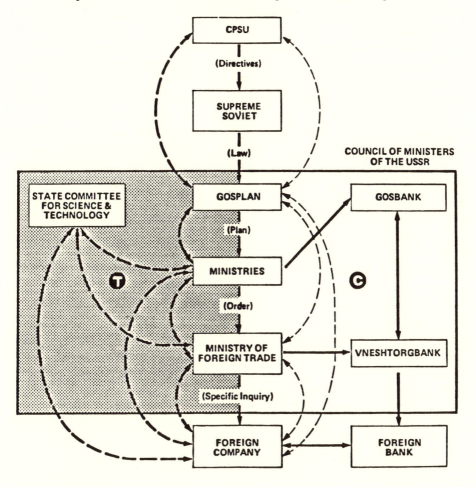

Source: USSR Ministry of Foreign Trade, Moscow, 1985.

Besides undertaking its planning role for the whole economy, Gosplan exercises important coordinating and control functions between operational ministries. It is consulted and takes part in the decision making for priorities, allocation of raw materials, import requirements, and expenditures of hard currency. It is in a position to identify new approaches to industrial problems for the ministries, a role in which it is also useful for foreign firms operating in the Soviet Union. The basic planning unit in the Soviet Union is the well-known five-year plan.

In some cases Gosplan officials make themselves available to Western business people specifically to learn of the latest developments in fields in which they have a particular interest. In general, however, their role is not active in this respect. They prefer to leave this to the State Committee for Science and Technology and to individual ministries. In any case, they are always eager to receive material on new projects and activities from Western firms.

Gosplan publishes a monthly magazine (in Russian) entitled *Planned Economy*, which contains authoritative articles on a wide variety of planning topics.

3. The State Committee for Science and Technology, which reports to the Council of Ministers, supervises and coordinates scientific-technical research and development in the Soviet Union. The committee plays an important role in selecting foreign suppliers of technology and equipment for priority industrial projects, and it works closely with many Western firms.

The State Committee for Science and Technology is one of the more important Soviet agencies for foreign firms operating in the Soviet Union. Founded in the late 1950s in response to the need for acquisition and application of new technology, it is responsible for a wide variety of operations reaching into every corner of the country's industrial structure.

Chairman of the committee is Gury I. Marchuk, who holds the title of academician of the Academy of Sciences, one of the most prestigious titles in the Soviet Union. Marchuk is assisted by ten to twelve deputy chairmen, each a recognized authority in one or more industrial branches. One of the best-known deputy chairmen is Dzherman M. Gvishiani, son-in-law of former Premier Kosygin.

The committee functions as a coordinating rather than an operational body. It has a large staff of experts in functional departments such as those for computer technology, chemical industry, light industry, and food. These experts maintain a continuing working relationship with their counterparts in the ministries, research institutes, and other agencies responsible for economic development.

Contacts between these experts and Western firms are developed and maintained through the committee's foreign relations department, which is organized along geographical lines and headed by Dimitry N. Pronsky. Staff members of the area sections make contacts for a firm, assist it in staging seminars and symposia, arrange exchanges of information and specialists, and are helpful in making the firm known to Soviet industrial end users.

Recently, the committee developed the practice of concluding so-called cooperative agreements with Western firms in different branches. There are now more than 300 of these agreements, of which more than 80 are with U.S. firms. The agreements outline the general features of cooperation—such as exchanges of information and technical specialists, joint R&D, acquisition of know-how and licenses, and joint project development—and specify individual areas where such cooperation is desirable.

The USSR State Committee for Foreign Economic Relations is active largely in developing countries, where it delivers plants, machinery, equipment, technical assistance, and engineering know-how and design, sometimes in collaboration with Western firms.

Finally, the USSR State Committee on Material-Technical Supplies operates only domestically. It distributes and sells to industrial consumers chemical products, machinery, and equipment through two associations: Soyuzglavkhim (products) and Soyuzglavneftekhimmash (machinery).

With a framework agreement of this type, the Western firm is at liberty, with the assistance of committee experts, to come to working arrangements with individual Soviet ministries. These arrangements are formalized as protocols attached to the original agreement.

The major advantage for a Western firm in concluding a cooperation agreement with the committee is that it opens up easier access to a range of Soviet ministries, committees, institutes, and other organizations. Committee assistance is particularly helpful in the case of multinational corporations with interests that cut across different Soviet ministerial jurisdictions. In the case of certain key industrial ministries, such as radio and electronics industries, committee assistance is almost indispensable. Conversely, in the absence of an agreement, a company may find its long-term objectives at best more difficult to attain.

Similarly, a working arrangement with a ministry within the agreement framework has various benefits. The ministry is, for example, in a position to arrange visits to factories and enterprises under its jurisdiction. In the case of one firm in the energy field, a comprehensive tour of major production facilities in different parts of the Soviet Union was organized. The company's executives and specialists got to know many of their Soviet counterparts and acquired a better feel for long-range business prospects.

Access to research institutes sometimes also has interesting results. A manufacturer of metallurgical products found that scientists of one research and design institute had developed laborsaving processes that, with some adaptation, could be used in his own operations. Committee officials have, in fact, been stressing the advantages to both sides of coupling the extensive Soviet industrial research effort with the practical experience of Western firms. From the Soviet viewpoint this makes sense, since putting innovations into production is often a weak point.

Once a cooperation agreement has been signed and projects with individual ministries are under way, the committee can arrange for accreditation for an office in Moscow and otherwise facilitate doing business in the Soviet Union. As a rule, these facilities are not available to non-accredited firms.

Some Western firms have expressed hesitation about the legal status of cooperation agreements. Since the agreement merely provides an umbrella for development of mutually interesting projects in specific fields, it does not have binding force in the event that the working parties are unable to come to agreement on details. In general, the legal side of a business relationship is not particularly emphasized in the Soviet Union. In the Soviet scheme of things, the development of a good personal relationship on a businesslike basis is considered a prerequisite for ironing out most disputes.

THE STRUCTURE AND ORGANIZATION OF
CHEMICAL AND PETROCHEMICAL INDUSTRIES

In the past 30 years chemical and petrochemical sectors have been, and continue to be, a good market for Western firms. There is an ongoing and very active demand for complete plants, machinery, equipment, and engineering expertise, as demonstrated by two large chemical fairs and the number of specialized exhibits held in Moscow during the past few years. In 1985 the Soviet Union imported more than $1 billion worth of machinery and equipment from Western suppliers for the chemical industry.

Eight major Soviet ministries and committees are directly concerned with administration of the chemical and petrochemical sectors:

USSR Ministry of Chemical Industry
    Minister: V. V. Listov

USSR Ministry of Oil Refining and Petrochemical Industry
    Minister: V. S. Fedorov

USSR Ministry of Chemical and Oil Machinery Construction
    Minister: K. I. Brekhov

USSR Ministry of Foreign Trade
    Minister: B. I. Aristov

USSR State Committee for Foreign Economic Relations
    Chairman: S. A. Skachkov

USSR State Committee on Material-Technical Supplies
  Chairman: N. V. Martinov

USSR State Planning Committee
  Chairman: K. V. Talyzin

USSR State Committee for Science and Technology
  Chairman: G. I. Marchuk

Of the ministries, two are key in an operational sense—those for the chemical industry and those for the oil-refining and petrochemical industry. Although the titles give an idea of the division of responsibility between them, there are, nevertheless, some areas, such as synthetic fibers, where both have an active interest in the same products.

The USSR Ministry of the Chemical Industry has had eleven main product departments, which are currently being converted into all-Union or countrywide production associations merging the ministerial-level managers and experts with the manufacturing enterprises and factories. The areas covered are:

—Basic chemicals

—Organics and non-organics

—Nitrogen

—Mining-industry chemicals

—Dyes and organic products

—Paints and varnishes

—Plastics

—Chemical fibers

—Chloric acid and reagents

The new associations are designated by the word *Soyuz* (Union) prefixed to a contraction of the product group. Thus *Soyuzkhimplast* stands for Union Association for Plastics and *Soyuzkhimvolokno* for Union Association for Synthetic Fibers.

An interesting feature of Chemical Ministry operations is the so-called Department of Product Compensation formed to look after payment from imports of plants, technology, and equipment by means of end-product deliveries—an aspect of doing business with the Soviet Union that is increasing in importance. Until now this activity had been handled administratively by the USSR Ministry of Foreign Trade and its foreign trade organizations.

The Chemical Ministry is the first production ministry to have a department authorized to deal directly with foreign firms. Its establishment does not mean the exclusion of the Foreign Trade Ministry, which still has responsibility for price negotiations and other aspects of export-import operations. Nevertheless, for foreign firms there is an advantage in gaining direct access to experts of the consuming organizations.

Like the Chemical Ministry, the Ministry for Oil Refining and Petrochemicals is converting its main departments into production associations. Until now, production departments of this ministry were the following:

—Oil-refining and petrochemical industry
—Tire industry
—Shale-oil industry
—Rubber industry (two departments)
—Carbon-black industry
—Fat-substitutes industry

Associations formed so far include (the terminology and functions parallel those of the Chemical Ministry): Soyuztekhuglerod (carbon black), Soyuz-remshina (tire recapping), and Soyuzneftekhim (petrochemicals).

Both the Chemical Ministry and the Ministry of Oil Refining and Petrochemical Industry have a large number of scientific research and design institutes that play a role in the decision-making process. Some of the more important of these institutes are one for the oil-refining and petrochemical industry (VNIIPINEFT); three for the rubber industry (GIPROKAUCHUK, VNIISK, and NIIRP); the rubber and latex industry (NIIR); monomers for synthetic rubber (NIIMSK); the tire industry (NIISHP); plastics (NIIPM); and polymers (VNII-POLIMER).

The USSR Ministry of Chemical and Oil Machinery Construction is essentially a supplier of plants and equipment to the Soviet Chemical and Oil Refining and Petrochemical Ministries. It also engages in export activities through the Ministry of Foreign Trade and the State Committee for Foreign Economic Relations.

The ministry has departments for pump manufacture, oil-drilling machinery, oil-refining and chemical machinery, delivery of complete lines, compressor and refrigerator machinery, and industrial fittings.

Exports and imports of chemical products as well as machinery and equipment for the chemical industry are the responsibility of the USSR Ministry of Foreign Trade. Products are handled by the FTO Soyuzkhimexport, and machinery and equipment are sold and purchased by the FTO Techmashexport. The operations of the Techmashimport are controlled by the ministry's main Department for Imports of Machinery and Equipment from Capitalist

Countries. Although contacts through this department and subordinated FTOs constitute the normal route for large contracts, functional ministries are responsible for decisions on purchases and cooperation.

Of the Soviet state committees listed, the most important are those for planning and for science and technology. The State Planning Committee is the main Soviet agency in the planning field. It has a section for the chemical industry that supervises planning of its development in the economy in conjunction with the operating ministries and other governmental bodies involved, including, especially, research institutes of the USSR Academy of Sciences.

The State Committee for Science and Technology possesses essentially coordinating functions that cut across all other governmental bodies having a function in the chemical and petrochemical sector. Its major interest is the acquisition of up-to-date technology. With this in mind, it concludes cooperation agreements with foreign firms that provide for, among other things, consideration of technical exchanges, know-how transfer, licensing, and other appropriate collaborative activities between the Western partner and the Soviet chemical and petrochemical industry.

3

SOVIET BUSINESS OUTLOOK AND BEST EXPORT PROSPECTS

THE Soviet Union's difficulties in increasing hard-currency export earnings, continuation of a policy to reduce its percentage of trade with the West, and disinclination to finance its hard-currency trade deficit will limit expansion of Western exports to the USSR. According to the American Embassy in Moscow, prospects for U.S. exports directly relate to Soviet import priorities, Soviet bilateral trade requirements, the ability of firms to channel shipments through third-country clearing accounts, and U.S. export-control regulations. High on this list of products are oil and gas equipment, agricultural machinery and equipment, agricultural chemicals, food-processing and packaging equipment, mining equipment, scientific instruments, and medical equipment.

   The performance of the Soviet economy during the past eighteen months has been mixed. Although 1984 saw continued modest growth in industry, stagnating agricultural output held growth of national income below the level of 1983. In the first quarter of 1985, harsh winter weather reduced industrial growth to the slowest rate of the five-year-plan period (1981-85). However, a rebound in the second quarter and a more vigorous style of leadership under General Secretary Gorbachev improved the prospects for the Soviet economy in 1985.

In industry, the main trends of the past 18 months include: rapid growth in the output of the high-tech goods and the machine-building sectors, lagging production in basic industries such as ferrous metals and construction materials, and slow growth in the consumer-goods sector.

The energy sector performed poorly in 1984. Oil production declined for the first time, slipping to 613 million metric tons from 616 million metric tons the previous year. The slump continued into 1985, with output through mid-year running some 4% below the 1984 pace. The coal industry is scrambling to maintain output at levels attained in recent years. Nuclear-power programs continue to limp along well behind schedule. The natural gas industry maintained its record of rapid growth in 1984, with no slowdown in sight in 1985.

In foreign trade, the Soviet Union recorded a record trade surplus in 1984, despite softening oil markets, where it earns 60% of its hard currency (see Table 3.1). Sharp cutbacks in machinery and equipment imports from the West provided some breathing space for record grain imports (See Table 3.2). Problems in oil production and transportation reduced oil exports precipitously in early 1985, presaging some deterioration in the hard-currency trade account in 1985. Returning to the Euromarket for the first time since 1979, the Soviet Union negotiated more than $1 billion in credits at very favorable terms in 1984. Borrowing continued apace through mid-1985, with further improvements in terms. At the end of 1984, Soviet net hard-currency debt was about $10 billion.

The Soviet Union has been a $27 billion to $28 billion hard-currency market for several years. Given the softness of world energy markets and heavy Soviet reliance on energy sales to earn hard currency, the level of hard-currency imports is not expected to increase (although there may be year-to-

Table 3.1
Soviet Exports by Main Groups of Merchandise, 1984
(74.4 Billion Roubles; $91.8 Billion)

	Percent
Chemicals, Fertilizers, Rubber	3.5
Consumer Goods	1.8
Machinery and Equipment	12.5
Mineral Fuels	54.4
Ores, Metals, and Products	7.2
Wood and Related Products	2.8
Other	17.8

Source: V/O Vneshtorgreklama, ministry of Foreign Trade of the USSR, Moscow.

Table 3.2
Soviet Imports by Main Groups of Merchandise, 1984
(65.3 Billion Roubles; $80.7 Billion)

	Percent
Chemicals, Fertilizers, Rubber	4.5
Consumer Goods	11.7
Foodstuffs and Raw Materials	
for Their Production	22.5
Machinery and Equipment	36.6
Mineral Fuels, Electricity	6.1
Ores and Concentrates, Metals	8.3
Other	10.3

Source: USSR Ministry of Foreign Trade, Moscow, 1985.

year variances related to the scheduling of deliveries for major products). The import patterns that have been evident throughout the decade are expected to continue: Soviet agricultural purchases will amount to $10 billion to $12 billion per year, ferrous metals and chemicals $5 billion to $6 billion, consumer products $1 billion, and machinery and equipment (including major project imports) $9 billion to $12 billion. Soviet difficulties in increasing hard-currency export earnings will constrain purchases from Western countries beyond these levels.

THE FIVE-YEAR PLAN
AND BUREAUCRATIC STRUCTURES (1986–90)

The five-year-plan goals include the development of an agro-industrial complex to ensure constant and adequate food supplies to Soviet consumers, rapid development of fuel and energy resources, modernization of long-distance transportation, renovation of machine-building and metalworking industries, redirection of steel production into a wider variety of better quality products, and introduction of measures to conserve the use of fuels and metals.

Due to a shortage of incremental investment funds and the vast amount of incomplete capital construction now on hand, Soviet planners will be trying to achieve these results with a growth in investment funds half that of the last five-year plan. The rhetorical focus is on quality rather than quantity, "intensification" (usually defined as higher productivity from existing facilities, rather than additional production lines), and more rational use of resources and manpower rather than the addition of new resources or labor.

To most Western commentators, five-year-plan targets of the Soviet Union are a convenient way of measuring economic progress or the lack of it. For the business person searching for commercial links with the Soviet Union, the plan can be of far more pragmatic use, because these plans list the priority sectors of economic development—often with surprising detail about the kinds of equipment sought, import substitution, or export-oriented industries to be established. Beyond this they also indicate the degree to which a country intends to pursue trade with industrialized countries.

Thus, for instance, the Soviet Union's eleventh five-year plan, which covers the period from 1980 to 1985, made it clear that foreign trade was to grow by at least 30% during those five years. Remarks made by Secretary General Mikhail Gorbachev on various official occasions have reinforced the impression that the Soviet Union expects to continue to rely on trade with the West to modernize key sectors of its industrial plants, improve its agricultural production, and exploit its natural resources.

The plan furthermore gives specific instances of new development goals, which, compared to those of previous plans, indicate where opportunities for Western technologies exist. Thus offshore exploration is going to play a larger role in the Soviet Union's oil-production plans. Intercity telephone services are to be expanded. In the consumer sector the plan even details the kinds of appliances, such as freezers, two-door refrigerators, color television sets (including portables), videotape recorders, and automatic gas ranges, to be manufactured in greater numbers.

The 1986-90 five-year plan will likely emphasize the machine-building sectors, energy, and agribusiness. Hard-currency imports required to meet economic objectives in these sectors will be high on the priority list, with equipment imports for the oil and gas industries near the top. The Soviet Union is committed to maintaining its hard-currency earnings from oil and gas sales, and demand will be strong for equipment suitable for use in hostile environments, particularly in offshore Arctic conditions.

The long-term Soviet Food Program will continue to engender a secondary emphasis on imports related to increasing agricultural productivity and reducing storage and processing losses. Agricultural chemicals are among the best prospects for U.S. exporters. Market opportunities are also expected for food processing and packaging equipment. Because of the high costs of most agricultural machinery, Soviet interest in prospective licensing ventures will be stronger than demand for final product imports, although there are some export opportunities for implements. Other sectors offering the best prospects include machinery and equipment for increasing productivity in the consumer goods and other light industries, mining equipment for the nonferrous metallurgy and coal industries, general-purpose chemicals, scientific instruments, and medical equipment.

Recent Soviet purchases reveal much about the priorities assigned to hard-currency allocations. Annual hard-currency outlays have been about $1.3 billion for oil and gas equipment, $900 million for metalworking machinery and equipment, $170 million for analytical and scientific instruments, $130 million for food-processing and packaging equipment, $115 million for mining equipment, $70 million for medical equipment, and $30 million for agricultural machinery and equipment.

PROJECTS UNDER THE SOVIET PLAN
(1986–90)

Major projects under the 1986-90 plan will result in substantial deliveries in the oil and gas machinery and equipment and metalworking machinery and equipment sectors. Chemical and mining equipment also figure into the deliveries for these projects. Among these major projects are the Astrakhan II sour-gas project, the Blagoveshchensk polyester plant, the Sahkalin offshore oil and gas project, the Moskvich and Gorky automotive projects, the Zima PVC plant, the Kursk pesticide plant, and the Karchaganak sulfur and liquids project. Contract awards form the Barents offshore oil- and gas-exploration project will probably be made somewhat later in the five-year plan.

Other projects in the food-processing, ferrous-metallurgy, chemical, agricultural machinery, coal-slurry, and building-materials sectors will also be included in the 1986-90 plan. Deliveries for these projects are apt to cause surges in hard-currency imports for certain industry sectors in given years. The outlook for U.S. firms to play a role in these major projects is mixed, depending in part on the state of overall relations between the two countries. In some cases, Moscow may sign contracts with non-U.S. Western firms with the understanding that they will subcontract to U.S. companies for specific equipment or services.

One difficulty in forecasting Soviet imports of industrial equipment is the fluctuation of Soviet agricultural import requirements. There has been an inverse relationship between agricultural product hard-currency imports and machinery and equipment hard-currency imports for a number of years. When poor harvests require more hard currency to be allocated to the purchase of agricultural products, machinery and equipment purchases have been cut back. Grain imports from all sources were 55 million metric tons (mmt) in the 1985-86 grain-marketing year (July 1-June 30), and current-year purchases are estimated to be 37 mmt. With the signing of the Long-Term

Grain Agreement between the United States and the USSR, the Soviet Union is obligated to purchase at least 9 mmt of grain each year (U.S. fiscal year October 1-September 30) through September 1988. Up to 1 million tons of the requirement may be met through purchases of soybeans and/or soybean meal in a ratio of two-to-one, grain-to-soybeans. In the 1984-85 year, Soviet grain purchases from the United States were approximately 19 mmt. (For a list of top U.S. exports to the USSR in 1979-83, see Table 3.3)

Bilaterialism in Soviet trade has not been a serious problem for U.S. exporters, but the countries importing Soviet oil and/or gas are pressing more forcefully their concerns about their mounting trade deficits. Foremost among them are France, Italy, West Germany, and Austria. U.S. exporters are most apt to encounter difficulties when product-quality differences are marginal and especially if the competing firm from one of these countries is also able to offer a more attractive financing package. The relative appreciation of the dollar has also complicated the task of U.S. exporters.

The following projects are included in the next five-year plan:

—A huge chemical complex at Saratov for production of nylon 66 tire cord and hexamethylene-diamine salts. Secondary products might include acids and enhanced oil-recovery chemicals.

—A major chemical complex near Ufa in Bashkiria to produce polyester fibers and dyestuffs.

—A polyolefin facility at Buddenovsk.

—An acrylic acid and acrylate plant with emphasis on additives for the steel industry.

—A steel plant at Orel (west of Moscow) and a metallurgical complex at Volzhsk to produce large-diameter pipe.

—Oil and gas development at Kazakhstan and sulfur-from-gas projects at Tenghiz.

—Completion of the Astrakhan complex for extracting sulfur from gas, with an overall goal of stopping hard-currency sulfur imports and beginning exports of 1 million tons of sulfur by 1987.

—Further expansion of oil and gas extraction at Sakhalin in the Far East.

—A number of new gas pipelines, including one from Western Siberia to the Czecho-slovak border.

—A second stage of the Vostochniy Port facilities, particularly for coal handling and shipment.

—Completion of the South Yukutia coal complex, where plans call for new coal exports to Japan of some 5 million tons from this region.

—New production capabilities for bleached sulphate cellulose at Bratsk and Ust-Ilimsk and new plants at Solombal, Arkhangelsk, and Kotlass for softwood non-bleached sulphate cellulose.

Table 3.3
Top U.S. Exports to the USSR, 1979–83 (Millions of Dollars)

1979 Exports Commodity	Value	1980 Exports Commodity	Value	1981 Exports Commodity	Value	1982 Exports Commodity	Value	1983 Exports Commodity	Value
Yellow Corn	1,402	Yellow Corn	602	Yellow Corn	782	Yellow Corn	819	Wheat, Unmilled	801
Wheat, Unmilled	812	Wheat, Unmilled	336	Wheat, Unmilled	773	Wheat, Unmilled	802	Yellow Corn	391
Gold Bullion	548	Anhydrous Ammonia	95	Phosphoric Acid	166	Phosphoric Acid	268	Phosphoric Acid	215
Soybeans	489	Gold Bullion	86	Light Fuel Oils	81	Soybeans	171	Soybeans	157
Phosphoric Acid	93	Palladium	55	Anhydrous Ammonia	78	Anhydrous Ammonia	89	Anhydrous Ammonia	86
Palladium	62	Tracklaying Tractors	51	Tracklaying Tractors	57	Tracklaying Tractors	51	Cotton	61
Anhydrous Ammonia	56	Soybeans	45	Parts of Track-laying Tractors	49	Pressure Sensitive Tape	36	Pressure Sensitive Tape	59
Pressure Sensitive Tape	50	Pressure Sensitive Tape	42	Tallow	49	Petroleum Coke	34	Light Fuel Oils	49
Molybdenum Ore	41	Parts of Track-laying Tractors	39	Unwrought Nickel	38	Copper Ore	34	Palladium	42
Barley	31	Uranium Fluorides	35	Parts of Tractors	35	Insulating or Transformer Oils	28	Urea	38
Unwrought Nickel	29	Tallow	28	Petroleum Coke	33	Parts of Track-laying Tractors	26	Tallow	22
Parts of Oil and Gas Drilling Equipment	28	Unwrought Nickel	21	Palladium	31	Palladium	25	Nickel	19
Parts of Track-laying Tractors	28	Petroleum Coke	20	Copper Ore	25	Unwrought Nickel	12	Parts of Industrial Gas Turbines	17
Metal Coins	25	Metal Coins	18	Pipehandlers	24	Urea	10	Parts of Track-laying Tractors	16
Platinum Group Metals	16	Phosphoric Acid	17	Gold Bullion	21	Gasoline	10	Parts of Tractors	15

Source: USSR Division, U.S. Department of Commerce.

—Expansion of the Yenisei pulp and paper plant and Sukpa forestry complex and construction of a third stage at the Amursk facility.

—Creation of new industrial regions in Eastern Siberia and the Soviet Far East supported by vast investments, with the zone along the newly completed Baikal Amur railway having top priority.

—Development of the South Aldan iron ore deposits, including plants to process ore into pellets.

—New plants to process Udokan copper and Siberian zinc, lead, tin, and molybdenum.

In addition to these projects, the USSR's long-term program for land reclamation and drainage announced in October 1985 calls for investments of some 50 billion roubles. Land areas totaling 7 million hectares will be drained and prepared for irrigation. This will require massive quantities of heavy machinery. Industry has been instructed to plan for a supply of:

—35,000 excavators

—32,000 bulldozers

—10,000 heavy-duty wheel tractors

—4,400 tread tractors

—22,000 scraper-surfacers

—11,000 stump pullers and brush cutters

—6,300 truck-mounted cranes

—High-powered earth-moving equipment

—High-capacity trucks

—Centrifugal vertical pumps

—Other specialized equipment

To support these undertakings, new irrigation and sprinkler systems and various water-measuring devices will also have to be produced.

4

FORMS OF INDUSTRIAL COOPERATION

INDUSTRIAL cooperation between U.S. firms and Soviet enterprises is a general term that includes at least seven vehicles for accomplishing mutually advantageous trade. Starting with the forms that involve less extensive and less complex cooperation and moving to the forms that involve more extensive and more complex cooperation, the seven vehicles are:

—Science and technology agreements
—Licensing agreements
—Leasing agreements
—Turnkey projects
—Compensation arrangements
—Joint tendering
—Joint equity ventures

In an effort to establish a framework for industrial cooperation, the United States and the USSR have signed a number of agreements since 1972 that attempt to foster favorable conditions for mutually advantageous trade. In addition to the Seventh Principle of the 1972 Basic Principles of Relations, there are other agreements that provide for industrial cooperation: the 1972 U.S.-USSR Science and Technology Agreement; the 1974 U.S.-USSR Long-Term Economic, Industrial, and Technical Cooperation Agreement; and the Final Act of CSCE—Basket I.

In the brief period of U.S.-USSR trade since 1972, science and technology agreements, patent and licensing agreements, and turnkey projects have been the most widely used forms of industrial cooperation between U.S. firms and Soviet enterprises. The science and technology (S&T) agreements, which 58 U.S. firms presently have with the State Committee for Science and Technology (SCST), generally call for exchanges of scientific-technical information, production samples, and seminars, as well as for joint efforts in research and development. An S&T agreement is usually followed up by a protocol with an industrial ministry (e.g., the All-Union Chemical Industry). However, not many major accomplishments have resulted from S&T agreements thus far. Perhaps for this reason the SCST has indicated its desire to sign S&T agreements with U.S. firms only if there is a high degree of certainty that concrete cooperation in a specific field will occur.

Although patents and licensing agreements have been another field of active cooperation, estimates of Soviet purchases of U.S. licenses are not readily available, since most are acquired through turnkey projects or purchases of machinery and equipment. However, it is known that a substantial number of U.S. firms have signed contracts to provide equipment and technology for complete plants to be constructed in the USSR. Soviet enterprises have not constructed turnkey plants in the United States; they have, however, registered more than 450 patents with the U.S. Patent Office and sold licenses to at least twenty U.S. firms.

V/O Licensing is the Soviet agency charged with the purchase, sale, and promotion of licenses abroad. Experience indicates that firms interested in licensing activities with Soviet enterprises should also make contact with the ultimate end-user ministry, as well as the SCST. It is also desirable when seeking licensing arrangements to contact the appropriate Soviet industrial ministry.

Even after the potential for the sale of a license is identified, mutual interests established, and negotiations undertaken, the process generally will move forward very slowly. Soviet authorities may insist on exploring each detail before including it in a contract in order to arrive at as precise an agreement as possible.

It cannot be overemphasized that U.S. companies interested in licensing arrangements with Soviet enterprises should secure the services of an experienced attorney or consultant for assistance in drafting the contract and negotiating its provisions. This assistance can be especially useful with provisions covering matters such as the type of technical property rights to be licensed, training of technicians, flow of new improvements, duration of contract, marketing territory, compensation, arbitration, termination, and cancellation. Further details on preparation of patent and trademark applications and filing fees should also be secured in consultation with competent legal counsel.

In recent years four newer forms of industrial cooperation—leasing agreements, compensation arrangements, joint tendering, and joint equity ventures—have been devised to overcome constraints inherent in the earlier forms. These constraints relate to financing, Soviet hard-currency earnings, quality and managerial control, ownership rights, profit sharing, and a number of other issues. Under a *leasing agreement*, a U.S. firm, usually in conjunction with a private financial institution, owns the leased equipment, and the Soviet enterprise uses the equipment while making lease payments. At the end of the lease, the Soviet enterprise has the option of purchasing the equipment for a nominal amount, usually a dollar. The one barrier that has prevented leasing agreements from being used more widely is the prohibition against Western ownership in the USSR. In December 1986, however, a USSR deputy foreign trade minister indicated that the creation of a joint equity leasing company in the West might surmount this problem.

A *compensation arrangement* in the context of U.S.-USSR trade is a set of transactions involving mutual but not simultaneous deliveries of goods over an extended period, usually financed by Western credits. A compensation arrangement differs from a straight barter deal in that Soviet goods do not directly pay for the import of U.S. plants and equipment. Rather, its most basic form, a U.S.-USSR compensation arrangement consists of at least two concurrent but unlinked sales contracts with attendant financing agreements. For example, a U.S. supplier sells equipment and technology to a Soviet foreign trade organization (FTO). This transaction is financed by Western government-supported or private credits. At the same time, a Soviet FTO (possibly, but not necessarily, the same as the first one) contracts to sell to a Western customer (probably, but not necessarily, the supplier of the equipment and technology) products that will generate sufficient hard currency to repay the credits with which the goods were purchased by the first FTO. Frequently, the compensation agreement provides that the Soviet counterdeliveries consist of goods produced by the facility in the USSR that is built with the U.S. machinery and technology. The USSR Ministry of Foreign Trade currently lists an ammonia complex and the International Trade Center, both supervised by the Occidental Petroleum Company, as being the only two U.S.-USSR compensation arrangements. Other U.S.-USSR compensation projects are possible, but problems related to sufficient U.S.

financing, mutually satisfactory pricing formulas for return products, and quality control and management inputs by U.S. firms must be resolved before compensation arrangements can fulfill their potential.

The next form of industrial cooperation, *joint tendering*, involves an agreement between a U.S. firm and a Soviet enterprise to engage in the construction of a project or the manufacture of a product, usually in a third country. Typical examples have included Soviet enterprises providing hydroelectric equipment, whereas U.S. firms have contributed engineering-construction services for power facilities in several countries. This form of cooperation provides for joint control of many aspects of the projects, an arrangement that presently is not possible for such a project located in the USSR.

The most extensive form of industrial cooperation is a *joint equity venture*. In third countries, the USSR currently has more than 50 Soviet-owned companies, including Nafta B, a Brussels-based petroleum company; Moscow Narodny Bank, a London-based commercial bank; and many less-developed-country-based fishing companies. In the United States there are two joint equity ventures, the U.S.-USSR Trade and Economic Council, Inc., and the U.S.-USSR Marine Resources, Inc. The first company was established in 1973 to promote bilateral trade and economic cooperation between the United States and the USSR. The U.S.-USSR Marine Resources differs from the service-oriented U.S.-USSR Trade and Economic Council in that it was formed, in 1976, to catch, process, and store hake, a type of fish. The USSR presently does not allow joint equity ventures such as the U.S.-USSR Marine Resources between U.S. firms and Soviet enterprises in the Soviet Union. Soviet trade specialists from the USSR Academy of Sciences have indicated, however, that compensation arrangements with U.S. firms might gradually evolve into a limited form of a joint equity venture.

In terms of dollar volume of imports from the West and the projected return product flow, the USSR is more involved in countertrade, through compensation arrangements, than are all of the other Eastern European countries combined. According to Soviet officials, about 15% of Soviet trade turnover with the West in 1976 was directly related to countertrade arrangements. Soviet hard-currency earnings from compensation deals were estimated to increase from $1.5 billion in 1978 to nearly $4 billion in 1985.

From statements made by former Soviet President and Party General Secretary L. I. Brezhnev and former Council of Ministers Chairman A. N. Kosygin, it is apparent that compensation arrangements are viewed as an important method of conducting trade with the West. An early indication of Soviet interest in compensation arrangements was a 1974 restructuring in the Soviet Ministry of Foreign Trade that created a special department under

Deputy Minister V. N. Sushkov called the Main Administration for Compensation Arrangements with the West (MACAW). The function of this department is to coordinate compensation arrangements among different industrial ministries.

As a result of directives issued by the Soviet Council of Ministers (implementing a resolution approved by the Central Committee of the Communist Party in 1976), FTOs have been reorganized this year to operate on a profit and loss basis. The FTOs' boards are restructured to include representatives of foreign trade, appropriate industrial ministries, associations, and production enterprises to coordinate requirements in export markets with production quality and planning at home.

The reorganization provides for the establishment with FTOs of firms specializing in certain product lines to handle two-way trade and allows for the creation of incentives, in the form of material funds and benefits, to encourage profitable export trade. As a result of the Soviet drive to develop foreign trade activities, Western companies exporting to the USSR can expect added pressure for CT arrangements.

The USSR has reported signing more than 50 compensation arrangements involving about 60 projects with the West. The compensation transactions range from raw materials to manufactured goods. The most important agreements, however, both in value and volume, are in the areas of natural gas, fertilizers, chemicals, timber, and coal, indicating Western preference for raw materials, semiprocessed goods, and certain chemical products. (See Figure 4.1 for a model of a counterpurchase/compensation transaction.)

This Western preference is also reflected in the amount of return product the Western firm accepts as repayment for its machinery, equipment, and financing. For raw materials, especially natural gas, the amount is well over 100%; for semiprocessed and chemical products it is about 100%; and for manufactured goods it is usually much less than 100%. Compensation arrangements requiring annual counterdeliveries of plant production in the range of 20-30% would recover for the Soviet party the entire cost of the Western-supplied plant in a few years.

A Soviet compensation agreement usually involves three documents: (1) a contract between the Western exporter of machinery and equipment and the importing Soviet FTO; (2) a financing agreement between a Western bank and/or government agency and the Soviet Foreign Trade Bank (Vneshtorgbank); and (3) a contract between the Soviet FTO exporting a return product and the Western firm importing it. Sometimes a general protocol outlining the basic framework of the compensation agreement may also be signed by the Western firm and MACAW.

Figure 4.1

Model of a Counterpurchase/Compensation Transaction

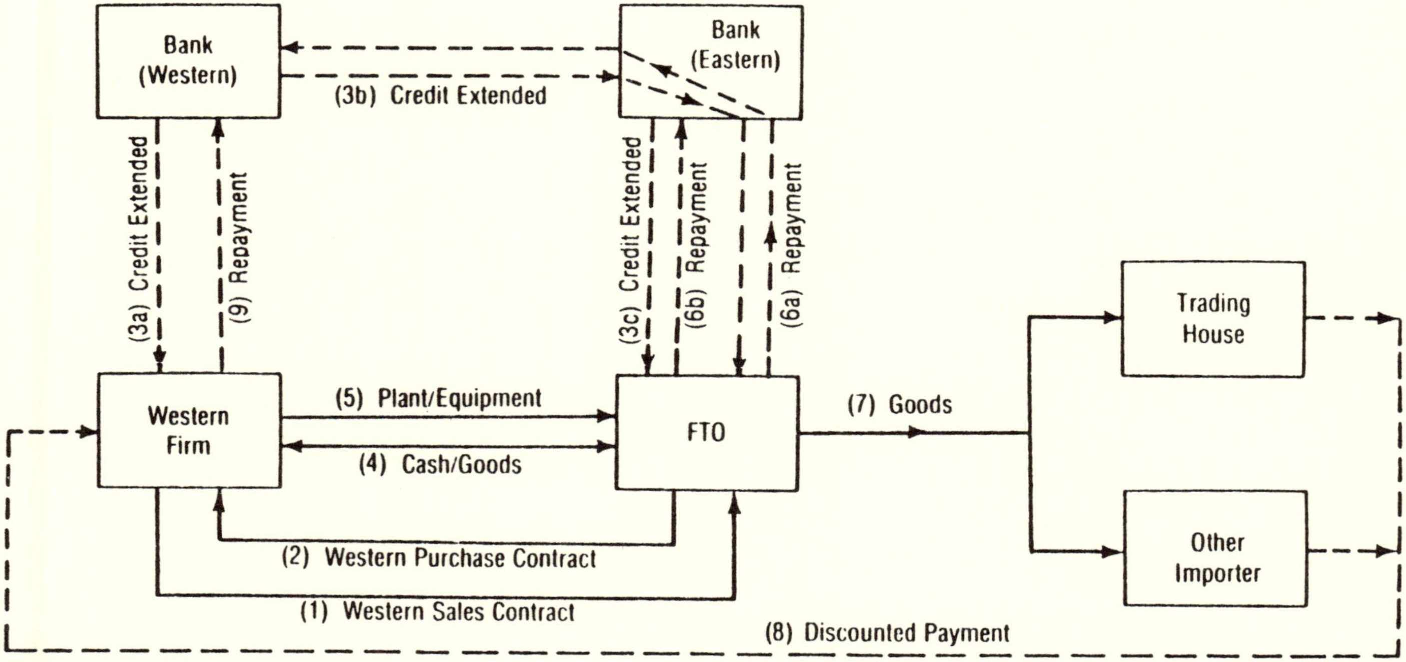

Note ---- Indicates payment and credit lines

Source: Countertrade Practices, Department of Commerce.

A number of important points are included in the above documents. The main contract usually sets forth marketing rights for both sides. Typically, the USSR will ask for the entire CMEA (Committee of Mutual Economic Assistance) area, as well as other selected countries.

The method of price calculation for the return product is also contained in the main contract. The price of the return product is usually based on some mutually agreed-upon index of representative prices, with the likely possibility of a discount. This index is adjusted every six to twelve months. Some Western firms believe it is also advisable to internationalize large-scale compensation projects in the Soviet Union by establishing a consortium of participating firms from different Western countries. Such a strategy may help to insulate the project from the uncertainties of bilateral political relations.

From all of the available evidence, it seems that the USSR will be increasing its reliance on compensation arrangements and that it plans for such transactions to account for an increasing portion of Soviet trade with the West in the years ahead. The Soviets hope to accompany this policy with a shift from the present concentration on natural resource development to that of expansion of their intermediate and finished-goods industries. They also are studying modes of cooperation that would provide the Western party with a vested interest (short of an equity position) in the joint enterprise and thereby provide for continuing managerial and quality-control assistance, as well as technology updating.

OVERCOMING COMPETITIVE CONSTRAINTS

Innovative approaches to overcoming competitive constraints may entail sourcing (making contacts) through a West European subsidiary, sourcing through a clearing-account country (chiefly Finland, Yugoslavia, or India), or developing a workable countertrade proposal. U.S. components and intermediate products are frequently processed or assembled in Western Europe for eventual shipment to the Soviet Union. If local content requirements can be met, clearing-account possibilities may be opened for products to which the Soviets have not allocated hard-currency resources. Countertrade transactions remain difficult to negotiate, especially when multiple end-use ministries or foreign trade organizations are involved in the transaction. Limited market-expansion opportunities exist for companies that are able to identify and use products supplied by the same ministries/organizations that are receiving the imported goods.

Subcontracting and licensing opportunities are also likely to increase. Many of the major projects planned for 1986-90 offer substantial subcontracting possibilities for American firms, which might compete for contracts as parts of a consortium. Since hard-currency constraints restrict equipment-purchase options, Soviet organizations have displayed greater interest in licensing production technology in many industry sectors. Technology sales on a fee basis are also beginning to play a more important role in Soviet trade.

In assessing the Soviet market, U.S. companies must analyze more than Soviet economic trends. American firms must consider U.S. export-control regulations, competitive pricing, and competitive financing. Even though each of these constraints may present difficulties, U.S. firms can compete in a number of the high-priority import sectors. A major advantage is that Soviet end users retain a high regard for the quality of American products.

5

SETTING UP A BUSINESS OFFICE IN THE USSR

A COUNTRY that will be conducting a great deal of business with the USSR may find it advantageous to establish an accredited office in Moscow. Among other benefits, an official representative office allows the firm to implement contracts with Soviet commercial organizations more readily and to obtain information of possible future projects. Since the negotiation of the 1972 Trade Agreement, Soviet policy has been to accord U.S. companies applying for accreditation treatment no less favorable consideration than that given to firms of other countries. In addition, in Article IV of the 1974 U.S.-USSR agreement to facilitate economic, industrial, and technical cooperation, the Soviets agreed to expedite the acquisition or lease of suitable business and residential premises by American firms and to facilitate the importation of essential office equipment, the hiring of local staffs, and the issuance of visas, including multiple entry-exit visas, to qualified representatives of the company.

Six Soviet organizations have the authority to accredit foreign corporations:

Ministry of Foreign Trade
32/34 Smolenskaya-Sennaya Pl.
Moscow 121200, USSR

State Committee for Science and Technology
11 Ulitsa Gor'kovo
Moscow 103009, USSR

State Bank of the U.S.S.R. (Gosbank)
12 Neglinnaya
Moscow 103016, USSR

Ministry of the Maritime Fleet
1/4 Ulitsa Zhdanova
Moscow 10325, USSR

Ministry of Civil Aviation (Aeroflot)
27 Leningradkiy Prospekt
Moscow 125167, USSR

Main Administration for Foreign Tourism (Intourist)
16 Prospekt Marksa
Moscow 103009, USSR

The Protocol Departments of the Ministry of Foreign Trade and of Intourist or the Foreign Relations Departments of the other organizations receive and are responsible for the accreditation applications and are the main points of contact for firms concerning office matters after accreditation is granted.

Although Gosbank, Intourist, and the Ministries of Civil Aviation and the Maritime Fleet process and accredit only foreign banks, travel organizations, airlines, and shipping companies, respectively, the jurisdictions of the Ministry of Foreign Trade (MFT) and the State Committee for Science and Technology (SCST) in this area are not as clearly defined.

Generally, MFT accredits companies that are engaged in ordinary commercial transactions or compensation projects and are doing a substantial annual volume of business with Soviet organizations. SCST, on the other hand, generally accredits only firms that have signed science and technology cooperation agreements and whose potential commercial deals would involve primarily substantial amounts of technology cooperation. In deciding which organizations to apply to for accreditation, U.S. companies should take into consideration these loosely defined criteria. It should be noted, however, that 23 of the 26 companies with official offices in Moscow have been accredited by the MFT, and most firms should probably approach this ministry first.

Soviet officials have indicated that there is no set minimum level of sales required before accreditation can be granted. On the other hand, a company's level of trade with the USSR and its previous dealings with Soviet organizations are two important factors considered by the Soviets when they examine an application for accreditation. There are additional factors that Soviet organizations weigh heavily when a firm seeks a permanent Moscow office: the necessity of installing, servicing, and maintaining equipment sold to the USSR; providing operating instruction or training; the potential for future business; and the degree of interest in a particular firm by its Soviet partner foreign trade organization (FTO). In many cases the size of the company and its international reputation will play a role in the accreditation process.

A corporation derives many specific benefits from having an accredited office in Moscow: permanent office space and apartments for its staff; the assistance of the USSR Department of Services to the Diplomatic Corps (known by its Russian initials UPDK); permission to install a telex and hire local personnel; listings in business directories; and importantly, multiple entry and exit visas for its American representative. Western firms usually import their own office equipment and supplies, some of which are not subject to duty. An employee of a permanent office may also import a car, household appliances, furniture, and other conveniences.

The Soviets have authorized accredited U.S. firms to employ up to five American or other non-Soviet personnel, but the exact number is always defined in the accreditation agreement. In practice, most accredited U.S. companies employ only a representative and a deputy representative, although company technicians can reside in Moscow on a long-term but limited basis. The company may employ an unlimited number of Soviets.

Although the application process is relatively easy, accreditation can and usually does take a long time (at least a year) to obtain. If official permission to open an office is received, the company often must wait many months to obtain permanent office and housing space because of the severe shortage of these facilities in Moscow. In the interim, accredited firms operate out of hotel rooms.

Details on how to apply for an accredited office through the MFT are contained in an attachment to an October 18, 1972, letter from former Soviet Foreign Trade Minister Patolichev to then Secretary of Commerce Peterson. The documents specified in paragraphs 2, 3, and 4 of these instructions comprise the actual application for accreditation. The power of attorney required in paragraph 3 should be a document signed by an officer of the corporation (e.g., president, treasurer, secretary) authorizing an individual of the firm to discuss, negotiate, and make all necessary arrangements in connection with opening an office in Moscow. The power of attorney referred to in paragraph 7 should authorize an individual of the company to be its legal representative in the USSR with all appropriate power to discuss and make commitments on commercial matters with Soviet organizations.

If any of the required information is not included, the Protocol Section of MFT will consider the application incomplete and may, or may not, inform the company that this is the case.

The instructions stipulate that the application material be "certified in accordance with established procedure by consular offices of the U.S.S.R. abroad." The procedure in the United States requires that the information enumerated in subparagraphs a, b, c, and d of paragraph 2 be witnessed by an officer of the corporation. These documents must be notarized, and then a local county clerk must certify the authority of the notary public. Next the secretary of state of the state in which the company is incorporated must certify the county clerk's stamp and signature; all of this material is then forwarded to the U.S. Department of State's Authentication Office, which, for $2.50, places its seal on the papers and signs the secretary of state's name. At this stage, the documents are properly authenticated and certified so that they may be presented to the Consular Division of the Soviet Embassy in Washington (1609 Decatur Street, NW, Washington, DC 20011), which puts the last seal on the application. It is now ready for acceptance by the Protocol Department of the Ministry of Foreign Trade.

Accreditation is normally granted for one year, and a firm must file an application annually to renew this permission. In addition, the accredited office must submit a quarterly report to the MFT concerning its activities, commercial contacts with Soviet organizations, its export and import transactions concluded, and the status of their implementation. According to the MFT, accreditation can be terminated under the following conditions: (a) after the expiration of the agreed terms; (b) if the foreign company ceases its operations abroad; (c) if the ministry finds that the office is violating the terms of its permission; or (d) if the office's activities run counter to the interests of the USSR.

WHAT THE USSR BUSINESS OFFICE COSTS

One Western firm with 115 square meters of office space and 150 square meters of apartment space in the Soviet World Trade Center complex paid the following expenses for 1985. This calculation does not include the salary and benefits for the firm's Moscow representative. They are:

	US$
Office rental (including parking garage, fee for 5 square meters of kitchen space, electricity, and maintenance)	$ 60,000
Telex, telephone, and postal expenses	15,000

Apartment rental	32,000
Office supplies, car expenses, and miscellaneous expenses	11,000
Soviet staff salary (including two secretaries, a driver, and a maid)	34,000
Travel allowances (including four trips to the West)	22,000
Entertainment	7,000
Total	$181,000

In addition, when a firm signs a space rental contract with Sovincenter, the organization responsible for administration of the Soviet World Trade Center in Moscow, it must also sign a second contract for interior design and furnishings. One company with 210 square meters of office space paid $87,000 for materials and furnishings and an additional $81,500 for labor and installation charges to outfit its offices. Certainly, there are advantages to using the Moscow World Trade Center. The complex is a complete business and residential center and offers conference, symposia, and banquet facilities and an adjoining first-class hotel with a pool. In addition, the Ministry for Foreign Trade and several Foreign Trade Organizations are nearby.

APPLYING FOR AN ACCREDITED OFFICE

WASHINGTON, D.C.
October 18, 1972

DEAR MR. MINISTER,

I have the honor to confirm, as was stated by my delegation in the course of the negotiations leading to the conclusion today of the Agreement Between the Government of the United States of America and the Government of the Union of Soviet Socialist Republics Regarding Trade, that while the Trade Representation of the Union of Soviet Socialist Republics in Washington established pursuant to Article 5 of said Agreement, its officers and staff members may engage in appropriate activities to promote trade generally between the two countries for the purpose of said Agreement, as is customary in international practice, United States legislation in force, i.e., Title 22 of the United States' Code, Sections 252-254, makes it inappropriate for the Trade Representation, its officers and staff to participate directly in the negotiation, execution or fulfillment of trade transactions or otherwise carry on trade.

I have the further honor to confirm that at such time as the United States of America shall have become a party to the Vienna Convention on Diplomatic Relations, dated April 18, 1961, and its domestic legislation shall have been revised to accord fully with the terms of Articles 29 through 45 of said Convention, regarding diplomatic privileges and immunities, my Government will be prepared to give favorable consideration to amending the Agreement Between the Government of the United States of America and the Government of the Union of Soviet Socialist Republics Regarding Trade by deleting the second and third sentences of paragraph 3 of Article 5, thus permitting officers and members of the administrative, technical and service staffs of the Commercial Office of the United States of America in Moscow and the Trade Representation of the Union of Soviet Socialist Republics in Washington to participate directly in the negotiation, execution and fulfillment of trade transactions and otherwise carry on trade.

Please accept, Mr. Minister, the assurances of my highest consideration.

Sincerely yours,

/s/
PETER G. PETERSON

MR. N. S. PATOLICHEV
  Minister of Foreign Trade of the
  Union of Soviet Socialist Republics

WASHINGTON, D.C.
October 18, 1972

DEAR MR. MINISTER,

I have the honor to acknowledge the receipt of your letter of this date, with attachments, which reads as follows:

Dear Mr. Secretary:

This is in response to your request for information on the procedures established by the Ministry of Foreign Trade for the accreditation of offices of foreign companies including United States companies, and on the facilities made available to such companies once accreditation has been approved. Such information is attached hereto.

United States companies will receive treatment no less favorable than that accorded to business entities of any third country in all matters relating to accreditation and business facilitation. Applications by United States firms for accreditation will be handled expeditiously. Any problems arising out of these applications that cannot readily be resolved through the regular procedures shall be resolved through consultation under the Joint U.S.-U.S.S.R. Commercial Commission at the request of either side.

As you have been advised, the U.S.S.R. Chamber of Commerce and Industry and the State Committee of the Council of Ministers of the U.S.S.R. for Science and Technology are establishing a large trade and economic exposition center which will include display pavilions of the various participating countries. The United States has been invited to have such a pavilion. Further, to meet the growing interest of foreign firms in establishing a permanent residence in Moscow, we have decided to construct a large trade center containing offices, hotel and apartment facilities and are asking United States companies to make proposals for and cooperate in the development and building of the trade center. The trade center will be used for, among other things, housing and office facilities for accredited United States companies.

Prior to the availability of these facilities, however, office facilities of an appropriate size in buildings accessible to trade sources will be made available as soon as possible once a United States company is accredited. The facilities to which such firms shall be entitled are explained in the attached information.

It is recognized that from time to time United States businessmen may have problems regarding such facilities which they are unable to resolve through discussions with various foreign trade organizations or other organizations. In such cases officials of my Ministry, as well as those of the State Committee of the

Council of Ministers of the USSR for Science and Technology, shall be available through their respective protocol sections for assistance in resolving these problems.

Please accept, Mr. Secretary, the assurances of my highest consideration.

Sincerely yours,

/s/
N. PATOLICHEV

MR. PETER G. PETERSON
Secretary of Commerce
  of the United States of America

I have the further honor to inform you that I have taken cognizance of the contents of the above letter and its attachments.

Please accept, Mr. Minister, the assurances of my highest consideration.

Sincerely yours,

/s/
PETER G. PETERSON

MR. N. S. PATOLICHEV
Minister of Foreign Trade of the
  Union of Soviet Socialist Republics

Attachment to letter of N. Patolichev to Secretary Peterson, October 18, 1972

SUMMARY OF BUSINESS FACILITIES FOR FOREIGN COMPANIES

An accredited company will be authorized to employ at its office not more than five American or other non-Soviet personnel, as well as Soviet personnel if desired. If requested, such communications facilities as telephones, extensions, telex equipment will be made available promptly. The name, location, and function of an accredited office will be listed in the latest issue of suitable business directories if such are published. Subject to the requirement that such equipment be exported when no longer needed by its office and subject to applicable customs regulations, accredited offices will be permitted to import, as promptly as desired, typewriters, calculators, dictation and copying equipment, one stationwagon-type automobile, as well as other equipment for the purpose of efficient and business-like operation of the office.

Subject to applicable customs regulations, each non-Soviet employee will be permitted to import a passenger car, household utilities, appliances, furniture and other necessary living items at any time within a year after the arrival of the employee in Moscow. In addition, suitable housing for such employee and family will be made available as soon as possible.

Normally, such employees and members of their families will have visas prepared for exit from and entry into the Soviet Union within three to five days. In the case of a business or personal emergency, however, a special effort is made to issue visas more promptly, and, in the case of demonstrated need, the question of granting a multiple entry and exit visa shall be examined very carefully.

INSTRUCTIONS ON THE PROCEDURE FOR THE ISSUANCE OF PERMITS FOR THE OPENING OF OFFICES OF FOREIGN FIRMS IN THE USSR AND FOR THE REGULATION OF THEIR ACTIVITY

1. Permits for the opening of offices of foreign firms in the U.S.S.R., referred to hereinafter as "Office(s)," may, in accordance with legislation in force in the U.S.S.R., be issued to foreign firms that are known on the world market and that have affirmatively presented themselves in the capacity of trade partners of Soviet foreign trade organizations with whom they have concluded especially large commercial transactions. In this connection it will also be considered that the Offices will effectively assist Soviet foreign trade organizations in the development of Soviet exports, including machinery and equipment, and also in the import of machinery and equipment that is technologically modern, and in familiarization with the newest achievements of world technology.

2. A foreign firm interested in opening an Office shall submit to the Protocol Section of the Ministry of Foreign Trade, referred to hereinafter as the "Protocol Section", an application containing the following information:

a) the name of the firm, the date of its formation, and the place of its residence;

b) the subject matter of its activity, the organs of its administration, and the persons representing the firm according to its charter (the articles of incorporation or the articles of agreement of the firm);

c) the date and place of ratification or registration of the charter (the articles of incorporation or the articles of agreement of the firm) on the basis of which the firm operates;

d) the charter capital of the firm;

e) with which Soviet foreign trade organization the firm has concluded a transaction for the performance of which the firm requests a permit for the opening of an Office, the subject matter and amount of the transaction, and the period of operation of the transaction;

f) with which other Soviet foreign trade organizations the firm has commercial relations.

The information enumerated in subparagraphs "a", "b", "c", and "d" must be confirmed by documents (by-laws, charter, articles of incorporation or articles of agreement, an extract from a trade register, etc.) attached to the application in the form of notarized copies certified in accordance with established procedure by consular offices of the U.S.S.R. abroad.

NOTE: Besides the indicated information and documents, a firm shall submit, upon inquiry by the Ministry of Foreign Trade, also other information and documents concerning the firm's activities.

3. The representative of a foreign firm presenting in its name a petition for the opening of an Office in the U.S.S.R. shall give to the Protocol Section a properly prepared power of attorney.

4. In the permit for opening an Office, issued by the Protocol Section in the accompanying form, there shall be indicated:

a) the objective of opening the Office;

b) the conditions under which the firm is permitted to have the Office;

c) the period for which the permit is issued;

d) the number of personnel at the Office who are foreign citizens and employees of the firm.

5. On questions of the purchase and sale of goods the Office may communicate with Soviet organizations that do not have the right to operate in foreign trade only through the Ministry of Foreign Trade and shall conduct its activities in observance of the laws, decisions of the Government, instructions, and rules in force in the U.S.S.R.

6. Every quarter the Office shall send to the Protocol Section written information on the Office's activities, its commercial contacts with Soviet organizations, its export and import transactions concluded, and the course of their performance.

7. The person who is authorized to be the head of the Office shall give to the Protocol Section a properly prepared power of attorney from the firm, and shall inform the Protocol Section in a timely fashion of his replacement and also of the dates of arrival in the U.S.S.R. and of departure from the U.S.S.R. of personnel of the Office.

8. An Office opened in accordance with the procedure established by the present Instructions shall apply, on questions of the furnishing to it of day-to-day services, to the Ministry of Foreign Affairs of the U.S.S.R., the Administration for Services to the Diplomatic Corps.

9. The activity of an Office shall terminate:

a) upon expiration of the period for which its permit was issued;

b) in the event of termination of the activity abroad of the firm having the Office in the U.S.S.R.;

c) upon decision of the Ministry of Foreign Trade in the event of violation by the Office of the conditions under which the firm was permitted to open the Office in the U.S.S.R., or in the event of a declaration that the Office's activity does not correspond to the interest of the U.S.S.R.

6

ADVERTISING IN THE USSR

AMERICAN firms desiring to bring their organizations and/or products to the attention of Soviet end users can advertise in Soviet trade publications and American journals circulated in the USSR or through direct mailings to plants and institutes.

Firms in most cases must work through the foreign trade organization (FTO) V/O Vneshtorgreklama, which handles foreign commercial advertising in the USSR and Soviet commercial advertising abroad. American companies can deal directly with Vneshtorgreklama headquarters in Moscow.

Advertisements can be placed in specialized Soviet journals and newspapers such as *Automotive Industry*, *Paper Industry*, and the *Economic Gazette*. (See Tables 6.1 and 6.2; Table 6.3 presents guidelines for advertising in Eastern Europe.) Although ads by foreign firms usually include company addresses, interested Soviet readers are officially referred to the State Public Scientific-Technical Library for further information. According to Vneshtorgreklama, television advertising is appropriate only for the announcement of trade fairs.

American firms can also reach Soviet end users through ads in various U.S. journals distributed in the USSR by special arrangement. In some cases these publications are special Russian-language editions, for example, Petroleum

Table 6.1
Soviet Newspapers: Description and Advertising Rates

TITLE	CIRCULATION AUDIENCE
BULLETIN OF FOREIGN COMMERCIAL INFORMATION ("BIKI")	4.700 foreign trade organisations staff, economists
ECONOMIC GAZETTE	900.000 (3 regional editions) 300.000 (1 regional edition) management, economists
EVENING LENINGRAD	150.000 residents of Leningrad
MOSCOW NEWS	780.000 total 600.000 in English 121.000 in Russian 27.000 in French 19.000 in Spanish 13.000 in Arabic Broad sections of readers
MOSCOW NEWS INFORMATION (IN ENGLISH)	120.000 (30.000 in the USSR) tourists to the USSR, English scholars in the USSR
SOVIET TRADE	1.300.000 shop assistants and management, economists, salesmen, employees
REGIONAL AND LOCAL NEWSPAPERS	—
SUPPLEMENT TO "EVENING MOSCOW"	235.000 residents of Moscow
SUPPLEMENT TO "EVENING LENINGRAD"	100.000 residents of Leningrad

FREQUENCY	PAPER SIZE / TYPE AREA (mm)	PRINTING* FEATURES	RATE PER PAGE (rbls)	
156	300 x 450 260 x 405	intaglio 2.25	1c 815	
52	285 x 400 260 x 380	offset 2.25	2c 10950 (3 regional editions) 2c 3650 (1 regional edition)	
312	420 x 570 380 x 525	offset 3.00	1c 6500	
52 (supplement 25)	300 x 420 245 x 385	letterpress (offset in Russian edition) 2.25	1-2c 9680 8150 3560 1960 1805 1695	supplement 1c 8800 7410 3235 1780 1640 1540
52	300 x 420 245 x 385	letterpress 2.25	1c 4000	
156	420 x 570 390 x 540	letterpress 2.25	1c 11000	
—	—	—	1c 9.000	
104	295 x 430 260 x 380	offset 2.25 bleeding	1-2c 5300	
52	— 260 x 380	letterpress 2.25	1-2c 5000	

Type of printing used, minimal available type height (mm), bleeding availability

Source: Advertising Services to Foreign Companies in the USSR, Press Media, V/O Vnesh-torgreklama, Moscow, 1985.

69

Table 6.2
Selected Soviet Journals: Description and Advertising Rates

TITLE	EDITORIAL CONTENTS	CIRCULATION AUDIENCE
ACCOUNTANCY	automation and mechanization of accountancy, calculators, data terminals and processors, type-writers, etc.	160.000 bankers, book-keepers, economists, etc.
AGRICULTURE ABROAD	see the title	18.500 engineering and research staff,. farm management
AGRICULTURAL CONSTRUCTION	materials, technology and technique for agricultural construction, branch economics	25.000 engineering and research staff, management
AGRICULTURAL ECONOMICS	see the title	60.000 farm management, economists, research staff
AGRICULTURAL SCIENTIFIC BULLETIN	theoretical and practical problems of agriculture, cattle-breeding, fodder production, plant protection and stimulation, mechanization and automation of the branch	8.500 agronomists, live-stock experts, research staff, management
AGROCHEMISTRY	soil science, fertilizers, chemical stimulants, herbicides, etc.	10.400 research staff
AERONAUTICS AND COSMONAUTICS	aviation and space equipment, aircrafts, gliders, parachutism	70.000 pilots, engineering staff, sportsmen
APPLIED BIOCHEMISTRY AND MICROBIOLOGY	theoretical problems of applied biochemistry and microbiology	1.500 engineering and research staff
ARCHITECTURE, CONSTRUCTION AND DESIGN	architecture, design, housing, building materials and tools, greenery-planting, etc.	6.000 architects, designers, decorators, housekeepers
ARCHITECTURE IN THE USSR	architecture, city-building, building constructions and materials	30.000 architects, projectors, research staff

Frequency	Paper size / Type area (mm)	Printing* features	RATE PER PAGE (rbls)			
			inside	cover 2	cover 3	cover 4
12	170 x 260 130 x 225	letterpress 3.00	1c 500	—	—	1c 580 2c 625
12	170 x 260	letterpress 2.25 bleeding	—	—	1c 380	1c 400
12	220 x 290 180 x 250	letterpress 2.25	—	—	1c 400 2c 440	1c 420 2c 460 3c 505 4c 590
12	170 x 260 125 x 215	letterpress 3.00	—	—	1c 460 2c 500 3c 550	1c 500 2c 550 3c 600
12	165 x 255 125 x 215	letterpress 2.25	1c 330 only 1/2 page available	—	1c 360	1c 385 2c 420
12	170 x 260 125 x 185	letterpress 3.00	—	—	—	1c 335
12	220 x 290 185 x 260	intaglio 2.25	1c 700	—	1c 770 2c 840	—
6	170 x 260 125 x 185	letterpress 3.00	—	—	—	1c 300
6	230 x 230 200 x 200	letterpress 2.25 bleeding on inside covers	1c 400	1c 440 2c 485 3c 530 4,5c 615	1c 440 2c 485 3c 530 4,5c 615	1c 470 2c 510 3c 560 4,5c 650
12	220 x 290 190 x 270	letterpress 2.25	1c 560	—	1c 615	1c 650

* Type of printing used, minimal available type height (mm), bleeding availability

Source: Advertising Services to Foreign Companies in the USSR, Press Media, V/O Vnesh-torgreklama, Moscow, 1985.

71

Table 6.3
Advertising in Eastern Europe: A Corporate Checklist

For most companies, advertising is a way of life . . . but what about Eastern Europe? What requirements must be considered when setting corporate policy or working with the state advertising agency in each Comecon country? Given below is a checklist of the chief elements that should be considered by regional managers before launching or evaluating the results of an East European advertising campaign.

Corporate policy

- Determine whether company products are actually suitable for advertising in Comecon.
- Remember that a successful campaign in the West may not be relevant to Comecon sales.
- Decide the purpose of a campaign. Is it to influence pending negotiations? Cultivate end-user specialists? Or build a groundswell of general consumer demand?
- Determine the target audience. Is it FTO purchasing officials? Enterprise directors? R&D officials? The general public?
- Remember that local officials will not authorize advertising for products that are unlikely to obtain import licenses.
- Establish headquarters consensus on the size of the advertising budget and length of the campaign.
- Don't anticipate immediate results. Two to three years may be necessary to get a message across.

Dealing with state ad agencies

- Treat the state advertising agency contract with the same care used in any other EE operation.
- For cost planning, anticipate that most ad agency fees are modest compared with high-flying agencies in the West.
- Request that the agency provide a client list as a guide for evaluation.
- Seek the opinion of other Western clients on agency performance and shortcomings.
- Before signing a contract, evaluate promotion materials prepared for other Western firms.
- Insist on a high-ranking agency official as permanent liaison; do not accept junior staffers who are rotated frequently.
- When selecting media, remember that by expenditure 50% of Western advertisements is targeted for technical-scientific periodicals; 20% for newspapers and magazines; and 20% for other media.
- Don't arbitrarily reject agency advice on advertising themes; agency officials can help tailor publicity to local market preferences and peculiarities.

Technical-scientific periodicals

- Remember that technical press advertising works best in countries with relative decentralization: Yugoslavia, Poland, Hungary.

- Specialized publication ads are also valuable in the Soviet Union because of its size and the difficulty in reaching decision influencers.
- Be prepared for selection problems due to the large number of different technical periodicals—estimated at 1,000 for all of EE.
- Make the advertisement serve as an information source: except for the USSR (where not allowed), include a detachable coupon enabling interested readers to write for catalogs.
- Don't forget to refer end-user readers to the FTO that actually imports company products.
- If an EE state sales agency is employed, list the agency's telephone and telex number.

General press and TV

- Ensure that the advertisement is direct and graphically appealing; many East European pictoral ads are vague and dull.
- Visual advertisement generally should avoid Western backdrops; an ad supposedly photographed in a Polish kitchen should not be shot in southern California.
- Exception: some visual ads—particularly for soft drinks and jeans—may seek to create a Western image with models deliberately photographed in London or Los Angeles.
- For TV, linkage of advertisements to program content can follow tried and traditional Western practice: e.g. shaving cream (produced by local licensee) promoted during soccer games.

Direct mail campaigns

- Note that Western companies are "recommended" —in practice required—to channel direct mail efforts through the state advertising agencies.
- Inspect suggested mailing lists submitted by the agencies. Ensure that addressee officials have not been rotated or replaced.
- Include only technical, not commercial, information for targeted end-users. Never quote prices or offers.
- Use the local East European language. Only a minority of addressees will read a Western language.
- Beware of the poor quality of East European paper and printing. If necessary, print brochures on quality paper in the West.

Source: Reprinted from the November 7, 1980, issue of *Business Eastern Europe*, p. 357, with the permission of the publisher, Business International Corporation.

Engineer Publishing Company's *Petroleum Engineer*, Gulf Publishing Company's *Hydrocarbon Processing*, McGraw-Hill's *Electronics*, and Miller Freeman Publishing's *World Coal* (the annual November survey issue). A number of American journals have agreements with the Soviets permitting photocopying of the English version, including advertisements, and distribution to institutions and technical specialists. At least one of them, *Datamation*, is permitted to insert special advertisements translated into Russian. The Welt Publishing Company has an arrangement with the USSR news agency TASS enabling it to place items on new products and processes in a Soviet bulletin on scientific-technical developments abroad.

Under an agreement with Vneshtorgreklama, Chilton International published in Russian a nine-volume encyclopedia of American engineering and industry for distribution to Soviet end users. U.S. firms purchased space in the company catalog section of each volume, such as Number I, *Metal Production, Machine-building and Metalworking*; and volumes on building and construction, oil and gas, food processing and packaging, and forest industries and pulp and paper.

Vneshtorgreklama offers an advertising mailing service directed toward Soviet end users. The coverage of a mailing campaign must be taken on faith: firms cannot follow up on their own, since Vneshtorgreklama does not provide end-user lists and requires that all Soviet responses to the foreign firm go through Vneshtorgreklama itself. Material distributed by the U.S. firm may not contain detachable coupons or invitations to forward requests for further information directly to the advertiser; however, it may refer end users to the USSR State Public Scientific-Technical Library for company catalogs and a company prospectus.

CATALOG-DISTRIBUTION SYSTEM

American firms can conveniently and inexpensively acquaint scientific-technical and production personnel in Soviet end-user organizations with their capabilities and products by distributing catalogs through the USSR State Public Scientific-Technical Library System. Information received by the system is passed through more than 85 industrial-information agencies, 15 republic divisions, and about 10,000 scientific-technical bureaus. These bureaus provide technical information services to end-user personnel, including officials, seeking and evaluating needed equipment.

Catalogs are placed in the main library and its branches. The library publishes abstracts of new catalogs in a biweeky bulletin, which has a circulation of about 40,000. End-user personnel then request copies of interest to them.

In addition, foreign firms advertising in Soviet publications now generally refer Soviet readers to the library for a copy of the firm's prospectus.

Library officials indicate that there is a great unsatisfied demand by Soviet industrial enterprises for U.S. catalogs. For a marketing effort, a minimum of 100 catalogs per company is needed to reach an adequate number of end users. With a very small investment, a firm is able to reach many potential end users in the USSR. Catalogs and brochures should be sent to the Division of Industrial Catalogues, State Public Scientific-Technical Library, Ploshchad Nogina 2/5, Moscow 103074, USSR, or mailed to the U.S. Commercial Office, American Embassy, APO New York 09862, for delivery to the library.

7

TRADE FAIRS AND EXHIBITIONS IN THE USSR

THE most convenient and effective way to acquaint Soviet traders, economic decision makers, and end users with U.S. products is through participation in various types of industrial exhibitions. These exhibitions are the primary commercial events in the individual commodity fields in the USSR. They attract most of the major Soviet buyers and influential government officials charged with maintaining and improving performance in the respective branches of the Soviet economy.

The Soviets distinguish between three types of international industrial exhibitions: major international exhibitions, which are large-scale fairs, where both Soviet and foreign participation is permitted; international specialized exhibitions, which are usually more limited in thematic scope; and foreign exhibitions, where participation is limited to foreign exhibitors.

Although some exhibitions are held in other cities of the USSR such as Leningrad, Kiev, and Kishinev, the major exhibitions are usually conducted in Moscow's Sokolniki Fair Grounds or at the new exhibit area of the Moscow International Trade Center, both located within easy access of most of the decision-making ministries. Major officials of the ministries, state committees, foreign trade organizations (FTOs), and technical and scientific institutes all make a point of attending these exhibitions. General trade fairs draw large crowds, whereas more specialized exhibitions usually attract key professionals.

All exhibitions in the USSR are sponsored or cosponsored by the USSR Chamber of Commerce and Industry, Soviet economic organizations or FTOs, and city councils. In some cases they are organized by the Soviet sponsors and in other cases by promoters in the United States or other Western countries. By special agreement, and usually under cosponsorship by the Soviet government and the exhibiting country's government, one-nation exhibitions are often organized to show Soviet buyers the commodities produced only in the exhibiting country. These exhibitions may carry a wide variety of capital and consumer goods or may be limited to the products of one industry. In the latter case, the exhibition is usually organized in the exhibiting country by an industry association interested in a given product line.

One-company exhibits that invite key target audiences are one of the best methods of reaching both the decision makers and the technicians in the USSR. A company that wishes to stage such a solo exhibition must obtain the cosponsorship of the corresponding FTO or ministry.

The Trade Promotion Division of the U.S. Department of Commerce sponsors U.S. participation in major international exhibitions in the Soviet Union at least twice a year. U.S. firms interested in obtaining information on Soviet trade fairs, applying for participation, or receiving permission to organize a solo exhibit should contact Expocentr, USSR Chamber of Commerce and Industry, Sokolnichesky val 1-a, Moscow 107232, telephone 268-7083, telex 7185 UIVTPP SU.

CONFERENCES, SEMINARS, AND EXHIBITS

Exhibitions in the USSR frequently are accompanied by conferences and seminars that explain the applications and functioning of the products exhibited and branch out into related topics within the general framework of the exhibition. Such seminars and conferences are most useful and enlightening to the Soviets.

Conferences and seminars not connected with exhibitions have some utility, but this is limited by Soviet requirements that the programs be held on a purely technical level and not be primarily a source of promotional materials for a given product line. The conferences and seminars, however, provide an opportunity for establishing informal contacts, which later can be used for commercial purposes.

The Trade Promotion Division of the U.S. Department of Commerce also sponsors seminars/exhibits in the U.S. Commercial Office in Moscow. They involve more specific themes than do trade fairs. The seminar portions are limited to problem-solving approaches or state-of-the-art presentations regarding their products, whereas the exhibit portions afford the U.S. participant the opportunity to display equipment and models. Representatives of appropriate ministries and FTOs, technicians, and end users are invited to attend these Commercial Office events.

Any American firm can stage its own promotion event—exhibit, seminar, conference, and so on—in the U.S. Commercial Office (USCO) when space is available. The USCO will provide all of the basic services that are available during Commerce-sponsored events, including assistance in publicizing the event. A firm may also arrange such promotion events at the U.S.-USSR Trade and Economic Council or through Vneshtorgreklama.

Companies use the Commercial Office's 1,170 square-foot exhibit area, which can seat 100 persons when participating in Commerce-sponsored seminar/exhibits or technical sales seminars. In addition, as long as space is available, any firm can use the USCO at any time for its own promotional events. Equipment and space are free; communications, receptions, interpreters, and freight forwarding are at cost. Commercial Office facilities also can be used for conferences, commercial negotiations, or receptions with Soviet officials. In connection with its promotional program, the USCO provides simultaneous translation equipment; slide, movie, and overhead projectors; chartboards; and easels.

Promotional materials detailing international exhibitions in the USSR and general conditions of participation in international exhibitions are shown on the following pages.

1986—1990 гг.

•

МЕЖДУНАРОДНЫЕ ВЫСТАВКИ
В СССР

•

INTERNATIONAL EXHIBITIONS
IN THE USSR

THE USSR CHAMBER OF COMMERCE AND INDUSTRY
ALL-UNION ASSOCIATION
EXPOCENTR

ДОБРО ПОЖАЛОВАТЬ
НА МЕЖДУНАРОДНЫЕ ВЫСТАВКИ В СССР!

Международные выставки в СССР пользуются широкой известностью среди деловых кругов различных стран мира.

Выставки предоставляют экспонентам благоприятные возможности:

— показать свои производственные достижения,

— осуществить широкую рекламу товаров,

— обменяться научно-техническим опытом с коллегами из других стран,

— заключить коммерческие сделки,

— установить новые деловые связи.

К услугам экспонентов:

— удобные выставочные площади,

— изготовление и художественное оформление стендов и офисов, готовые стенды,

— транспортировка и экспедиционная обработка грузов,

— машины и механизмы,

— квалифицированные переводчики,

— обслуживающий персонал.

Организаторы выставок готовы оказать необходимую помощь участникам и гостям международных выставок в СССР.

За справками просим обращаться по адресу: СССР, 107113, Москва, Сокольнический вал, 1а, В/О «Экспоцентр»

Телефон: 268-70-83

Телекс: 411185 ЭКСПО СУ

WELCOME TO THE INTERNATIONAL EXHIBITIONS IN THE USSR!

International exhibitions in the USSR enjoy great popularity among the business circles throughout the world.

The exhibitions offer the participants favourable opportunities to:

—show their achievements and products;

—launch a wide publicity compaign;

—exchange scientific and technological experience with their foreign colleagues;

—make commercial deals;

—establish new business contacts.

The exhibitors have at their disposal:

—well-equipped exhibition areas;

—stands and offices manufacturing and decoration, prefabricated stands;

—cargo transportation and forwarding;

—machines and mechanisms;

—well-trained interpreters;

—personnel.

The organizers of the exhibitions will render the participants and guests of the international exhibitions in the USSR every assistance they might need.

Address your inquiries to: USSR, 107113, Moscow, Sokolnicheski Val, 1a, V/O "Expocentr"

Telephone: 268-70-83

Telex: 411185 EXPO SU

1986 г.
4-я международная выставка „Системы и средства связи"

г. Москва   27 мая — 5 июня

Системы и аппаратура спутниковой и космической связи, аппаратура радиорелейных и тропосферных линий связи; системы и аппаратура передачи информации по кабельным, волноводным, волоконно-оптическим линиям связи; коммутационное оборудование и аппаратура передачи данных; системы и аппаратура радиосвязи; телевидение и радиовещание; электронно-вычислительные средства для автоматизации и управления сетями и аппаратурой средств связи; производство микросборок и функциональных устройств на новых физических принципах функционирования; новые методы конструирования и проектирования; компоненты и материалы для радиоэлектронных изделий, аппаратуры и систем передачи информации; оборудование и аппаратура для почтовой связи; бытовая радиоэлектронная аппаратура; автоматизированные комплексы и приборы контроля и измерения; технологическое оборудование и процессы; радиолюбительство.

1986
4th International Exhibition "Communication Means and Facilities"

Moscow   May 27—June 5

Systems and equipment for space and satellite communication; radio relay and troposcatter communication systems; systems and equipment for transmission through cable, waveguide and fibre-optics communication lines; commutator equipment and transmission systems; radio communication systems and equipment; television and broadcasting equipment; computers for automation and control over communication network and equipment; microassembly and functional devices based on new physical principles of operation; new design methods; components and materials for radio-electronic items, equipment and transmission systems; mail service equipment; domestic radio electronic equipment; automated units and control instruments; technological equipment and processes; radio amateuring.

3-я международная выставка „Железнодорожный транспорт"

ст. Щербинка Московской обл.   8—17 июля

Техника железнодорожного транспорта и системы управления; машины и оборудование для строительства и ремонта железнодорожного пути; автоматика, телемеханика, связь и вычислительная техника на железнодорожном транспорте; технология работы и системы управления эксплуатационной деятельностью железной дороги; научно-техническая литература.

3rd International Exhibition "Railway Transport"

st. Scherbinka near Moscow   **July 8-17**

Railway engineering and control systems; railways building and repair machines and equipment; automatic machines, telemechanics, communication and computers in railway transport; technology and railway functioning control systems; scientific and technological literature.

3-я международная выставка „Оборудование для продовольственных отраслей промышленности, торговли и общественного питания"

г. Москва   3—12 сентября

Поточные линии, машины и оборудование для переработки молока и молочных продуктов, производства масла, маргарина, мыла, переработки мяса, субпродуктов, изготовления полуфабрикатов, производства белковых продуктов, розлива пищевых жидкостей, сахарной и кондитерской промышленности, хлебопекарного и макаронного производства, переработки овощей и фруктов, фасовки и упаковки пищевых продуктов; средства транспортировки, погрузки и хранения упакованных и неупакованных продуктовых товаров; торгово-холодильное оборудование, оборудование для плодоовощных баз, механизации и автоматизации предприятий общественного питания и торговли.

3rd International Exhibition "Equipment for the Food Industry, Trade and Public Catering"

Moscow   September 3-12

Flow lines, machines and equipment for milk and milk products processing, production of butter, margarine, soap; meat and chitterlings processing, manufacture of semiproducts, protein products production, liquid products bottling, equipment for the sugar and confectionery industry, bakery, fruits and vegetables processing, foodstuffs wrapping and packaging; packed and non-packed foodstuffs transportation, loading and storage means; refrigerators for trade, equipment for storehouses, mechanization and automation of trade and public catering establishments.

1987 г.
2-я международная выставка
„Технология изготовления
строительных материалов
и конструкций“

г. Москва   27 мая — 5 июня

Средства автоматизации производственных процессов на предприятиях стройиндустрии; изделия химической промышленности для промышленного, сельскохозяйственного и жилищно-гражданского строительства; технологические процессы и оборудование для производства прогрессивных строительных материалов и конструкций, в том числе энергосберегающие; индивидуальные и групповые средства защиты работающих; механизированный инструмент для строительных и монтажных работ; строительные манипуляторы; микропроцессорная техника для бетоносмесительных, асфальтосмесительных и других установок; приборы для экспресс-диагностики, контроля расхода топлива, тахографы; строительные материалы; спецодежда строительных рабочих.

1987
2nd International Exhibition
"Building Materials and Constructions
Manufacturing Technology"

Moscow   May 27 — June 5

Production processes automation means at the building industry enterprises; chemicals for industrial, agricultural and construction engineering; technological processes and equipment for the manufacture of new building materials and improved constructions (including energy saving); individual and group protection means; building and assembly mechanisms; manipulators; microprocessors for concrete and asphalt mixers and other units; express diagnostic instruments, fuel meters, tachographs; building materials; overalls.

4-я международная выставка „Электротехническое оборудование и линии электропередачи"

г. Москва   15—24 июля

Электротехническое оборудование для производства и передачи электроэнергии; оборудование для добывающих отраслей промышленности, металлургии, машиностроения, станкостроения, сельского хозяйства; термическое оборудование; сварочное оборудование; электротехнические изделия; механизмы, приспособления и специальный инструмент для электромонтажных работ; электроконструкции; электромонтажные изделия и материалы; бытовые электроприборы и машины; научно-техническая литература.

4th International Exhibition "Electrotechnical Equipment and Power Transmission Lines"

Moscow   July 15—24

Electrotechnical equipment for power generation and transmission; equipment for the extractive industry, metallurgy, machinebuilding, agriculture; thermal equipment; welding equipment; electrotechnical items; mechanisms, devices and special purpose tools for wiring; electric constructions; wiring items and materials; domestic electric equipment and machines; scientific and technological literature.

6-я международная выставка „Химия"

г. Москва   10—19 сентября

Машины, оборудование и технологические схемы для производства новых химических материалов; контрольно-измерительная аппаратура и приборы в производстве синтетических материалов и изделий; машины, оборудование и технологические схемы для производства минеральных удобрений и химических средств защиты растений; оборудование и приборы для производства продуктов микробиологического синтеза; машины и оборудование для транспортировки, погрузочно-разгрузочных работ и хранения химических веществ; защита от коррозии; использование полимерных материалов в машиностроении, строительстве и на транспорте; научно-техническая литература.

6th International Exhibition "Chemistry"

Moscow   September 10—19

Machines, equipment and technology for the manufacture of new chemicals; control and measuring equipment and instruments in the manufacture of synthetic materials and articles; machines, equipment and technology for the manufacture of mineral fertilizers and plant protection chemicals; equipment and instruments for the manufacture of microbiological synthesis products; machines and equipment for chemicals transportation, handling and storage; corrosion resistants; use of polymer materials in machine-building, construction and transport; scientific and technological literature.

1988 г.
4-я международная выставка
„Аппаратура и приборы
для научных исследований"

г. Москва

Аппаратура, приборы и оборудование для научных исследований в области физики, химии, энергетики, машиностроения, биологии, медицины и охраны окружающей среды; научно-техническая литература.

1988
4th International Exhibition
"Scientific Research Equipment
and Instruments"

Moscow

Apparatus, instruments and equipment for scientific research in physics, chemistry, energetics, machine-building, biology, medicine, environment protection; scientific and technological literature.

3-я международная выставка „Строительные и дорожные машины и средства механизации строительно-монтажных работ"

г. Москва

Машины для производства земляных работ, разработки мерзлых грунтов и скальных пород, машины для свайных работ; погрузочно-разгрузочное оборудование; дорожно-строительные машины; машины для строительства мелиоративных систем; машины для строительства нефте- и газопроводов; машины для производства бетонных работ; строительно-отделочные машины; оборудование по обслуживанию, диагностике и ремонту строительных и дорожных машин; машины и механизмы для специальных строительных работ; ручной механизированный инструмент и средства малой механизации для монтажных и строительных работ; транспорт для бездорожья и полярных условий; унифицированные агрегаты, узлы и детали строительных и дорожных машин; научно-техническая литература.

3rd International Exhibition "Construction and Road-Building Machines and Erection Mechanization Means"

Moscow

Earth-moving machines, frozen soil and rock drillers, pile driving and extracting machines; handling equipment; road-building machines; land reclamation systems building machines; oil- and gas-pipeline laying machines; concrete placement machines; construction finishing machines; building and road-making machines maintenance, diagnostic and repair equipment; special purpose building machines and mechanisms; small-size erection and building tools; vehicles for impassable roads and the polar zone; unified plants, joints and components for construction and road-building machines; scientific and technological literature.

4-я международная выставка „Оборудование и технологические процессы в легкой промышленности"

г. Москва

Оборудование для первичной обработки натуральных волокон, производства, текстурирования и кручения химических волокон; прядильное оборудование для натуральных и химических волокон; ткацкое оборудование; красильно-отделочное оборудование; оборудование для производства нетканых материалов; оборудование для трикотажного, швейного и мехового производства, производства обуви и кожгалантерейных изделий; средства автоматизации технологических процессов; измерительные приборы и аппаратура.

4th International Exhibition "Equipment and Technological Processes in the Light Industry"

Moscow

Machinery for natural fibres preliminary processing, for man-made fibres production, texturing and twisting; spinning machinery for natural and man-made fibres; weaving machinery; dyeing and finishing machinery; machinery for non-wooven fabrics production; knitting, sewing and fur treatment machinery, shoe and haberdashery production machinery; automation means for production processes; measuring devices and apparatus.

1989 г.
3-я международная выставка
„Средства автоматизации
производственных процессов"

г. Москва

Электронные машины и комплексные системы для автоматизации управления технологическими процессами, производствами и объектами непроизводственной сферы; вычислительная техника, приборы и средства автоматизации, прогрессивное технологическое оборудование; научно-техническая литература.

1989
3rd International Exhibition
"Automation Means
for Production Processes"

Moscow

Computers and automatic complexes for production processes control, for plants and non-productive establishments control; computers, instruments, automation means, new production equipment; scientific and technological literature.

2-я международная выставка „Оборудование, приборы и инструменты для металлообрабатывающей промышленности"

г. Москва

Станки с программным управлением, в том числе многооперационные с автоматической сменой инструмента; автоматические линии; станки для силового и прецизионного шлифования; станки для электрофизикохимических, ультразвуковых, светолучевых и вибрационных методов обработки; кузнечно-прессовое оборудование с программным управлением; оборудование для изготовления изделий из металлических порошков; автоматические манипуляторы с программным управлением; контрольно-измерительное оборудование; приборы и инструменты.

2nd International Exhibition "Equipment, Appliances and Instruments for the Metal-Working Industry"

Moscow

Programmed control machines including multipurpose machines with automatic tools' substitution; transfer lines; machines for power and precision grinding; machines for electrochemical and physical treatment, for ultrasonic, light-beam and vibration treatment; machines for production articles of metal powders; automatic devices with programmed control; test equipment; appliances and instruments.

4-я международная выставка
„Машины, оборудование и приборы
для лесной, целлюлозно-бумажной
и деревообрабатывающей промышленности"

г. Москва

Машины для лесовосстановления и защитного лесоразведения; машины и средства борьбы с лесными пожарами и вредителями леса; машины и оборудование лесопильного производства; оборудование и механизмы для первичной обработки леса; оборудование и технологические процессы целлюлозно-бумажного производства; машины и оборудование деревообрабатывающего производства; средства механизации погрузочно-разгрузочных работ и пакетирования; технология и комплектное оборудование мебельного производства; дереворежущий инструмент и оборудование для его подготовки к работе; средства автоматизированного управления технологическими процессами и предприятиями; транспорт леса и продукции лесопереработки; контрольно-измерительная аппаратура и приборы; образцы продукции и научно-техническая литература.

4th International Exhibition
"Machinery, Equipment and Instruments
for the Pulp and Paper, Timber
and Wood-Working Industry"

Moscow

Machinery for reforestation and protective afforestation; means and machinery for forest fire and forest pests fighting; sawing equipment and machinery; equipment and mechanisms for timber preliminary treatment; equipment and production processes in the pulp and paper industry; machinery and equipment for timber treatment: mechanization means for timber handling and bundling; techniques and complete equipment for the furniture manufacturing; wood-cutting tools and maintenance equipment; automatic control for production processes and plants; timber and timber products transportation; control and measuring equipment and instruments; samples of materials and products: scientific and technological literature.

1990 г.
4-я международная выставка
„Здравоохранение, медицинская техника и лекарственные препараты"

г. Москва

Организация и основные направления развития здравоохранения; санитарно-эпидемиологическая служба; медицинская техника; электронная, диагностическая и физиотерапевтическая аппаратура; приборы и аппаратура, применяемые в отоларингологии, стоматологии, офтальмологии, гастроэнтерологии и в других областях медицины; лабораторная техника, медицинские инструменты, больничное оборудование; протезно-ортопедические изделия; лекарственные препараты; научно-техническая литература.

1990
4th International Exhibition
"Public Health, Medical Equipment and Drugs"

Moscow

Organization and main tendencies in public health service development; sanitary-epidemiological service; medical equipment; electronic, diagnostic and physiotherapy apparatus; apparatus and devices used in otolaryngology, stomatology, ophthalmology, gastroenterology and other branches of medicine; laboratory equipment, medical instruments, hospital equipment; prosthetic and orthopaedic articles; drug preparations; scientific and technological literature.

3-я международная выставка
„Оборудование, машины, приборы
и средства автоматизации
для угольной промышленности"

г. Донецк

Горно-проходческие машины и оборудование; очистное оборудование; шахтный транспорт; оборудование для механизации вспомогательных работ; машины и оборудование для открытых горных работ; оборудование углеобогатительных фабрик; комплексное использование угля и отходов обогащения; аппаратура и средства автоматизации и связи; охрана труда и техника безопасности; горноспасательное дело и борьба с подземными пожарами; научно-техническая литература.

3rd International Exhibition "Equipment, Machinery, Apparatus and Means of Automation for the Coal Industry"

Donetsk

Shaft-sinking machinery and equipment; purification equipment; shaft transport facilities; equipment for mechanization of auxiliary operations; machinery and equipment for open-cast mining; equipment for coal preparation plants; complex utilization of coal and preparation wastes; communication and automation apparatus and equipment; labour protection and safety measures; rescue and underground fire-fighting equipment; scientific and technological literature.

5-я международная выставка „Современные средства воспроизводства и использования водных биоресурсов"

г. Ленинград

Воспроизводство и охрана рыбных запасов; товарное рыбоводство; флот рыбной промышленности; судовая радиоэлектроника; орудия промышленного рыболовства; оборудование для добычи рыбы и морепродуктов; производство упаковочных материалов; оборудование для погрузочно-разгрузочных работ и транспортировки грузов; холодильное оборудование; охрана труда в рыбном хозяйстве; производство сетей, делей, канатов и изготовление рыболовных снастей; автоматизированные системы управления предприятиями, флотом, отраслью в рыбном хозяйстве.

5th International Exhibition "Modern Means of Reproduction and Exploitation of Water Biological Resources"

Leningrad

Reproduction and protection of fish resources; commodity fish-breeding; fishing fleet; radioelectronic equipment for ships; equipment for commercial fishing; equipment for fishing and sea food extraction; packing materials production; facilities for cargo handling and transportation; refrigerating equipment; labour protection in the fishing industry; manufacturing of fish-nets, hoists, ropes and fishing-gears; automatic control systems for plant, fleet and branch in the fish industry.

5-я международная выставка „Сельскохозяйственные машины, оборудование и приборы"

г. Москва

Почвообрабатывающие машины и оборудование; химия в сельском хозяйстве; машины и оборудование для мелиоративных работ; энергетические и транспортные средства и оборудование; средства малой механизации; уборка трав и силосных культур и производство зеленых кормов; агропромышленные комплексы; машины и оборудование для комплексной механизации работ в животноводстве и птицеводстве; научные исследования в области тракторного и сельскохозяйственного машиностроения машины для лесовосстановления и защитного лесоразведения;

5th International Exhibition "Agricultural Machinery, Equipment and Instruments"

Moscow

Tillers and implement; chemistry in agriculture; machinery and equipment for melioration; power generation, transportation means and equipment; small-scale mechanization; grass- and forage harvesting, green-cut fodder production; agro-industrial enterprises; machines and equipment for overall mechanization in cattle- and poultry breeding; scientific research in tractor and agricultural machine building; machinery for reforestation and protective afforestation.

Информацию о проведении международных **выставок** в **СССР** дают также следующие организации:

The following organizations will also supply information on the International Exhibitions in the USSR:

Vertretung der Handels- und Industriekammer
der UdSSR in Österreich
Opernring 4/2/6
A-1010 Wien
Österreich

Représentation de la Chambre de Commerce et
d'Industrie de l'URSS en Belgique
3, rue Joseph 11
1040 Bruxelles
Belgique

Predstavitelstvo Torgovo-promyshlennoj
palaty SSSR
Bul. Patriarha Eftimia 44
Sofia
Bulgaria

The British-Soviet Chamber of Commerce
2 Lowndes Street
London SW 1 X GET
England

Szovjetunio Kereskedelmi és Iparkamarja
Madyarorszagi Kepviselete
Nepstadion ut., 71
1143, Budapest, XIV
Magyar

Vertretung der Handels- und Industriekammer
der UdSSR in der DDR
Leipziger Str. 60, 05-03
108 Berlin
DDR

Representation of the USSR Chamber of Commerce
and Industry in India
Safdarjang Enclave a-1/6
111 0029 New Delhi
India

Camera di Commercio Italo-Sovietica
Via Locatelli
5-Milano
Italia

Przedstawicielstwo Izby
Handlowo-Promyslowej ZRSS w PRL
Al. Jerozolimskie 101 m. 3
02-011 Warszawa
Polska

Repressentasão de Camara do Comercio e Industria da URSS
em Portugal
Rua Actor Antonio Silva 5, 12° Esq.,
Lisboa 5, Portugal

Reprezentanta Camerci de Comert si Industrie a URSS
in R. S. Romania
Bucuresti
Sectorul 1, str. Alex. Sahia, nr. 48
Romania

The US — USSR Trade and Economic Council
1211 Avenue of The Americas
New York N.Y. 10036
USA

Suomalais-Neuvostoliittolainen
Kauppakanari
Ealevankatu 13 A 1
00100 Helsinki 10
Finland

Chambre de Commerce Franco-Soviétique
Avenue Franklin D. Roosevelt, 22
Paris 8e
France

Československo-Sovětska
Obhodni Komora
U Laboratoře 6, 16200
Praha 6
CSSR

Représentation de la Chambre de Commerce
et d'Industrie de l'URSS
Stauffacher Str., 28
8004 Zürich
Schweiz

Prestavnistwo TPP SSSR
ul. Generala Zhdanova, 16
Beograd
Jugoslavija

General Conditions of Participation
in the International Exhibition in the USSR

The organizer of the International Exhibitions in the USSR is Vsesojuznoje Objedinenije "Expocentr" of the USSR Chamber of Commerce and Industry.
Current account No. 60800024 with the USSR Bank for Foreign Trade, Moscow.
Address: V/O "Expocentr", 1a Sokolnichesky Val, Moscow, 107113, USSR.
Telephone: 268-58-74
Telex: 411185 EXPO SU
The address of specialized firms "Mezhvystavka", "Transexpo", and "Inform-reklama" is the same.

VALID FROM 1st JANUARY, 1983

International Exhibitions in the USSR are sponsored by Vsesojuznoje Objedinenije "Expocentr" of the USSR Chamber of Commerce and Industry in collaboration with economic organizations and Foreign Trade Associations and the Executive Committees of the City Soviets.

V/O "Expocentr" carries out all work involved in preparing, holding and closing of the Exhibition through specialised firms: the Firm of International Exhibitions in the USSR "Mezhvystavka", the Firm of Transportation and Forwarding Services "Transexpo", the Firm of Information Advertising Services "Informreklama", Department of Design of Foreign Exhibitions in the USSR "KOIV", as well as other departments of V/O "Expocentr".

The present General Conditions of Participation in the International Exhibitions in the USSR (hereinafter referred to as "the General Conditions of Participation"), valid from 1st January, 1983, are binding upon all Exhibitors.

The information on time and site of an Exhibition, as well as the normative documents: themes, Service Guide, Transport Conditions, Tariff for Transportation and Forwarding Services, application forms for participation are published separately and are considered as an integral part of the General Conditions of Participation.

§ 1. AIMS OF THE EXHIBITION

Demonstration of the latest achievements in technology and manufacturing of machinery, equipment, instruments, materials, and other products pertaining to the themes of the Exhibition.

Exchange of scientific and technological experience.

Assisting representatives of Soviet and Foreign business circles to establish contacts and expand trade, economic, scientific, and technological relations.

§ 2. OFFICIAL REGISTRATION OF EXHIBITORS

A firm (organization) wishing to take part in the Exhibition, will send to V/O "Expocentr" a filled in and signed application for participation in the Exhibition, in duplicate. Applications submitted after the deadline will be accepted only if free exhibition space is still available.

V/O "Expocentr" reserves the right to accept an application reducing the required display space, as well as to reject an application without stating grounds.

V/O "Expocentr" notifies the firm (organization) about their official registration as an Exhibitor, and about reservation of exhibition and storage space, not later than one month after the deadline for applications.

As an exception, V/O "Expocentr" reserves the right after confirmation of the application to shift a show space or change its size for technical or organizational reasons.

From the date of official registration of the firm (organization) as an Exhibitor, V/O "Expocentr" on the one hand, and the firm (organization) on the other hand, are regarded as having entered into contractual relations on the basis of the present General Conditions of Participation, and other normative documents, issued by V/O "Expocentr" for each Exhibition.

The firm (organization) will submit to V/O "Expocentr" before the deadline for applications, a list of exhibits, made out in duplicate according to the established form. Only exhibits mentioned in the list of exhibits and confirmed by V/O "Expocentr" can be displayed. In cases of changes in the firm's list of exhibits, the Exhibitor has to notify V/O "Expocentr" in due time.

Organization of a joint display of firms (organizations) is possible at the Exhibition with the consent of V/O "Expocentr". The Exhibitor organizing the joint display will submit to V/O "Expocentr" together with his application, a list of participants of the joint display showing their legal addresses, nationality, and display spaces.

The organizer of a joint display bears full responsibility for the observance of the General Conditions of Participation by all members of the display.

V/O "Expocentr" reserves the right to exclude any firm (organization) from the list of members of a joint display without stating grounds.

In case of changes in current prices for rent of exhibition space and various services, V/O "Expocentr" will inform the Exhibitor accordingly before the deadline for applications.

§ 3. EXHIBITION SPACE

Exhibition and storage spaces are leased to the Exhibitor for the period of installation, holding, and dismantling of the Exhibition.

The total sum of the rental for exhibition space will be remitted to the current account of V/O "Expocentr" with the USSR Bank for Foreign Trade in Moscow 30 days prior to the fixed date of mounting jobs start.

The exhibition space rental also includes:

a) cost of general lighting of the roofed exhibition space and open territory of the Exhibition;

b) cost of general exhibition safeguarding service;

c) cost of general cleaning of the exhibition grounds and central passageways in the pavilions and open-air space, and removal of garbage and construction waste from specially allocated places, during mounting, work, and dismantling of the Exhibition;

d) cost of issue of entry cards for Exhibitors in accordance with the list of personnel submitted by the firm, and depending upon the size of the rented space:

size of rented space	number of entry cards according to the size of the space rented
under 18 sq.m	3
19 sq.m to 36 sq.m	5
37 sq.m to 54 sq.m	7
55 sq.m to 100 sq.m	10

Exhibitors renting over 100 sq.m will get one extra entry card for every subsequent 20 sq.m. The number of issued entry cards will not be increased for the sake of co-Exhibitors or representatives of firms (organizations) accredited in the USSR. Additional entry cards may be purchased for 10 roubles each for the period of mounting, work, and dismantling of the Exhibition;

e) general advertising done by V/O "Expocentr";

d) cost of the Exhibitor's copy of the Official Catalogue of the Exhibition.

The Exhibitor may use the space allotted to him only in accordance with the aims and theme of the Exhibition.

The Exhibitor may not sublet the space allotted to him without the written consent of V/O "Expocentr".

The minimal exhibition space to be rented is 18 sq.m. Each incomplete sq.m is charged as full sq.m.

Exhibition spaces not occupied by the Exhibitor 48 hours prior to the Official opening of the Exhibition, will be regarded as free, and V/O "Expocentr" will have the right to use them. The sum received for rent of such spaces will not be returned to the Exhibitor.

§ 4. SERVICES

On the Exhibitor's application and at his expense V/O "Expocentr" will render the following services: arranging transportation of exhibition cargoes through the USSR territory; mounting and dismantling of exhibits; equipment and decorative design of stands and offices by designs of the Exhibitor; electrotechnical fitting and sanitary jobs; installation of telephones and teletypes; rent of furniture and equipment; decorative and photographic jobs; lease of stands; hiring of personnel; supplying auxiliary materials; organization of promotional activities, etc.

Applications for the necessary services must be submitted to V/O "Expocentr" by the Exhibitor two months prior to the fixed date of mounting jobs start (applications for personnel may be submitted to V/O "Expocentr" one month prior to the fixed date of mounting jobs start).

Applications must be signed by a person authorised for signing financial documents at the Exhibition. In case the applications are submitted later than necessary, V/O "Expocentr" will not guarantee fulfilment in due time.

If applications for services are submitted at the start of mounting or later, the rates for the following services will increase by 25%: building and rent of stands, installation of telephones, rent of furniture and equipment, construction and decorative jobs, fire-proofing of materials.

If applications for the above-mentioned services as well as applications for gas, compressed air, fuel and lubricating materials are submitted less than 48 hours prior to the required date of fulfilment, and if they are accepted, the rates will increase by 100%.

The payment for services in the amount shown in the proforma-invoice, must enter the current account of V/O "Expocentr" with the USSR Bank for Foreign Trade, Moscow, one month prior to the fixed date of mounting jobs start. Simultaneously the Exhibitor will notify V/O "Expocentr" about the number of the payment order of his Bank, specify the date and sum, and the names of persons, authorised for settling accounts at the Exhibition.

Orders for various services will be accepted by V/O "Expocentr" at the current rates and tariffs, on the condition that the funds specified in the proforma-invoice have entered the current account of V/O "Expocentr".

In case of cancellation of orders by the Exhibitor, the latter will compensate all actual expenses, and in case of refusing the ordered personnel the Exhibitor will pay damages at the rate of three days' salary of the personnel.

It is prohibited to hire interpreters or other personnel other than through V/O "Expocentr".

Expenses involved in participation in the Exhibition will be compensated on the basis of invoices of V/O "Expocentr" in accordance with the existing trade and currency agreements between the USSR and the Exhibitor's country.

If the Exhibitor's country does not have the above-mentioned agreements with the USSR, all accounts will be settled with freely convertible currency.

After the end of the dismantling the Exhibitor will check the mutual accounts with V/O "Expocentr", including the customs certificates of cargoes not presented for re-export.

The final account for participation of the Exhibitor in the Exhibition will be settled in 30 days starting on the date of presentation or postal dispatch of the V/O "Expocentr" invoice.

Any sum remaining after settling all accounts by the Exhibitor, will be returned to the Exhibitor's account in accordance with the indicated Bank's references and in the same currency as it was remitted, at the USSR State Bank exchange rate for the day of return.

If by the end of dismantling of the Exhibition, the Exhibitor fails to settle the presented invoices exceeding the sum remitted for services, V/O "Expocentr" has the right to retain any exhibits belonging to the Exhibitor, by way of compensation.

§ 5. PREPARATION AND DECORATION OF STANDS

Exhibition space is leased to the Exhibitor in a condition fit for installation and equipping of stands.

The Exhibitor may build his own stands and temporary constructions in the roofed as well as in the open exhibition areas. In such cases the Exhibitor should submit to V/O "Expocentr" the drawings of stands and temporary constructions, in duplicate, for co-ordination two months prior to the fixed date of mounting jobs start. No amendments to the approved design are allowed without a written consent of V/O "Expocentr".

The Exhibitor may invite firms of the third countries for carrying out of construction and decorative jobs only with the written consent of V/O "Expocentr".

All temporary constructions and stands will be erected within the boundaries of the space allotted to the Exhibitor. The height of stands must not exceed 2.5 metres.

Passageways for the public must be left unobstructed, not less than 3 metres wide. Throughout the work of Exhibition the Exhibitor should see that the exhibits are accessible for public inspection. Exhibits may not be taken out of the pavilion, or of the stand before the close of the Exhibition without the written consent of V/O "Expocentr". The arrangement of the exhibits on the stands should be done so that all exhibits thoroughly seen to the visitors, and it should meet the requirements of exhibition aesthetics. Everyday cleaning of exhibits and stands, as well as of the other rented areas, is done either by the Exhibitor, or against his order at his expenses.

All construction jobs in the pavilions connected with installation of stands and exhibits (laying of foundations, making openings in walls, etc.) as well as excavation on open grounds, may be carried out by the Exhibitor only with the written consent of V/O "Expocentr".

§ 6. MOUNTING AND DISMANTLING JOBS

The installation of exhibits and decoration is not to be started before the fixed date, and must be finished (including the removal of empty packing cases) not later than 24 hours before the opening of the Exhibition. Admittance of cargoes into the pavilion will be stopped 48 hours prior to the Official opening of the Exhibition.

The Exhibitor should not begin dismantling exhibits and decoration before the close of the Exhibition, and must complete the dismantling, restore the rented space to the original condition, and remove the exhibition goods not later than the fixed date.

Mounting and dismantling of exhibits and decoration must be done within the time-limits set by the exhibition schedule. In some cases, with the permission of V/O "Expocentr", the mounting and dismantling jobs may be done overtime, on the condition of additional payment for the watchman/guarding services during these hours.

Acceptance and handing back of the roofed and open-air exhibition spaces are officially registered by a statement, signed by the authorised representatives of V/O "Expocentr" and of the Exhibitor. Without the signed statement handing back of the exhibition area to the V/O "Expocentr" representative, the Exhibitor, his representative, or his forwarding agent will not be allowed to take cargoes away from the exhibition territory.

V/O "Expocentr" can accept goods for storage by the Exhibitor's letter and at his expense at a fixed rate, on condition that there is a customs clearance for storing them at the exhibition territory. The maximum period of storing the goods is one year only, starting at the date of entry in the USSR.

If the dismantling is not completed in time by the Exhibitor, or his authorised representative, or his forwarding agent, V/O "Expocentr" has the right to clear the area of the Exhibitor's property at the latter's expense, bearing no responsibility for damages during transportation, and to recover from him threefold rent for the exhibition and storage spaces, from the date when the lease expired to the date when the areas are cleared.

In case the storage accounts are not settled within three months, or if the Exhibitor rejects the exhibits left, the above exhibits are subject to realisation.

If the amounts received after realisation of the exhibits do not cover the storage expenses, V/O "Expocentr" has a right to demand compensation from the Firm.

§ 7. FIRE PREVENTION MEASURES, SAFETY REGULATIONS

The Exhibitor must observe the "General Fire Regulations" attached to the present Conditions of Participation and also fulfil the requirements of Safety Regulations valid on the territory of the Exhibition, and bears responsibility for its violation.

§ 8. TRANSPORTATION OF EXHIBITION CARGOES

All exhibition cargoes, including decoration, are to be delivered to the Exhibition before the fixed date of mounting jobs start. If the cargoes enter the exhibition territory 72 hours prior to the opening, or later, V/O "Expocentr" will not guarantee getting the exhibition cargoes ready for demonstration in time, and the transport/forwarding rates will increase by 50%.

Exhibition cargoes arriving as a private luggage of the foreign personnel of the exhibitions, will not be cleared by the customs. After the close of the exhibitions, such cargoes should not be re-exported as a private luggage.

Information and advertising materials, as well as representation food-stuffs and souvenirs must be packed and shipped separately from other goods.

Three sets of all printed matter (books, catalogues, posters, calenders, magazines, maps, etc.) for distribution at the Exhibition must be packed in separate boxes, labelled "Booklets" with the attached packing list in duplicate, and must be submitted to V/O "Expocentr" by the fixed date of mounting jobs start. Films, slides and tapes (one each) are packed in the same box.

Packing, marking, shipping and drawing up of the shipping documents for exhibition cargoes are done on the basis of the "Transport Conditions for the Exhibitors (Forwarders) at the International and Foreign Exhibitions in the USSR".

For transportation of the exhibition cargoes, the Exhibitor may use the services of Soviet transport organizations, and the services of transportation and forwarding agencies of the country from which the cargo was despatched, and those of agencies in the transit countries. The Exhibitor must inform V/O "Expocentr" of the name of his forwarding agent two months prior to the fixed date of mounting jobs start.

V/O "Expocentr" renders the Exhibitor (Forwarder), at the latter's expense all necessary services involved in transporting cargoes from the entry border stations of the USSR to the Exhibition site, and back. In this case the Exhibitor (Forwarder) has to deliver his exhibition cargoes to border station/port in due time, with regard to the time of their further transportation which is fixed by the Agreement on International Railway Freight Services.

Before the arrival of exhibition cargoes, the Exhibitor (Forwarder) sends his representative to receive arriving cargoes, to present them to the customs, to take care of their storage and to despatch them to their destination upon the closing of the Exhibition. The receipt of exhibition cargoes (on arrival) and the return of exhibition cargoes (in despatch) are effected by the acceptance certificate.

The movement of cargoes and empty packing cases within the territory of the Exhibition can be done by handling means, which the Exhibitor has to order through V/O "Expocentr".

Accounts connected with transportation of exhibition cargoes are settled by the Exhibitor himself, or by his entrusted forwarding agent, according to the current transportation/forwarding rates and in the order stipulated by paragraph 4 of the present General Conditions of Participation.

§ 9. CUSTOMS FORMALITIES

All exhibition cargoes (exhibits, stand equipment, etc.) are let in without import license in accordance with the USSR standing regulations. Upon the closure of the exhibition the cargoes are to be removed abroad or to get a formal permission to stay in the USSR before dismantling period is over.

Cargoes arriving or leaving the exhibition are submitted for customs inspection. Before the start of inspection the Exhibitor (Forwarder) via V/O "Expocentr" presents to the Customs packing lists (specifications), two copies in Russian made out for each case; or the customs declarations (in Russian or in German). The documents must contain a detailed list of cargoes including tools, devices, accessories, etc. Failure to list such cargo items or their listing under wrong names will make the Exhibitor (Forwarder) responsible according to the USSR Customs legislation.

The cargoes not inspected on the day of unloading or those inspected for shipment are marked with control bands, and sealed by the Customs representative, and are submitted to V/O "Expocentr" for bonded storage. If examination is done during loading or unloading, there will be no marking or sealing.

Technical means for the Customs formalities are supplied, marking is done by the Exhibitor (Forwarder) or by V/O "Expocentr" at their expense.

Examination of exhibition cargoes is done by the Customs at the territory of the Exhibition in the presence of representative of V/O "Expocentr" and of the Exhibitor (Forwarder) within three days after their presentation for inspection.

Reasonable quantities of food-stuffs and souvenirs for representation purposes may be exempt from customs.

Expensive souvenirs as well as food-stuffs and non-alcoholic beverages for the Exhibitor's stuff may be allowed by the Customs in reasonable quantities when the Customs duties are paid.

To have food-stuffs and souvenirs cleared the Exhibitor is to present a set for letter to the Customs. Letters are presented to the Customs in succession upon arrival of cargoes to the exhibition.

Gifts, souvenirs and food-stuffs are cleared during inspection of other cargoes of the firm that arrived to the exhibition. Cargoes not cleared by the Customs are submitted to V/O "Expocentr" for bonded storage.

The exhibits sold to Soviet organizations during the exhibition, left for testing or storage, must be officially registered at the exhibition Customs and V/O "Expocentr" or, on its instructions, at the exhibition Directorate otherwise they will be considered as cargoes not submitted for customs inspection for which V/O "Expocentr" will not bear any responsibility.

Before the dismantling period the Exhibitor (Forwarder) is to report to V/O "Expocentr" all cargoes that arrived to the exhibition giving contract numbers, shipping invoices, acts and other documents.

The exhibits, stand equipment, building and auxiliary materials for construction of stands and for demonstration of exhibits that are badly damaged, or used up during the exhibition may be cleared by the Customs upon presentation of a statement signed by the Exhibitor (Forwarder) and by the representatives of V/O "Expocentr".

If the exhibition cargoes are not moved abroad within the period specified by the USSR legislation, they are handed over without compensation to the State property according to the standing regulations.

Failure to present cargo documents and cargo for Customs examination, loss of cargoes, removal and damage of stamps or seals as well as opening, repacking or replacing of cargoes without the Customs permission will make the Exhibitor, his representative or, at his absence, the Forwarder, who fulfills customs and forwarding formalities, responsible according to the USSR Customs legislation.

§ 10. COMMERCIAL ACTIVITIES

At the Exhibition, a Commercial Centre is set up, consisting of representatives of the Foreign Trade Ministry and of the corresponding All-Union Foreign Trade Associations, for carrying on negotiations, business meetings, talks, and concluding trade transactions.

In accordance with the Soviet laws, the exhibits and equipment may be sold, and trade deals concluded, only through the All-Union Foreign Trade Associations. The retail sale of samples is prohibited.

The sold exhibits cannot be removed from the stands during the Exhibition.

§ 11. INFORMATION, CATALOGUE, ADVERTISING

The Exhibition is advertised in Press, Radio and Television.

Press Centre of the Exhibition assists the Exhibitor to arrange press-conferences, cocktails, meetings with Soviet and foreign press representatives and issues bulletins on preparation and holding of the Exhibition.

An Official Catalogue is issued by the opening of the exhibition in which a short annotation about the firm is to be published in Russian language by the Exhibitor at his expense. The text of the annotation may be published in the Official Catalogue for additional payment in English, French, German, Spanish and Italian. If the text of the annotation is not submitted to the Publisher of the Official Catalogue 2 months before the fixed date of the mounting jobs start, V/O "Expocentr" will place an annotation in the Official Catalogue about the firm on the basis of the available information and in this case will bear no responsibility for possible inaccuracies.

The Exhibitor or any other firm not taking part in the exhibition may have an advertisement published in the Official Catalogue the text of which should be submitted to the publisher by the same time as that for the annotation.

The address for forwarding the text of the annotation and other advertising materials as well as conditions of publication and payment will be advised to the Exhibitor by V/O "Expocentr" or the Publisher of the Official Catalogue.

The Exhibitor who is the sponsor of joint participation is not entitled to publish any advertisements in prospects containing the list of the joint exposition members.

During the Exhibition the Exhibitor is given an opportunity to deliver lectures and show films on the subject of the Exhibition within the framework of the scientific technical simposium. All expenses involved indelivering lectures and showing films are paid by the Exhibitor.

Formal applications to deliver lectures and show films should be submitted to V/O "Expocentr" two months prior to the fixed date of mounting jobs start.

Together with the application, the Exhibitor should send to V/O "Expocentr" three copies of texts or summaries of the lectures in Russian, German, English or French.

V/O "Expocentr" receives orders from the Exhibitor for conducting advertising arrangements such as: publications in the Press, specialised magazines and Information Bulletin of V/O "Expocentr"—"International and Foreign Exhibitions in the USSR", broadcasting over exhibition or city radio, television and in electronic news flasher; running of advertising films; making and setting up advertising billboards; mounting of posters and leaflets, etc.

The Exhibitor has the right to advertise his products within his display area. The advertising should relate to his products and meet the requirement of the aims and contents of the Exhibition. The conformity of the advertising to the aims and contents of the Exhibition is determined by V/O "Expocentr".

V/O "Expocentr" has the right to stop the distribution of advertising materials or other publicity arrangements if the contents fail to meet the above requirements, or hinder the normal work of the Exhibition.

The Exhibitor may install radio advertising facilities at his stand only with the consent of V/O "Expocentr".

§ 12. ENTRY TO THE USSR, REGISTRATION OF THE EXHIBITION PAPERS

Two months prior to the fixed date of mounting jobs start, the Exhibitor is to send a duly made out list of his staff, specifying the time periods of their stay at the Exhibition to facilitate V/O "Expocentr" to render timely assistance to the Exhibitor and his staff in obtaining the USSR entry visas and in registration of Exhibition documents.

Reception and service of the foreign personnel of the Exhibitions held in Moscow are carried out by V/O "Sovincentr" of the USSR Chamber of Commerce and Industry or VAO "Intourist".

For arranging accommodation and service of the Exhibitor's personnel we advise you to address V/O "Sovincentr" (123610, Moscow, Krasnopresnenskaya Nab., 12. Telex: 411486 SOVIN SU) not later than one month before the fixed date of mounting jobs start.

To arrange his trip to the USSR via VAO "Intourist" the Exhibitor is to address a tourist agency that cooperates with "Intourist" in his country.

Upon arrival in the city where the Exhibition is held the Exhibitor and his staff notify V/O "Expocentr" of their arrival and obtain the Exhibitor identity cards.

§ 13. LIABILITIES AND INSURANCE

In any case V/O "Expocentr" bears no responsibility for: a) loss or damage of the exhibits, or other property of the Exhibitor, his agents, employees, or his guests, including loss caused by fire, explosion, storms, floods, ligtning, and other disasters; b) personal injuries suffered by the Exhibitor's staff, agents, or other persons employed or invited by him, regardless of the manner in which these injuries were acquired. The Exhibitor bears legal responsibility arising from his participation in the Exhibition.

The Exhibitor has to compensate to V/O "Expocentr" all the losses caused by damage to the rented exhibition and storage spaces, stands, electric mains, plumbing, sewage, and V/O "Expocentr"'s property, as well as for other losses that can be suffered by V/O "Expocentr" due to the Exhibitor.

V/O "Expocentr" charges to the Exhibitor's account the compulsory insurance of the leased covered exhibition, storage and other spaces against fire for the period of mounting, work, and dismantling of the exhibition, and also civil liabilities for damages caused to health or property of the visitors to the Exhibition. The insurance is settled with the USSR Joint-Stock Insurance Company—"Ingosstrakh" (12, Pyatnitskaja St., Moscow).

The insurance premium against fire shall be paid by the Exhibitor at the rate of 20 copecks per 1 sq.m of leased indoor exhibition, storage, and other spaces, and against civil liabilities at the rate of 60 copecks per 1 sq.m of leased indoor and outdoor exhibition spaces. The above premium must be paid in full to the account of V/O "Expocentr" with the USSR Bank for Foreign Trade in Moscow, simultaniously with the remittance of rental payment. The insurance acquires validity only after the Exhibitor remits the full sum of insurance.

Other kinds of insurance are accomplished by the Exhibitor himself. Only those insurance policies will be considered acceptable, in which the insurance agency refuses to impose regressive demand on V/O "Expocentr". This pertains to all possible causes of damage provided for by the insurance policy.

Actions of the Exhibitor and of his staff must not disturb the accepted public order.

§ 14. LIABILITIES FOR POSTPONEMENT OF PAYMENTS AND NON-OBSERVANCE OF CONDITIONS OF PARTICIPATION

If the Exhibitor postpones payments of the final invoices for his participation in the exhibition 5 percent penalty of the monthly postponed amount will be collected from him. If the rental payment is not timely remitted V/O "Expocentr" has the right to cancel the application for participation in the exhibition.

If the Exhibitor seriously violates the General Conditions of Participation V/O "Expocentr" has the right to cancel the contract for participation in the Exhibition retaining the sums already remitted by the Exhibitor, and all invoices exceeding the sums of remitted amount of paying for services, are to be paid by the Exhibitor according to the standing regulations. All exhibition cargoes must be removed from the USSR territory within the time specified by V/O "Expocentr".

If V/O "Expocentr" seriously violates the General Conditions of Participation, the Exhibitor has the right to demand cancellation of the contract for participation in the Exhibition and refunding of the remitted money in accordance with paragraphs 3 and 4 of the present General Conditions, less the money spent by the Exhibitor's orders.

§ 15. REDUCTION OF EXHIBITION SPACE, WITHDRAWAL FROM PARTICIPATION

Should the Exhibitor reduce his exhibition space or refuse to participate in the Exhibition after the confirmation of his application (the date of the confirmed application mailing from V/O "Expocentr") is made by V/O "Expocentr" he has to pay V/O "Expocentr" the following amount of penalties:

a) 25 per cent of the rent for the allotted space if the Exhibitor gives notice of his space reduction not later than two months before the fixed date of mounting jobs start;

b) 50 per cent of the rent for the space not occupied by the Exhibitor if the notice of space reduction is given later than the above date but prior to the fixed date of mounting jobs start. 100 per cent of the rent for the space not occupied by the Exhibitor if the notice of space reduction is given later than the date of the mounting jobs start;

c) 50 per cent of the rent for the allotted space if the Exhibitor gives notice of his refusal not later than two months before the date of the mounting jobs start;

d) 100 per cent of the rent for the allotted space if the refusal to participate comes later than the above date.

§ 16. CANCELLATION OR POSTPONEMENT OF THE EXHIBITION

If the Exhibition dates are altered or the cancellation of the Exhibition comes from the reasons beyond the control of V/O "Expocentr", the latter sends a written notification to the Exhibitors. The obligations of V/O "Expocentr" ensuing from the General Conditions of Participation, will become invalid. V/O "Expocentr" has the right to retain the sums spent against the Exhibitor's instructions. The Exhibitor has no right to demand reimbursement.

§ 17. SETTLEMENT OF DISPUTES

If disputes and disagreements which might arise between V/O "Expocentr" and the Exhibitor, are not settled by bilateral negotiations, they were referred to the Foreign Trade Arbitration Commission of the USSR Chamber of Commerce and Industry, and are settled in accordance with the regulations of the proceedings in this Commission. The decision of the above Arbitration Commission is final and binding upon both parties.

Should a dispute arise from inadequate interpretation of the text of General Conditions of Participation in the International Exhibitions in the USSR, published in a foreign language, the reference is made to the Russian text.

Supplement

GENERAL FIRE REGULATIONS FOR FOREIGN FIRMS AND ORGANIZATIONS PARTICIPATING IN EXHIBITIONS HELD IN THE USSR

1. Foreign firms and organizations participating in international events and sponsoring foreign exhibitions in the USSR bear full responsibility for observing fire regulations and fire protection during the exhibition's installation, holding and dismantling.

2. The Exhibitor should submit to the Soviet management of the exhibition plan of his exposition not later than two months before the start of installation works.

In the indoor and outdoor expositions plans the Exhibitor should indicate:

a) the sizes and location of the exhibits, offices, and auxiliary premises (cinema halls, special rooms for film projectors, kitchens, dining-rooms, restaurants, bars, information bureaus, etc.);

b) arrangement of the main and emergency exits, fire-plugs, electric switchboards in conformity with the general plan of pavilion distributed by the Soviet management. Considerable space should be left and free access provided to secure proper use of the exits, fire-plugs and electric switchboards;

c) exhibits demonstrated in operation; operating principles for engines; types of fuel, gases, lubricants, raw materials;

d) conventional symbols for the drawings, together with all necessary explanations.

The Exhibitor should submit two copies of the exposition plans.

The explanations and inscriptions on the plans should be made in Russian.

3. The Exhibitors and Sponsors of the exhibitions should submit to the Soviet management of the exhibition in advance, but not later than a month before bringing inflammable, explosive and radioactive materials and exhibits to the USSR, information of all these exhibits, in order to take all coordinated necessary safety measures. The import of these exhibits is permitted only upon the consent of the Soviet management of the exhibition.

4. For decoration of the exhibition halls, and for constructing offices, podia, ceilings and barriers, only flame retardant materials should be used. All combustible materials should be fire-proofed. It is not allowed to use draperies made of combustible plastics that cannot be fire-proofed.

The use of combustible synthetics for decoration purposes (in the halls, lobbies, passages, staircases, etc.) is prohibited.

The Exhibitor should submit to the Soviet management of the exhibition the documentation stating the materials combustion ratio.

5. Carpeting must be properly fastened to the floor by perimeter and at the junctions.

6. Film projectors should be installed in special rooms with walls and ceilings made of fire-proof materials, and with isolated exits. The films (not more than one day's supply) should be stored in cans. The reels shown at the stands must be printed on fire-proof films.

7. It is prohibited to install turnstiles and thresholds in the passegeways and emergency exits. The passegeways must be at least 3 metres wide, and should allow circular movement of the visitors flow, and a free access to the emergency exits, electric switchboards, fire-plugs and fire-fighting means.

8. The use of electric or gas coffee- or tea-boilers will be allowed only in specially equipped places.

9. In the exhibition halls it is prohibited:

—to make store-rooms and work-shops;

—to store combustible and inflammable materials;

—to store gas fuels;

—to demonstrate operating equipment with the use of open fire.

10. In case permissible amperage of low-powered electric devices (electro-motors, transformers, etc.) is lower than the designed amperage of automatic safety device of the power network, it is necessary to provide additional protection. All electric installations must be earthed.

11. It is allowed to use cables with non-combustible or retarded combustible covering for open electric wiring, if there is no danger of its mechanical damage.

All joints and branches of wiring and cables should be welded, pressed, soldered, or should be effected with special clops. Cores of cables and wires should be safely insulated in places of joining.

12. Flexible wires in rubber cover, protected from mechanical damage should be used for connecting movable current collectors. When mounting electric fitting (sockets, switches, etc.) with combustible or almost non-combustible base, asbestos sheets should be placed under the base.

13. For illuminating exhibition halls, special electric lamps designed for type П-П premises (exposed to fire) should be used.

Diffusors made of organic glass, polystyrene, or some other inflammable materials should never be used with the lamps.

The distance between the lamps and surfaces should be not less than 40 cm.

14. The demonstration of equipment operating on gas or liquid fuel in the exhibition halls will be allowed only if the fuel is fed from a reservoir installed outside the building through pipelines, and if an exhaust system is provided.

Installation and show of such exhibits is to be approved by the Soviet management of the exhibition.

15. It is not allowed to store publicity materials and entertainment goods in pavilions. A day's supply of these materials can be stored in the offices.

The exhibits, spare equipment, wrappings, and packing cases should be stored outside the pavilions or in special places.

16. Smoking in the exhibition halls is allowed only in special places or in the negotiation premises.

17. Welding and other jobs fraught with fire may be carried out only by written permission of the Soviet management of the exhibition and on condition that all fire regulations are strictly observed.

18. All other problems of fire protection arising during the preparation, holding and dismantling of the exhibition are settled between the Exhibitor and the Soviet management of the exhibition immediately.

19. If the arrangement of the stands does not comply with the Fire Regulations, the Soviet management of the exhibition has the right to demand that the Exhibitor dismantles his stands.

20. Infringement of the present Fire Regulations is subject to penalty inflicted by the State Fire Inspectors.

V/O "Expocentr"   Should be submitted in two copies
The USSR Chamber of Commerce   by_____198__.
and Industry
USSR, Moscow, 107113
Sokolnichesky Val, 1a
Telex: 411185 EXPO SU
Telephone: 268-58-74

APPLICATION FOR PARTICIPATION

in international exhibition _____

Country_____

Firm (organization) _____

Address _____

Telex_____ Telephone_____

Current Account (No.) _____

_____
                              (name and address of the Bank)

Please register our firm (organization) as an Exhibitor of the Exhibition.
We hereby request exhibition space:
a) indoor_____sq.m*, b) outdoor_____ sq.m.
We hereby acknowledge all the clauses of the General Conditions of Participation in the International Exhibitions in the USSR and the Information Letter of the above Exhibition.

Director of the Firm (organization)_____
                                                    (name)

"_____"_____198__.   _____
                                                      (signature)

CONFIRMATION

V/O "Expocentr" of the USSR Chamber of Commerce and Industry informs you that your firm (organization) has been registered as an Exhibitor of the International Exhibition_____and that you have been allotted exhibition space:
a) indoor_____sq.m, b) outdoor_____ sq.m.

The rent for the exhibition space should be remitted to V/O "Expocentr" Current Account No. 60800024 with the USSR Bank for Foreign Trade, Moscow by "_____"_____198__ (one month prior to the fixed date of mounting jobs start)

Authorised by V/O "Expocentr"

_____   _____
      (signature)   (signature)

"_____"_____198__ .

_____
*The minimum size of allotted indoor exhibition sqace is 18 sq. metres (see the General Conditions of Participation in the International Exhibitions in the USSR, paragraph 3).

List of firms (organizations) exhibiting at our stand

Name of firm	National belonging	Juridical address	Exhibition space

Director of the Firm (organization)_____
(signature)

V/O "Expocentr"

_____

(the Exhibition name)

Should be submitted in two copies
prior to the deadline for participation
applying

LIST OF EXHIBITS

Country _____

Firm (organization) _____

_____

will send the following exhibits to the Exhibition

Exhibits	Type, model	Basic characteristics or functions of exhibits	Size	Weight, kg	Value of exhibits

Catalogues and proforma-invoices are enclosed

Director of the Firm (organization) _____

(name)

"_____" _____ 198__.

_____

(signature)

Should be submitted in two copies two
months prior to the fixed date of mounting jobs start

_____

(the Exhibition' name)

INFORMATION
for publication in the Official Catalogue
of the international exhibition

Country_____

Firm_____

Address _____

Telex _____ Telephone_____

Range of products _____

_____

_____

_____

_____

Please publish additionally in_____

(indicate languages)

Director of the Firm _____

(name)

"_____"_____ 198___.   _____

(signature)

V/O "Expocentr"

_____
(the Exhibition name)

Should be submitted two months prior
to the fixed date of mounting jobs start

LIST OF PERSONNEL

Country _____   Firm (organization) _____

Full name	Date and place of birth	Occupation	Responsibility at the exhibition	Passport No.	Date of arrival	Date of departure

Director of the Firm (organization) _____
                                              (name)

" _____ 198___.

_____
(signature)

8

NEGOTIATING PURCHASE OR SALES CONTRACTS

Iғ the U.S. firm is unfamiliar with the intricacies of working with the Soviets, it should seek qualified legal assistance as soon as contract negotiations are envisioned. Partially because of the enormous bureaucratic structure that must review any agreement, the Soviets negotiate in literal terms. As a result, topics that are taken for granted or given relatively cursory treatment in U.S. contracts must be spelled out explicitly. Performance criteria for U.S. firms will be expressed in fine detail.

Because a broad segment of the Soviet bureaucracy is involved in a given project, negotiation periods are often long, arduous, and demanding. Actual negotiating time on a project will usually range from a few weeks to a few months for straight sales and from one to several years on turnkey plants or licensing arrangements and more complicated sales.

Continuity is of extreme importance in developing a working business relationship with Soviet agencies, and wherever possible the same individual should be clearly identified as the U.S. project manager who participates in all discussions on the subject. He or she should be supported by a strong technical staff that is prepared to deal with a wide range of sophisticated and inclusive questions from the Soviet side. Although the presence of a senior executive of the firm is not required at all sessions, the Soviets are sensitive to rank, and an occasional visit from such an executive may prove helpful in resolving the more intricate issues. Although competence in the Russian language is desirable, it is not essential.

The Soviet negotiating team usually includes representatives of the foreign trade organization (FTO) and the end-user ministry. For negotiations on major contracts, representatives of other organizations may also participate.

For major contracts, the Soviets come to the bargaining table with a substantial background of knowledge of the general product category, usually backed by information of the U.S. firm, its product line, some of its more recent projects undertaken elsewhere in the world, and prices and concessions granted on these projects.

On the U.S. side it will probably prove extremely difficult to acquire comparable data concerning either the FTO or the end-user ministry. Although it has generally been possible to obtain some minimally acceptable level of technical data, Soviet technicians and higher level officials alike are reluctant to comment on broader issues that, in the state-controlled economy, become matters of government policy.

Soviet FTOs generally are required by the Ministry of Foreign Trade to obtain at least three Western price quotations on a particular commodity before entering into a purchase contract, and during the initial phase of negotiations the FTO will generally seek to acquire as many quotations as possible. It does so through inquiries addressed to potential suppliers or through the Market Research Institute of the Ministry of Foreign Trade. Although information supplied by this agency may fail to provide for important qualitative or technical differences among products, it is frequently used by the FTO as background material for discussions.

In discussions with the leading competitors, the Soviets may employ any or all of the following negotiating techniques during the initial phase:

1. The FTO may conduct concurrent discussions with several competing suppliers to secure the most favorable quotation. For this reason, the U.S. firm should open discussions by quoting a price that allows some margin for reduction in subsequent negotiations.

2. Using the advantage of its control over Soviet imports, the FTO may request a quotation of large quantities with the attendant quantity discount. In a subsequent session, the Soviets may then reduce the size of the potential order, while attempting to hold the U.S. supplier to the lower per-unit cost quoted earlier.

3. The Soviets may open negotiations with the weakest of the Western competitors. If this firm accepts certain demands, it may be difficult for subsequent firms to object to them.

4. The Soviets may seek a final agreement on price as the first item on the

agenda. Once this has been established FTO representatives will seek to include as many "extras" (such as training of Soviet personnel in the U.S. plant) as possible, while holding the supplier to the previously agreed upon price. Therefore, the U.S. negotiator should obtain precise specifications on all aspects of the project before tabling a final price.

5. Soviet negotiators may delay the proceedings to a point at which their U.S. counterparts can no longer afford to play a waiting game. The U.S. negotiating team should, therefore, come to the talks prepared for extensive delays stemming from both the complex, structured nature of the Soviet bureaucracy and the possible intent of the Soiet negotiators to stall for time. The U.S. group should establish in advance some realistic timetable for the negotiations, and it should decide whether it will negotiate beyond that point or will drop the negotiations after having given clear advance notice of its time limits and intent.

Under certain circumstances, the end-user ministry may specify both the particular equipment required and the specific supplier. This normally occurs in areas where the indicated supplier is offering a unique product. In these instances, the first phase of the negotiations may be dispensed with and the second phase of final contract negotiations immediately initiated. (Although the second phase is generally of shorter duration, it can be extremely demanding.)

STANDARD CONTRACT

One result of the Soviet foreign trade system is that negotiatons for major contracts tend to be bifurcated. Preliminary technical discussions with a Soviet end user may be carried on for months with very little consideration of specific commercial issues. Contract terms other than price may not even be discussed at this stage, since they are not of consuming interest to the Soviet scientists and technicians involved. The situation changes once technical discussions have been successfully concluded and the actual contracting party, the FTO, enters the arena.

When negotiations with an American firm reach the stage of strictly commercial matters, the FTO normally offers one of its own form contracts and urges its adoption. Most FTOs have several variations of their purchase form contracts, each suitable for a different type of transaction. The forms may range from a simple two-page agreement for the purchase of equipment on display at an exhibit in Moscow to a complex agreement for construction of a turnkey plant, including the licensing of the technology to be employed in the plant.

The extent to which an American company will succeed in modifying the standard form contract or in substituting its own proposal depends on the type of transaction involved and the relative bargaining position of the parties. According to its own charter, an FTO may contract only in writing, and the written contract must be signed by two authorized representatives of the organization. Indeed, every U.S.-Soviet contract contains a clause stating that the written agreement supersedes all oral negotiations preceding it and that "all amendments and addenda to the contract are valid only when in writing and signed by both parties." Because the Soviets do not recognize oral agreements as binding, the U.S. company should be sure that every possible contingency is provided for in the written contract.

The provisions of FTO form contracts cover only the basic commercial terms of the transaction. Often there are extensive appendixes, running a hundred pages or more, to cover matters such as technical specifications of the equipment being purchased, its installation in the Soviet Union, and the training of Soviet personnel.

The form contracts of the various FTOs are not identical, but they appear roughly similar in approach. The basis for this approach can be found in what are known as COMECON General Conditions.

The General Conditions constitute a unification of international trade law governing trade within COMECON, the Council for Mutual Economic Assistance, which consists basically of the USSR and Eastern Europe. Although the General Conditions have no direct application in U.S.-USSR trade, it is interesting to note that a number of clauses in FTO form contracts appear to have had their origin in the corresponding sections of the General Conditions.

Rather than covering all of the typical clauses in U.S.-Soviet contracts, the analysis below is restricted to three provisions that seem to cause concern to U.S. companies: arbitration, force majeure, and penalties.

Although all import orders will be issued by the FTO, and substantial sales may be concluded without reference to other organizations, the firm is advised to include contacts with several other Soviet entities as part of its market development effort. The principal outside contact should be the actual or potential end user of the product—either the relevant ministry or, more rarely, its producing enterprise—especially when the demand is known to exist. Where relatively sophisticated products and exacting user standards are concerned, this communication is necessary. Direct contact with an industrial ministry may be initiated by addressing inquiries to its Foreign Relations Department. Other contacts might include representatives of the Ministry of Foreign Trade and the State Committee for Science and Technology.

In the absence of known import requirements, the U.S. firm may generate demand for a product through conferences with the potential end user. In addition, by participating in or arranging technical sales seminars under the auspices of either the U.S. Commercial Office in Moscow, the U.S.-USSR Trade and Economic Council, or Soviet organizations, the firm would be able to bring its products and services to the attention of Soviet end users and other specialists in the USSR, who could later initiate purchase requests. Other methods of generating Soviet interest and demand over the long term are the use of the State Scientific-Technical Library system of the State Committee for Science and Technology and the various forms of advertising below.

The following ten rules are useful guides for U.S. business people who are thinking of entering the Soviet market:

—Do not begin unless you are prepared to make a substantial front-end investment without early return.

—Do not begin unless you are prepared to negotiate the first transaction for one to three years.

—Do not begin unless you are prepared to commit substantial amounts of senior executive time.

—Do not begin unless you are prepared to walk away from a negotiation at any time. If you go to Moscow with the idea that you must come home with a contract in your pocket, the chances are that you will make a very bad deal.

—Do not negotiate concessionary terms in order to establish a position; you will simply lose respect. Each transaction must stand on its own.

—Do not reject unusual transactions out of hand. Barter, long-term barter, switch transactions, and compensation arrangements can be profitable.

—Concentrate on personal relationships and the establishment of mutual trust and respect. These things, as well as quality performance, are the bases for subsequent business.

—Good advance work is imperative. Do not make a trip to Moscow without adequate preparation.

—Negotiate contracts with a maximum degree of specificity. The Soviets have the reputation of living up to the letter of a contract but of being unsympathetic toward items that were inadvertently overlooked.

—U.S.-USSR trade is not without limits; it is not about to soar into the tens of billions. It is a good potential market but one that takes a great deal of time and effort and one that should be considered with cold objectivity.

Upon advance request, commercial officers and local staff assist business people in making or confirming appointments with appropriate officials in Soviet foreign trade organizations, ministries, the State Committee for Science and Technology, the Chamber of Commerce and Industry, and research institutes. The U.S. Commercial Office (USCO) maintains an up-to-date list of all Soviet officials involved in foreign trade.

It is a good idea to bring along a sufficient number of business cards printed in both English and Russian. English-language guidebooks and phrase books may prove useful, as will a pocket English-Russian dictionary if you have some knowledge of Russian.

STRIKING A DEAL WITH THE SOVIETS

Success in business dealings with the Soviet Union requires an understanding of Soviet negotiating strategy and tactics. The Soviets drive a hard—and slow—bargain. But there is a reason for it. Although negotiations with the Soviets may at first seem painfully slow, if an American exporter "passes the test" the first time through, he can expect profitable dealings for many years to come.

The key to reaching the Soviet, and other East European, markets is understanding how to negotiate with representatives of centrally planned economies. In my ten years' experience in direct management and marketing in the Soviet Union, East Europe, and the United States, I have learned that the Soviets view the negotiating process as a test of potential suppliers. They believe that a company that survives a complex and drawn-out negotiating process is more likely to be a good supplier than one that balks at delays.

I cannot stress enough the importance of understanding how the Soviets negotiate. First, it is important to realize the distinction between formal state-to-state negotiations with the Soviets—such as those that former Undersecretary of Commerce Lionel H. Olmer conducted in January 1985 in Moscow—and commercial trade negotiations.

The distinction is important because the Soviets approach the two types of talks differently. The state-to-state negotiations take place on several levels, with formal group-negotiating sessions between all members of both delegations augmented by private discussions between the leadership of each negotiating team. As often as not, these talks are held outside the Soviet Union, usually in a neutral third country such as Switzerland.

Commercial trade negotiations, on the other hand, are far more likely to be held in Moscow. Soviet delegations to these talks are usually larger than their counterparts in state-to-state negotiations. There are few, if any, private meetings between the Soviet and American business leaders.

PRIORITIES

In commercial trade negotiations, Soviet priorities are different from those of other international traders. Eyes are not focused on a corporate bottom line. Consequently, contract negotiators from the Soviet foreign trade organizations are not intent on quickly concluding a profitable business deal. Soviet negotiators, in fact, will resist pressures to accelerate the pace of negotiations so as not to exceed the scope of the bargaining instructions they have received from the production ministries—on whose behalf they are negotiating. Commercial negotiations with the USSR, in fact, can take longer than state negotiations.

Indeed, before commercial trade negotiations even begin, the Soviets prepare a comprehensive game plan that resembles a chess strategy. Their game plan usually contains clearly stated Soviet goals for the negotiations—and anticipated U.S. responses to the various Soviet moves. A deputy minister is usually responsible for the game plan, which can also include an outline of the team leader's authority to negotiate, a complete list of participants, and extensive data on the potential supplier's company and the members of the U.S. negotiating team.

Once negotiations begin, Americans new to the process are usually surprised at the number and variety of delays that can occur. Americans may be shaken by an apparent lack of Soviet professionalism. In particular, the Soviets seem unreliable about responding to correspondence, even when they initiate an exchange of letters. (Soviet copying machines also seem to be a frequent bottleneck.) But such delays should not be taken personally. They are part of the Soviet negotiating strategy.

As a rule, the Soviets are also very cautious about releasing any technical data—even data crucial to a U.S. company's preparation of price quotes, equipment specifications, and the like.

Although the Soviets seem to expect rational, consistent behavior from their American counterparts, they themselves do not always feel bound by Western business norms. Long-scheduled meetings may be canceled on extremely short notice; when meetings do take place as scheduled, the Soviets are likely to put a new person in charge of their delegation without any explanation.

Yet another difference between the Soviets and Western business people is that the Soviets require formal negotiations for literally every purchase. There is no such thing as a simple purchase-order agreement with the Soviets.

SOVIET ASSUMPTIONS

There is a logic to all of the delays in negotiations. It is based on two Soviet assumptions about American business people. The first is that Americans regard compromise as both desirable and inevitable. The second is that Americans feel frustration and failure when agreements are not reached promptly.

The Soviets, therefore, believe that any delays—whether petty harassments such as failure to attend scheduled meetings or understandable reluctance to release technical information—will ultimately yield major concessions from the Americans, who expect at least some compromise and who are eager to reach an agreement. Although the strategy is not always successful, it is deeply ingrained in the Soviet consciousness, and it is impossible to avoid.

Despite the frequent delays, the Soviets usually know exactly what they want before the negotiations begin. This does not mean that changes cannot be worked out during the negotiations. But any change is an invitation for further delay, since it must be approved by at least one, and in some cases several, ministries.

HIERARCHY

Still, not all negotiations with the Soviets are somber, unproductive affairs. In particular, the technical discussions that mark the opening sessions of any commercial negotiations tend to be dominated by low- to mid-level specialists who are not permanent members of the negotiating team. The mood at these sessions tends to be relaxed, with everyone joining in, contributing opinions and questions.

However, once the negotiations reach their later stages, the Soviet penchant for discipline and hierarchy takes over. The Soviets are deeply sensitive about age, rank, and protocol. In the interests of maintaining negotiations, it is helpful for Americans to show the appropriate levels of respect.

Americans must also be cautious about interministerial cross fire. This can develop when production ministries, the end users, start sensing that the foreign trade organization charged with negotiating a contract with the U.S. supplier is dragging its feet. Foreign trade organizations, in turn, can feel threatened when the production ministries attempt direct contacts with the Americans.

The administrative support in areas such as typing, copying, and various other clerical tasks is uniformly below Western standards. (At times, clerical support can be so bad that it is not at all clear that it is not part of the waiting-game strategy. Often it is.) There are also cases in which the abrupt cancellation of a meeting has served as an excuse to bring in a new hard-line negotiator to head the Soviet delegation. Again, the purpose behind each of these maneuvers is to obtain the "big concession," predicated on the assumption that Americans expect to compromise.

Another common tactic involves changing a team's leadership without any explanation to the U.S. side. This tactic is used to switch from "hard-line" to "soft-line" negotiations and vice versa.

A Soviet negotiating team may also try to involve the U.S. negotiators in intramural bargaining. This can happen if the negotiating team is worried about selling the terms of the agreement to its superiors. In these cases, the Soviet negotiators will ask for help in "packaging" their arguments on behalf of the contract.

DUAL MEETINGS

Still another Soviet tactic is to play competing Western firms against one another by inviting representatives of each one to come to Moscow for negotiations at the same time. Selective information is used from one set of negotiations in an effort to influence the course of the other. The Soviets have even been so crude as to say that unless certain conditions are met, the contract will be awarded to a competitor who "just happens to be in town."

In addition, the Soviets also like to accept the language of particular clauses "in principle," while intending to make an issue of the language at a later time. They will, on occasion, accept a multimillion-dollar contract—and then quibble over small details, or a few dollars, so as to impress their superiors that "no details have been overlooked."

On rare occasions, the Soviets will negotiate without intending to conclude an agreement, merely practicing for future negotiations with a particular company. On those rare occasions when the Soviets do agree to negotiate outside their home turf, their behavior tends to be more flexible. Negotiators in the United States usually have more authority to make their own decisions. Opportunities for business entertainment are also greater when negotiations are held in the West, but the Soviets place very little emphasis on personal contacts between their negotiators and their U.S. counterparts.

The final product of these negotiations is usually a highly detailed agreement. The Soviets pursue detail far more diligently than their counterparts in international trade. Although some agreements in the West can be negotiated over the telephone and confirmed by telex, the Soviets will accept such arrangements only in dire circumstances.

In contrast with the rest of the agreement, however, the Soviets seek extremely generalized guarantee and warranty statements. This is because the Soviets believe that less precise language in these areas will cover any future claims they may have. (Warranties can be difficult to work out because of Soviet reluctance to allow on-site inspections.)

Despite all of the negotiating hurdles, a majority of U.S.-Soviet agreements benefit both sides. Because the Soviets prefer to do business with companies they are familiar with, in many cases an initial contract has served as the basis for years of future business. This is not all that surprising—given the structure of Soviet negotiating teams. The same group of negotiators can stay together for a decade or more, with only the end-user experts changing. This continuity gives the Soviets the advantage of a collective memory for the details of previous negotiating sessions. They are quick to sense a change in American attitudes and proposals.

Once Americans begin to understand how the Soviets think, the chances for final agreement—and future opportunities—increase.

9

FOREIGN TRADE
AND PAYMENTS

SOVIET enthusiasm in the early 1980s for large-scale import of Western technology and equipment as a means of modernization and bypassing domestic bottlenecks has been tempered by subsequent Soviet difficulties in absorbing sophisticated Western technology, by foreign exchange constraints, and by the use of economic sanctions by some Western trade partners. The USSR is determined not to become overly dependent upon the West in general or upon particular countries. Slower growth and possible near-term stagnation in Soviet hard-currency income, due to soft markets for Soviet energy and gold, have also contributed to the more selective Soviet import policy.

But when Soviet technology is inadequate—for example, in the exploitation of sour-gas or oil fields, when domestic production is insufficient—for example, with large diameter pipe, or when prompt construction is crucial—for example, with a railroad depot near Leningrad, the Soviets will opt for Western imports. Except in the most urgent cases, they then seek sharp competition among several Western firms.

The Soviet government is financially conservative and wary of large-scale borrowing to finance imports, keeping its net debt and debt-service ratio at a relatively low level (under 20%).

The Soviet Union's ability to finance imported Western technology depends essentially on three closely related factors: the surplus left on its convertible-currency export earnings after paying for other high-priority imports; the availability (and terms) of Western credits; and the extent to which it succeeds in negotiating countertrade agreements for future exports from convertible-currency countries to balance these imports.

When it comes to convertible-currency trade, the Soviet Union's merchandise imports exceed its merchandise exports, resulting in a persistent deficit on its overall trade balance. Net interest payments are negative too. Offsetting the deficit on these two items, however, are arms sales to developing-country market economies, gold sales, and net foreign borrowings. The Soviet Union's ability to finance purchases from the West has been enhanced by a variety of developments—improvements in its terms of trade as a result of increases in world oil prices, higher gold prices on world markets and greater opportunities for arms sales to the Third World. On the other hand, a number of adverse changes have also occurred such as poor harvests, which have made it necessary to import additional grain, and the cost of servicing the country's convertible-currency debt.

The USSR has tended to enjoy a high credit rating in international financial markets because it has held down its repayments on convertible-currency debt to some 15-17% of total convertible-currency receipts (from merchandise exports, arms sales, and so on).

Countertrade agreements are one of the devices used by the USSR to step up its convertible-currency earnings. These agreements enable the Soviet Union to repay credits advanced for the import of Western machinery and equipment with the convertible-currency proceeds of exports generated by the imported technology. Industries such as natural gas, chemicals, forestry products, and metallurgy account for most of industrial countertrade agreements.

Along with developing countries and other less industrialized ones, the Soviet Union suffers from a shortage of hard currency to finance its purchases in the West. Compared to the situation in deals between Western countries, a disproportionate amount of time has to be spent in helping the Soviet trading partner find ways to finance a project even if he has expressed a clear interest in some Western equipment or technology. Western governments have been facilitating exports to the USSR through generous lines of credits and credit guarantees, which, however, usually have to be blended with some private financing. The countries with the largest credit lines are France, Britain, Italy, Japan, and Canada.

Even when official credits are available, the Soviet Union purchaser may often ask a Western supplier to enter into a counterpurchase agreement through which sufficient hard-currency revenues can be generated to pay back the credits. Known as compensation deals, or buy-back, or counterpurchase, these arrangements—an outgrowth of the old barter agreements—have created considerable confusion, when companies new to the market fail to realize that Western bankers will not permit a buy-back or compensation agreement to be linked to the financing of the delivery contract. Two distinct agreements are necessary, one for the purchase and another for the counterpurchase. The payment on one cannot be made dependent on payments for the other. Knowing about this distinction can help a Western company in its approach.

Some of the larger traders with the USSR have set up subsidiaries that specialize in marketing compensation and counterpurchase goods in the West. This is relatively easy when it comes to raw materials such as oil, metals, or petrochemical feedstocks. Manufactures and some other commodities may require the intervention of switch traders, whose forte is a thorough knowledge of special markets for goods that are hard to sell; some of their solutions are creative. In any case, a newcomer to the market would be well advised to get in touch with one of them as he nears the crucial part of his negotiations with a foreign trade organization.

When official credits are not available and the Soviet partner cannot get financing from his country's foreign trade bank, the supplier can offer deferred-payment terms. Experienced traders in the USSR handle many of their shorter medium-term deals, for example, from one to two and a half years, in this manner and even some longer-term ones. They have also found a way of discounting their promissory notes with Swiss, German, or Austrian banks, which have developed a market for this paper without recourse to the seller if collection of the payments fails or proves difficult. The rates on this form of financing, known as forfaiting without recourse, are somewhat higher than straight commercial banking credits. But forfait rates have the advantage of being fixed and give the supplier a way of including a calculable discount cost in his bid to the purchaser.

The Soviet Union has made abundant use of all of these instruments to finance it hard-currency deficits. Western analysts are certain that the Soviet Union's reserves, particularly of gold, serve as a quiet guarantee of the entire trading bloc's debt to the West. Besides South Africa, which sells between three and four times as much, the Soviet Union is the only major supplier of gold to the world's free market and earns between $500 million and $1 billion a year from its sales in Zurich and London. It has proved difficult to estimate the Soviet Union's actual reserves of gold.

SOVIET-OWNED BANKS IN THE WEST

The Soviet Union wholly owns six banks in Western Europe: Moscow Narodny Bank Ltd. in London, established in 1919, with branches in Beirut and Singapore; Banque Commerciale pour l'Europe du Nord (Eurobank) in Paris, acquired in 1925; Wozchod Handelsbank A.G. in Zurich, etablished in 1966; Ost-West Handelsbank A.G. in Frankfurt/Main, established in 1972; Donaubank in Vienna, established in 1974; and the Bank Russo-Iran in Teheran, established in 1923. The stock capital of these banks is active outside the USSR.

These banks derive most of their funds from sources external to the Soviet Union. As fully chartered deposit and credit institutions under the laws of their host countries, these Soviet banks over the years have attracted increasing amounts of deposits in various currencies. They collect funds on current and deposit accounts from both domestic and foreign banks, including the Foreign Trade Banks of the socialist countries. Moscow Narodny Bank and Eurobank in particular serve as collection and payment agents for official foreign trade and banking organizations.

The Soviet banks in the West provide many commercial banking services similar to those offered by any large Western bank handling international payments. For example, among its services, Ost-West Handelsbank A.G. in Frankfurt/Main operates current accounts, accepts time deposits at market conditions, and opens, confirms, and advises on letters of credit. Wozchod Handelsbank A.G. in Zurich provides commercial banking services but does not accept savings deposits. Moscow Narodny Bank in London also handles a large volume of documentary credits, primarily for the Soviet Union. Soviet banks in the West on occasion have made local loans and participated in local enterprises. They also have purchased Western-government gilt-edged securities and municipal bonds.

As commercial banks, they believe that to some extent they have an advantage over most other Western banks in view of their contacts with socialist ministries, Foreign Trade Organizations, and other socialist entities involved in East-West trade. Many of these socialist organizations are, after all, stockholders of the Soviet banks in the West. On behalf of the Soviet Union and other socialist countries' banks as well as on their own account, Soviet banks in the West engage in various operations in convertible currencies, including Eurodollars and dollars held outside the United States. Moscow Narodny Bank, Eurobank, Wozchod Handelsbank A.G., and Ost-West Handelsbank A.G. have become important dealers in the international monetary, exchange, and bond markets, especially the Eurocurrency markets. Moscow Narodny Bank is credited with being one of the founders of the Eurodollar market in the late 1950s and remains active in operations with Eurodollar certificates of deposit. The Soviet banks in the West also serve as agents for gold sales by the USSR.

The major focus of the Soviet banks in the West is the financing of East-West trade. The banks handle transactions involving short- and medium-term financing of trade with the socialist countries.

Western exporters of plants and equipment cannot always obtain from their own government-supported export credit programs the entire amount of medium-term financing needed. Soviet banks in the West often finance the remaining uncovered 5% to 20%, while smaller export transactions may be financed completely by them. In such transactions, interest rates are determined case by case. For example, Ost-West Handelsbank usually charges a specific spread above the Deutsche Bundesbank's discount rate. If the bank's own resources are insufficient for financing a specific transaction, it will often form a consortium with other Soviet banks in the West or with other Western banks. The Soviet banks in the West have managed several financing consortia for sales to socialist countries and have acted as joint managers of other international banking syndications.

For transactions with the socialist countries, these banks do not insist upon Western export credit insurance, which generally is required by other Western commercial banks for export credits. Instead, a guarantee from the relevant Foreign Trade Bank is sufficient.

Soviet banks in the West can also provide guarantees for bills of exchange drawn by Western exporters to a socialist country and for the acceptance of commercial paper issuing from the various foreign trade organizations or other socialist exporting entities. Such guarantees are made either by an endorsement on the bills or by a separate payment guarantee.

Payment on cash-against-documents terms is increasingly used in East-West trade, especially between Western firms and Soviet foreign trade organizations when sufficient experience and mutual trust have contributed to the development of a solid trading relationship. Some Western firms that have such a relationship with a Soviet trading partner feel at ease with a cash-against-documents arrangement. The other Western firms generally prefer to use the irrevocable letter of credit.

Until good business relations have been well established with the Soviet Union, the U.S. business person inexperienced in Soviet-American trade is advised to require payment by irrevocable letter of credit rather than cash-against-documents. To obtain payment on a cash-against-documents basis, a Western exporter presents the shipping documents to his commercial bank. For cash against documents on sight terms from the Soviet Union, payment is usually completed within 30 to 45 days after the documents are received in Moscow. In payment against acceptance of a draft, the Western exporter's draft accepted by the Soviet importer is usually endorsed by the relevant foreign trade bank. The Western importer normally obtains the guarantee or endorsement of a large Western commercial bank when arranging payment on a cash-against-documents basis with the Soviet exporter.

SOVIET INSURANCE COMPANIES IN THE WEST

The Soviet Union wholly owns three insurance companies in the West, chartered under the laws of their host countries: Garant-Versicherungs A.G. in Vienna; Schwarzmeer und Ostsee A.G. in Hamburg; and Black Sea and Baltic Company Ltd. in London. Black Sea and Baltic is a member of the British Insurance Association and underwrites credit risks on exports to the Soviet Union and East European countries without relying on Export Credits Guarantee Department (ECGD) coverage.

The Soviet insurance companies in the West cover export credit risks as well as other risks for Western firms engaged in East-West trade with the Soviet Union and other Eastern European countries. The Soviet insurance companies in the West grant complete coverage to the Western exporter without requiring that he retain a certain percentage of the risk for his own account. This feature can be particularly attractive to the Western Exporter who would like to obtain insurance for the financed portion of an East-West trade transaction that Western-government-supported credit insurance programs do not cover.

Normally, there are no specific limits on the amount of liabilities or on the length of the credit period covered. Reinsurance arrangements with major Western insurance companies as well as with the East European state insurance companies permit the Soviet insurance companies in the West, especially Garant in Vienna, to underwrite East-West trade risks without limitation on amount of liability of length of credit maturities involved. Most Western banks provide financing on the basis of Soviet-owned insurance company guarantees.

Black Sea and Baltic, and especially Garant, provide 100% insurance of gross invoice value against all risks arising in the COMECON importing countries and resulting in a delay of payment or non-payment of a due amount. The risks usually appear when a particular East European country has a temporary shortage of hard currency. When a Western-government-supported export credit insurance agency such as Herms in Germany or the ECGD in England will not insure a particular transaction for various reasons or when the procedure takes too long, Western exporters may use Garant or Black Sea and Baltic for insuring sales to any eligible East European country.

The Soviet insurance companies in the West provide political risk coverage against war and revolution as well as insurance against the impossibility of

Western delivery resulting from interference or other action by the government of the Eastern European country. If the appropriate East European State Bank guarantees the East-West trade transaction, Garant will also cover the commercial risk of the Eastern European buyer's unjustified failure or refusal to accept the Western goods. Additional coverage includes preshipment cover (manufacturing risk) for specially fabricated equipment for a single export order, goods manufactured in unusually large amounts, or products that take an abnormally long time to manufacture. The Soviet insurance companies in the West, especially Schwarzmeer, also issue transportation insurance.

Garant offers a machinery erection and machinery guarantee, which is of interest to the Western exporter engaged in construction of a turnkey plant or other major construction project in Eastern Europe or the Soviet Union. Within the terms of the insurance, this policy covers named risks of damage to insured goods during the assembly and guarantee period for which the Western exporter is liable under his contract with the East European importer. Garant determines the percentages of cover and the premium rates for this policy on a case-by-case basis.

Insurance from Soviet insurance companies in the West, as from other Western insurers, normally follows the currency of the East-West trade contract. However, the insurance may be written in any currency indicated by the Western exporter, provided the premium is paid in the same currency. Any losses are also paid in the currency of the policy. Premium rates are generally competitive with those of other private Western insurers but slightly higher than the political and commercial risk coverage issued by Western-government-supported export credit insurance and guarantee programs.

10

PROPERTY RIGHTS
AND PROTECTION IN THE USSR

THE USSR State Committee for Inventions and Discoveries is the Soviet "Patent Office," which administers the laws on patents, inventors' certificates, trademarks, and industrial designs. Foreigners must apply for such rights through the Patent Bureau of the USSR Chamber of Commerce. The bureau requires a power of attorney from the foreign applicant to transact all matters connected with filings and prosecutions on his behalf. The bureau also collects all government filing and registration fees, as well as its own agent fees.

Having adhered to the latest revision adopted at Stockholm in 1967, the USSR is a member of the "Paris Union" International Convention for the Protection of Industrial Property. Thus U.S. nationals are entitled to receive the same treatment under that country's patent, trademark, and industrial design laws as that country extends to its own nationals. U.S. citizens are also entitled to a "right of priority" for patent and trademark applications. Under this procedure, a U.S. national has one year, after first filing a U.S. patent application in the United States, in which to file a corresponding patent application in the USSR and receive on the latter the date that appeared on the first filed U.S. application. He can thus preserve his earlier U.S. filing date for the later Soviet applciation. Other advantages to U.S. citizens include protection against arbitrary cancelation of their USSR patents and rights to register a trademark without first acquiring a U.S. registration for it.

PATENTS AND INVENTORS' CERTIFICATES

A Soviet patent vests in the owner rights to prevent others from using the invention or from importing products that it covers. The Soviet law applicable to patents is "The Statute on Discoveries, Inventions, and Innovation Proposals" effective January 1, 1974. Compared to inventors' certificates, patents play a lesser role in the Soviet industrial property system.

The inventor's certificate, awarded by the state to a party upon his application for an invention considered useful, entitles him to certain payments based on the invention's use and certain privileges, such as a promotion or a better job. The state assumes complete ownership of the invention.

Although the owner of a patent registration receives a legally recognized right to prevent its use by others, he himself cannot, in the absence of private enterprise, produce the patented product. Thus inventors' certificates, not patents, are the principal form of recognition acquired by inventors in the USSR. Foreigners, however, prefer patents in view of the recognized ownership rights therein and their role as legal bases for negotiating licensing agreements. Foreigners also find it important to acquire Soviet patent rights, since the owner of a Soviet patent is in a legal position to prevent importation of products that it covers.

Patent applications are examined for novelty and usefulness of the product. If granted, a patent registration is issued for a duration of fifteen years from the application filing data. Soviet law does not provide for compulsory working or licensing, and the only possibility available to the patent owner for remuneration is licensing or sale of his patent rights to the state.

TRADEMARKS

The "Statute on Trademarks," as amended, in effect since June 23, 1972, provides protection for product and service marks. Under this law trademarks must be registered in the USSR before they can be enforced. There is no prior-use requirement, the first applicant being entitled to registration. A registered trademark vests exclusive rights therein to the owner and is enforceable by him against its unauthorized use by others, including importers.

Not registrable as trademarks are terms commonly used as generic names for the product containing false or misleading information on the product's origin and "conflicting with public interest." An approved application is registered with no opposition period. Furthermore, marks are registered for the period indicated by the applicant up to ten years from application filing date and may be renewed for another ten-year period. Registration can be licensed or assigned.

INDUSTRIAL DESIGNS

Industrial designs may be registered in the form of a certificate patent. The "Law Concerning Industrial Designs" became effective July 9, 1965. The certificate conveys no right of ownership but enables payments and privileges to the owner if the design is used. Design patents can be licensed or assigned.

COPYRIGHTS

The Soviet Union adheres to the Universal Copyright Convention (UCC) effective May 27, 1973. Thus American writers and publishers of books, plays, and music are now entitled to receive protection in the USSR for their works published after May 27, 1973, and Soviet writers and publishers are entitled to the same treatment in the United States. Under Soviet law, copyright protection will be granted for the life of the author and for twenty-five years after his death. American authors or publishers desiring to secure such UCC protection for their works in the USSR need show on such works only their name, year of first publication, and the letter "c" in a circle. The same applies for Soviet works in the United States. The Soviets adhere to the original UCC text adopted in 1952 but not to the later revision adopted in 1971.

Copyright protection under the convention will not be extended retroactively by the Soviets for U.S. works published before May 27, 1973, nor vice versa by the United States for Soviet works in this country. The USSR established "The Copyright Agency of the USSR" (VAAP), which officially began operation on January 1, 1974. That agency's principal function is to represent Soviet authors abroad. In this connection, it acts as their agent for dealings with foreign parties regarding the publishing and translation abroad of works by Soviet authors. It also administers Soviet copyright owners' royalty accounts, receiving their royalties and paying them for works published abroad. Proposals for publishing and translation arrangements with Soviet authors should be addressed to VAAP, 6B Bronnaya, Moscow, 103104, USSR.

11

U.S. REGULATION OF EXPORTS IN SOVIET-AMERICAN TRADE

THE U.S. Department of Commerce exercises control over most exports from the United States (principal exceptions are arms and munitions controlled by the Department of State and nuclear material controlled by the Nuclear Regulatory Commission and the Energy Research and Development Administration).

Export controls exercised by the Department of Commerce are imposed for national security, foreign policy, or short-supply reasons. The primary objective in imposing licensing controls on exports to the USSR and other Communist countries is to prevent the export of goods and technology that would be detrimental to the national security of the United States.

Exports to Communist countries are subject to the provisions of the Export Administration Act of 1985, as amended. Under this act, many categories of goods may not require individual licenses; other exports require validated export licenses. Based upon applications submitted by U.S. exports, the licenses are issued by the Office of Export Administration (OEA), Department of Commerce, Washington, D.C. Export controls extend not only to exports of goods and technology from the United States but also to reexports of U.S.-origin technology and materials from foreign countries and the use of U.S.-origin components or technology in foreign-made products exported to third countries.

Validated export licenses are required for a wide variety of sensitive products, including certain numerically controlled machine tools, lasers, communications and navigation equipment, computers and computer peripherals, semiconductors and equipment used in their manufacture, electronic instruments, and special groups of chemicals. To determine whether a specific type of commodity requires a validated export license, an exporter should check the Commodity Control List. This list is part of the Export Administration Regulations, which can be ordered from the U.S. Government Printing Office or examined at any Commerce Department District Office or the Office of Export Administration.

In addition to controlling the export of selected commodities, the Commerce Department also requires that validated export licenses be obtained to transfer to Communist countries unpublished technical data related to the design, production, or use of articles or materials. A transfer of technical data may occur in some of the following ways: (1) actual shipment of plans, models, blueprints, manuals, and so on; (2) oral exchanges of information; (3) visual inspection by foreign nations of U.S.-origin equipment; and (4) application of personal knowledge or technical experience acquired in the United States to situations abroad.

The general policy of the Commerce Department is to approve applications to ship commodities or technical data whenever it can be determined, on a case-by-case basis, that the end use is non-strategic; that the end user is engaged in essentially peaceful activities; and that the transaction will not prove detrimental to U.S. national security.

Applications for export licenses and requests to reexport or otherwise dispose of U.S. commodities located abroad should be submitted on forms (DIB-622P and DIB-699P, respectively) available from the Office of Export Administration or Commerce Department District Offices. Besides the appropriate application form, customers of the exporter (both consignee and purchaser) should complete and sign a form entitled "Statement by Ultimate Consignee and Purchaser" (Form DIB-629P). Additionally, requests to incorporate U.S.-origin components in foreign goods that will be exported to the USSR should be submitted by letter. In all of the above three instances (applications for export licenses, requests to reexport, and request to incorporate U.S.-origin components), exporters should include technical specifications on the products to be exported. In most instances a product brochure is sufficient, but in certain areas additional information is required.

The Export Administration Act obliges the Department of Commerce to seek information and advice from various executive-branch departments and agencies. The Commerce Department may have to refer applications to the

Departments of State and Defense, the Energy Research and Development Administration, the National Aeronautics and Space Administration, and other concerned agencies. This may be done informally or, for the more difficult cases, through a formal interagency committee. Interagency referral can involve extensive technical review and policy consideration. If the ultimate decision is to approve the application, the Commerce Department must then consult the other countries that maintain similar strategic controls (the NATO countries, except Iceland, and Japan) to obtain their concurrence. Every effort is made to process all applications within 90 days of receipt. If additional time is required, the exporter is advised of the problems involved and is given an estimate of the time necessary to complete processing.

American companies interested in participating in Soviet trade fairs should be aware that a validated export license is required when controlled goods are to be exhibited in the USSR, even if a final sale is not contemplated. Since the licensing process can be time consuming, the exporter is advised to submit his export applications as far in advance of the fair or show as possible.

MOST-FAVORED-NATION TARIFF TREATMENT

Under present legislation, the Soviet Union is barred from receiving most-favored-nation (MFN) tariff treatment and, consequently, is subject to the substantially higher statutory tariff rates. MFN treatment for Communist countries was revoked in 1951 at the time of the Korean War. The Trade Act of 1974 provided that MFN status could be extended to the Soviet Union and other Communist countries only if they adhere to standards of free emigration as stated in the Jackson-Vanik amendment. In January 1975 the Soviet Union refused to accept this condition.

To date, Soviet exports to the United States have been largely raw and semiprocessed materials and have been relatively unaffected by the absence of MFN status, since U.S. tariff rates tend to escalate relative to the degree of processing. However, the structure of Soviet exports is changing, reflecting a higher degree of processing in some items and greater emphasis on intermediate manufactures and some finished products. The directives of the 26th Soviet Communist Party Congress and the current five-year plan regarding the development of trade with the West emphasized the need and desirability of this change. U.S. failure to extend MFN treatment will tend to inhibit the diversification and growth of Soviet exports to the United States. In addition, it could prove a deterrent to possible U.S.-USSR industrial-cooperation agreements, which often call for future imports of Soviet semimanufactured products.

12

SOVIET CUSTOMS PROCEDURES AND SYSTEM OF TARIFFS

THE following information on Soviet customs procedures was supplied by the Main Customs Administration, Ministry of Foreign Trade.

1. Office equipment can be imported duty free during a one-year period after the issuance of official accreditation. If a foreign company receives its permanent office space only after a substantial delay, the one-year period will be calculated from the date when the permanent office space is formally accepted by the company.

2. One automobile can be imported for each office duty free provided that at the time of importation the office in question supplies a written guarantee that the vehicle will be reexported from the USSR. Spare parts for that vehicle can be imported duty free at the time the vehicle is imported. Spare parts imported for the vehicle subsequent to its importation into the USSR are subject to duty. For the use of members of the office staff, one vehicle per family can be imported duty free, again provided that the staff member supplies a written guarantee of reexport. Spare parts for these vehicles are handled in the same manner as office vehicles. One set of winter tires can be imported for each vehicle duty free at the time the vehicle is brought into the USSR.

3. Office supplies are subject to duty as are food products, souvenirs, and give-away items.

4. In "reasonable" quantities, brochures and calendars can be imported without payment of duty.

5. Construction materials, plumbing equipment, and other items imported for offices and apartments are subject to payment of duty.

6. Material for exhibitions can be imported without duty on the condition that they will be reexported from the USSR. Items imported for exhibition and sold to Soviet foreign trade organizations must be cleared through customs before delivery.

7. Spare parts for office equipment and expendable supplies for motor vehicles such as oil and lubricants are subject to payment of duty.

8. Equipment that is "ruined" can be written off and disposed of in the USSR even if the company in question originally undertook to reexport these items.

9. No duties are charged on personal belongings brought into the country by members of office staffs.

10. Unaccompanied personal baggage is not subject to duty during a one-year period following the owner's arrival in the USSR.

11. Household goods can be imported without duty during a one-year period following the owner's arrival in the USSR.

12. No items brought into the USSR by either offices or individuals can be sold within the USSR, whether or not these items were originally subject to duty.

13. The mode of transportation used for bringing a given item into the USSR has no impact on its tariff status.

14. Goods imported from countries that do not give most-favored-nation (MFN) treatment to the USSR are subject to non-MFN rates for the purposes of Soviet tariffs; however, these rates apply only to "commercial" shipments. Shipments for offices and individuals, if subject to Soviet duties, are granted the lower MFN rate.

15. There is no provision in Soviet customs practice for allowing goods to enter duty free on the grounds that the items in question are not produced in the USSR or available for sale in the USSR.

SYSTEM OF TARIFFS

Foreign access to the Soviet market is controlled directly by administrative means through the USSR foreign trade monopoly. The USSR state foreign trade apparatus effectively insulates the Soviet domestic economy from external economic forces without having to depend upon a system of tariffs.

Generally, therefore, tariffs appear to have little or no effect on Soviet import decisions and apparently have not thus far had a tangible impact on U.S. exports. In 1961 the USSR introduced a double-column tariff, which provides for higher tariffs on imports from countries that do not extend MFN treatment to the USSR and lower tariffs on imports from all other countries. The declared purpose of the tariff system is to defend the "MFN principle" by introducing an apparent countermeasure against countries discriminating in trade against the USSR. The higher tariffs are at present applied to all U.S. imports, a situation that can be expected to continue until the United States extends most-favored-nation (MFN) treatment to the USSR.

In actual practice the foreign trade organization (FTO) that imports dutiable goods usually pays the customs duties, since FTO form contracts typically contain a clause that makes the buyer responsible for all "dues, taxes, and customs duties levied on the territory of the buyer's country."

For temporary exports to the USSR no duty is charged as long as the exporter signs a written declaration certifying that he will reexport his goods. Goods for a display at an exhibit or for demonstration to or testing by a Soviet organization or institution would be considered temporary exports.

PART TWO

The Structure of Soviet Foreign Trade Operations and Orders of a Business Transaction

13

COMMERCIAL LETTERS

LETTERS

1.   London, 12th Oct., 19 ...

V/O "Sojuzexport",
Smolenskaya-Sennaya, 32/34,
Moscow, 200,
U. S. S. R.

Dear Sirs,
      We shall be obliged if you will send us your latest catalogue
of Passenger Cars and Motor Cycles.

                                    Yours faithfully,
                                        A. Smith & Co., Ltd.

2.   Moscow, 15th Oct., 19 ...

Messrs. A. Smith & Co., Ltd.,
20, Moorgate Street,
London, E. C. 2,
England.

Dear Sirs,
      In accordance with your request, we have pleasure in sending

you, under separate cover, our latest illustrated catalogue of Passenger Cars and Motor Cycles.

We hope that the catalogue will be of interest to you.

Yours faithfully,
V/O "Sojuzexport"

3.   London, 3rd January, 19 ...

Dear Sirs,

Order No. 1016

We enclose our cheque for £1,020 . 10s. 8d. in final settlement of your invoice dated the 20th December, 1961, for the goods shipped by S. S. "Svir" against our Order No. 1016.

Yours faithfully,

. . . .

Encl.: Cheque.

4.   Moscow, 6th January, 19 ...

Dear Sirs,

Order No. 1016

We acknowledge with thanks receipt of your letter of the 3rd January enclosing your cheque for £1,020.10. 8d. in final payment of our invoice dated the 20th December, 1961, for the goods shipped by S. S. "Svir" against Order No. 1016.

Yours faithfully,

. . . .

5.   Moscow, 2nd March, 19 ...

Dear Sirs,

S. S. "Clyde". Contract No. 25

We attach a copy of the Charter-Party for the S. S. "Clyde" chartered by us for the transportation of 5,000 tons of Manganese Ore sold to you c. i. f. Manchester under Contract No. 25

Please acknowledge receipt.

Yours faithfully,

. . . .

1 Encl.

6.   Manchester, 3rd March, 19 ...

Dear Sirs,

Manganese Ore. Contract No. 25

With reference to Contract No. 25 for the sale to us of 5,000 tons of Manganese Ore c. i. f. Manchester, we would ask you to inform us whether you have already chartered a vessel for the transportation of the ore from Poti to Manchester.

Yours faithfully,

. . . .

7.   Moscow. 5th March, 19 ...
Dear Sirs,

S. S. "Clyde". Contract No. 25

In reply to your letter of the 3rd March, we refer to our letter
of the 2nd March in which we advised you of the chartering of
the S. S. "Clyde" and with which we sent you a copy of the Charter-Party for this vessel.

Yours faithfully,

·   ·   ·   ·   ·   ·   ·   ·   ·   ·   ·

8.   Manchester, 5th March, 19 ...
Dear Sirs,

5,000 tons Manganese Ore. S. S. "Clyde"

We thank you for your letter of the 2nd March enclosing
a copy of the Charter-Party for the S. S. "Clyde". We request
you to keep us informed of the position of the vessel. We should
also be obliged if you would advise us by cable of the date of the
vessel's sailing from Poti and the quantity of ore loaded.

Yours faithfully,

·   ·   ·   ·   ·   ·   ·   ·   ·   ·   ·

EXPRESSIONS OF REGRET. APOLOGIES. CORRECTION OF ERRORS

1.   Moscow, 18th August, 19 ...
Dear Sirs,

M/V "Leninogorsk". Order No. 2331

We confirm our telephone conversation of this morning during which we informed you that you had omitted to enclose with
your letter of the 15th August the invoice for the goods shipped
by M/V "Leninogorsk" against Order No. 2331.
Please send us the invoice by air-mail.

Yours faithfully,

·   ·   ·   ·   ·   ·   ·   ·   ·   ·   ·

2.   London, 18th August, 19 ...
Dear Sirs,

Order No. 2331

With reference to our conversation by telephone today with Mr.
M. G. Petrov, we regret that through a clerical error our invoice
for the goods shipped by M/V "Leninogorsk" was not enclosed in
our letter to you of the 15th August.
We send you the invoice herewith and apologize for the incon-
venience you have been caused .

Yours faithfully,

·   ·   ·   ·   ·   ·   ·   ·   ·   ·   ·

Enclosure.

3.   Moscow, 21st October, 19 . . .

Dear Sirs,

Portable Gas Turbines. Order No. 1716

We thank you for your letter of the 18th October enclosing your confirmation of our Order No. 1716 for 2 Portable Gas Tur· bines. We would like to draw your attention to an error which we noticed in the order confirmation, viz. the nominal rating of the turbines is indicated as 130 b. h. p. instead of 150 b. h. p.

For order's sake we would ask you to acknowledge receipt of this letter.

Yours faithfully,

. . . .

4.   Birmingham, 24th October, 19 . . .

Dear Sirs,

2 Portable Gas Turbines. Order No. 1716

We acknowledge with thanks receipt of your letter of the 21st October and very much regret that through a typing error the nominal rating of the Portable Gas Turbines was indicated in the confirmation of the order as 130 b. h. p. instead of 150 b. h. p.

We thank you for pointing out this mistake to us.

Yours faithfully,

. . . .

5.   Sheffield, 16th November, 19 . . .

Dear Sirs,

Diesel Locomotive Model 12 AC

We have received your cablegram of the 14th November reminding us of our promise to send you additional technical data concerning our Diesel Locomotive Model 12 AC described in the "Engineering" of the 10th October, 1960.

We regret that the information has been so delayed that you had to send us a reminder. Please accept our apologies for the delay which was due to pressure of work in our Technical Department.

We send you herewith the technical data required by you and trust that they will prove useful to you.

Yours faithfully,

. . . .

Enclosure.

CORRESPONDENCE IN CONNECTION WITH THE PURCHASE
OF CAVIAR

Messrs. Brown & Co., Ltd., of 12 Moorgate Street, London, E. C. 2., were interested in the purchase of caviar from the U.S.S.R. for immediate shipment as well as for shipment at regular intervals during 19 .... On the 12th of January they sent a letter to the U.S.S.R. Chamber of Commerce, Moscow, asking to be informed of the name and address of the organization engaged in the export of caviar from the U.S.S.R. (Letter 1). The U.S.S.R. Chamber of Commerce forwarded the letter to V/O "Sojuzexport" and informed the company accordingly (Letter 2). On receipt of the letter V/O "Sojuzexport" informed Messrs. Brown & Co., Ltd., that they could not offer the company any caviar for immediate shipment, stating that they intended to begin negotiations for the sale of caviar of 19 ... preparation at the beginning of March. They therefore requested Messrs. Brown & Co., Ltd., to inform them of the quantities, the assortment and the time of shipment required by the company (Letter 3). In their reply Messrs. Brown & Co., Ltd., promised to send the required information in a few days (Letter 4).

LETTERS

1.   London, 12th January, 19 ...

The U.S.S.R. Chamber of Com-
   merce,
Ul. Kuibysheva 6,
Moscow,
U. S. S. R.

Dear Sirs.

We are interested in the purchase of Caviar of U.S.S.R. origin for immediate shipment as well as for shipment at regular intervals during 19 .... We shall appreciate it if you will inform us of the name and address of the organization engaged in the export of this product from the U.S.S.R.

We thank you in advance for your trouble.

Yours faithfully,
Brown & Co., Ltd.

2.   Moscow, 15th January, 19 ...

Messrs. Brown & Co., Ltd.,
12 Moorgate Street,
London, E. C. 2,
England.

Dear Sirs,

We have received your enquiry of the 12th January and forwarded it to Vsesojuznoje Objedinenije "Sojuzexport", Smolenskaya-Sennaya 32/34, Moscow 200, who are the sole exporters of Caviar from the U.S.S.R. and who, no doubt, will contact you direct.

> Yours faithfully,
> The U.S.S.R. Chamber of Commerce

3.   Moscow, 16th January, 19 ...

Air-Mail
Messrs. Brown & Co., Ltd.,
12 Moorgate Street,
London E. C. 2,
England.

Dear Sirs,

Your letter of the 12th January has been forwarded to us by the U.S.S.R. Chamber of Commerce for reply. We thank you for your enquiry, but regret to inform you that at the present time we are not in a position to offer you any Caviar with immediate shipment. As to Caviar for shipment at regular intervals during 19 ..., we wish to state that at the beginning of February we intend to start negotiations with our Customers for the sale of Caviar of 19 ... preparation. We shall be therefore obliged if you will let us know the quantities, the assortment and the time of shipment required by you and we shall be glad to send you our quotations.

> Yours faithfully,
> V/O "Sojuzexport"

4.   London, 18th January, 19 ...

V/O "Sojuzexport",
Smolenskaya-Sennaya 32/34,
Moscow 200,
U. S. S. R.

Dear Sirs,

We acknowledge with thanks receipt of your letter of the 16th January. We note that at the beginning of February you intend to begin negotiations with your Customers for the sale of Caviar of 19 ... preparation. We shall be pleased to send you in a few days particulars concerning the quantities of Caviar, the assortment and the time of shipment required by us.

We hope that we shall have the pleasure of establishing business relations with your organization.

Yours faithfully,
Brown & Co., Ltd.

CORRESPONDENCE CONNECTED WITH AN INVITATION OF A REPRESENTATIVE OF A FOREIGN FIRM TO MOSCOW

1.   London, 15th July, 19 ...

V/O "Sojuzimport",
Moscow.

Dear Sirs,

We refer to the recent discussions we had with Mr. S. M. Stepanov of the Trade Delegation of the U. S. S. R. in London on the possibility of our supplying V/O "Sojuzimport" with machines manufactured by our company and distributing Soviet Machine-Tools in Great Britain.

To examine this matter in detail, our Managing Director Mr. James Robinson is prepared to travel to Moscow at the beginning of August, 19 ..., and have personal discussions with members of Sojuzimport.

At the suggestion of Mr. Stepanov we enclose a list of points which we would like to be discussed in Moscow.

We look forward with interest to your reply.

Yours faithfully,

Enclosure.   . . . .

2.   Moscow, 18th July, 19 ...

Dear Sirs,

We thank you for your letter of the 15th July on the possibility of developing mutual trading relations between your company and V/O "Sojuzimport".

We shall be very pleased to meet your Managing Director Mr. James Robinson and negotiate with him here in Moscow.

As to the time of Mr. Robinson's visit, we regret that our Vice-President Mr. V. D. Ivanov and the Manager of our Export Department Mr. M. G. Petrov, who are dealing with this matter, will be away from Moscow at the beginning of August. We suggest therefore that Mr. Robinson should visit Moscow after the 15th August if this time is convenient for him.

We should be obliged for an early reply.

Yours faithfully,

. . . .

3.   London, 22nd July, 19 ...

Dear Sirs,

We have received with pleasure your letter dated the 18th July in response to ours of the 15th July concerning the development of mutual business relations between V/O "Sojuzimport" and ourselves.

We greatly appreciate your invitation to Mr. J. Robinson to visit you for the purpose of discussing this matter. The time of the visit suggested by you, viz. after the 15th August, is quite convenient for us. Mr. Robinson proposes flying to Moscow about the 20th August , and we will advise you of the exact date after his flight has been arranged.

Yours faithfully,

. . . .

LETTERS EXPRESSING GRATITUDE FOR ASSISTANCE AND HOSPITALITY

1.   London, 28th August, 19 ...

Dear Mr. Ivanov,

Having returned home from Moscow, I would like to thank you and your associates for the hospitality and kindness shown me during my stay there.

Following the conversation I had with you finally in Moscow on the 26th August, I look forward to receiving your offer for the various machines selected by me for which, I believe, there should be a good demand in this country .

I had a most pleasant and interesting trip and trust if you should come to England that I can be of similar assistance to you.

Yours very sincerely,

. . . .

2.   London, 14th May, 19 ...

Dear Sirs,

With reference to the visit Mr. ..., Director of ..., and Mr. ..., Chief Engineer of ..., had the pleasure of paying you on the 12th May, we would like to thank you for the assistance and hospitality afforded them and for your kindness in showing them round your works.

We look forward to further co-operation with you in the future.

Yours faithfully,

Trade Delegation of the
U.S.S.R. in the U.K.

14

ENQUIRIES AND OFFERS

ENQUIRIES

When a Buyer wants to know at what price and on what terms he could buy the goods required by him, he usually sends out enquiries to firms, companies or organizations manufacturing such goods or dealing in them. Often the Buyer asks the Seller to send him illustrated catalogues, price lists or other publications and, if possible, samples or patterns of the goods he is interested in. When asking the Seller to send him a quotation (*or* to make him an offer), the Buyer gives as far as possible a detailed description of the goods required by him.

EXCHANGE OF LETTERS IN CONNECTION WITH AN ENQUIRY FOR CATALOGUES OF MACHINE-TOOLS

1.   Stockholm, 1st June, 19 ...

Dear Sirs,

We have seen your advertisement in "Soviet Export" and shall be obliged if you will send us your General Catalogue of Machine-Tools.

                         Yours faithfully,

                      . . . .

2.   Moscow, 4th June, 19 ...

Dear Sirs,

We thank you for your enquiry of the 1st June and are pleased to send you, by parcel post, two copies of our General Catalogue of Machine-Tools. We have marked with V the types of machines available now for sale and if you will advise us which models are of interest to you, we shall be glad to send you their detailed description with drawings.

                              Yours faithfully,

                              . . . .

3.   Stockholm, 8th June, 19 ...

Dear Sirs,

We acknowledge with thanks receipt of your letter of the 4th June and of two copies of your General Catalogue of Machine-Tools sent by you by parcel post.

The Catalogue is of considerable interest to us. We are particularly interested in your Grinding Machines shown on pages 9—12 of the Catalogue and shall appreciate it if you will send us detailed descriptive literature relating to these machines.

                              Yours faithfully,

                              . . . .

4.   Moscow, 12th June, 19...

Dear Sirs,

We thank you for your letter of the 8th June and in compliance with your request are glad to send you, under separate cover, brochures and leaflets in duplicate relating to our Cylindrical Grinding Machines, Models 3152, 3160, 3161, 3164, 3164A. To our regret we are unable to send you any publications covering Models 3151, 3162 and 3163 as they are out of print. A new impression is being printed and as soon as the publications are received from the printing works, we shall not fail to send you some copies.

                              Yours faithfully,

                              . . . .

ENQUIRY FOR PEROXIDE OF MANGANESE ORE

                              London, 15th February, 19...

Dear Sirs,

Peroxide of Manganese Ore

We are in the market for Peroxide of Manganese Ore containing minimum 89% of MnO_2.

We would ask you to inform us by return post whether you are in a position to supply us with 1,000 tons of such ore for

immediate shipment quoting us your lowest price and best terms.
Your price should include delivery c.i.f. London.

Yours faithfully,

. . . .

ENQUIRY FOR CAVIAR

London, 23rd January, 19...

Dear Sirs,

With reference to the previous contracts concluded with your
organization, we shall be glad to receive your offer for the sale
to us of Caviar of 19... catch.

We require the following quantities of barrelled caviar, viz.:

Beluga Caviar . . . . 5,000 lbs.
Osetrova Caviar . . . . 4,000 lbs.
Pressed Caviar . . . . 3,000 lbs.
Total 12,000 lbs.

We should like the shipment of the Caviar to begin in May
and continue at regular intervals until the end of 19 . . . .

We hope to receive your offer as soon as possible.

Yours faithfully,

. . . .

ENQUIRY FOR COTTON TEXTILES

Ottawa, 25th May, 19...

Dear Sirs,

At the suggestion of Mr. A. B. Ivanov, the Commercial Coun-
sellor of the U.S.S.R. Embassy in Canada, we write to enquire
whether you could supply us with Cotton Piece Goods.

ENQUIRY FOR A DIESEL ENGINE

Moscow, 5th May, 19...

Dear Sirs,

We require a 6 Cylinder Diesel Engine of 900 H. P. and would
ask you to send us your tender in accordance with the specification and technical conditions enclosed, stating:

1. The lowest price of the engine without foundation plate.
2. The price of the foundation plate.
3. The time of delivery.
4. The terms of payment.
5. The overall dimensions and weight of the engine.
6. The number of cases necessary for the packing of the engine, their measurements and weights.
7. The cost of packing for sea transportation.

We also request you to send us a list of spare parts stating
the price of each part separately.

The price for the engine should be quoted by you both free on rail your works and free on board English port.

Your offer should be accompanied by specifications, drawings and publications giving a full description of the engine as well as by a list of firms to whom you have supplied Diesel engines similar to that required by us.

Your tender with all enclosures should reach us by the 20th May at the latest.

Yours faithfully,

· · · · · · · · · · · · ·

2 Enclosures.

ENQUIRY FOR A PORTABLE AIR COMPRESSOR

Bombay, 12th October, 19...

Dear Sirs,

We require for the expansion of our plant a Portable Air Compressor, Model KCE-6M, as shown on page 25 of your catalogue and would ask you to send us your quotation. The machine must be delivered complete with all essential accessories and tools together with manuals in English for service and maintenance.

We have already received quotations from three manufacturers who are offering us compressors of a similar design, for delivery in 5—6 months. As, however, most of the equipment for our plant was purchased in the Soviet Union, we should prefer to obtain this additional machine from your organization. We should be prepared therefore to place this order with you if the Compressor could be delivered in January, 19..., at the latest. and if, of course, you could quote us a competitive price.

Your immediate reply will be very much appreciated.

Yours faithfully,

· · · · · · · · · · · · ·

ENQUIRY FOR MACHINERY FOR COAGULATING, EXTRACTING AND DRYING SYNTHETIC RUBBER

Moscow, 20th October, 19...

Dear Sirs,

We refer to the recent discussions with your Managing Director Mr. A. B. White here in Moscow, and in accordance with the agreement reached we request you ·to send us your tender in triplicate for two sets of Machinery for Coagulating, Extracting and Drying Synthetic Rubber as per specification enclosed.

The price, net weight and overall dimensions of each machine and each item separately must be indicated in the offer. Your quotation should also include two sets of rapidly wearing out parts.

We request you to enclose with your offer copies of your publications and drawings containing a full technical description of each machine included in the tender.

We await your quotation with interest.

Yours faithfully,

. . . .

Enclosure.

ENQUIRY FOR MACHINE-TOOLS

London, 15th October, 19...

Dear Sirs,

During our visit to the Brussels Universal and International Exhibition we were very impressed by the U. S. S. R. Pavilion and had the opportunity of seeing the various machine-tools exhibited there. We examined with interest a Jig Boring Machine, Model ЛP-87 and consider that there should be a good demand for this machine in the U. K. We are members of the British Association of Machine-Tool Merchants and have many contacts with the users of this type of machine.

We should therefore be grateful to you if you could send us a detailed quotation together with booklets fully describing the machine. Please state in your quotation what time of delivery you could guarantee and what resale discount you could grant.

We look forward with interest to receiving your answer.

Yours faithfully,

. . . .

TYPICAL SPECIFIC ENQUIRY

V/O Machinoimport

Ref. No. 509/2623   Smolenskaya Pl. 32/34
                                     Moscow G-200

                                     November 7, 1985

Mr. Smith
American International
U.S.A.

Re: 509-1-258

Dear Sir:

Please send us three copies of your proposal for workover rigs in accordance with the enclosed technical requirements and include in your quote a breakdown of firm prices, FOB Port, as well as your best delivery dates.

We would also ask that you include in your quote a normal complement of spare parts for two years' operation.

For all equipment quoted, please give separate weights and all necessary technical characteristics and materials of which it is made and attach to the proposal the necessary technical literature, brochures, and catalogues describing the equipment.

Also, please let us know when we may expect to receive your quote. Thank you very much.

Sincerely yours,

V/O MACHINOIMPORT

Enc: As described above, 4 pp.

TECHNICAL ENQUIRY

For the import of a 125-ton-capacity unitized rig for workover operations on offshore oil, gas, and gas-condensate wells.

I. Technical Requirements

1.1 Itemization

Complete unitized rig for routine and major repair of offshore wells at a depth of up to 6,000 m

1.2 Main objectives

Major and routine repairs, testing, and completion of deep wells with total flaring of the product on selected rigs in offshore oil and gas fields

1.3 Technical characteristics

1.3.1	Load on the hook	125 t.f.
1.3.2	Drawworks:	
	Tension on moving end of the rope	15-16 t.f.
	Minimum power	680 hp
	Minimum drum diameter	490 mm
	Hook-lift speed	
	Min.	0.2 m/sec.
	Max.	2.0 m/sec.
1.3.3	Derrick:	
	Telescoping, height from substructure to crownblock axis	29-31 m

Rigging	5 × 6
Maximum diameter of pulley rope	28 mm
Minimum number of lift speeds	4

1.3.4   Pump:

Minimum power	520 hp
Minimum capacity	15 liters/sec.
Minimum working pressure	400 atm
Drive—individual	

1.3.5   Rotary:

Minimum power	120 hp
Maximum number of rotation speeds	3
Maximum rpm	120
Minimum rpm	25

1.3.6   Maximum rig weight   40

1.4   Design requirements

1.4.1   Drive for rig mechanisms must be provided by an internal combustion engine.

1.4.2   Rig design must provide for mechanization of tripping, installation of the rig in working position, and rigging operations.

1.4.3   The rig must provide for installation of blowout-prevention equipment on the wellhead for a pressure of 700 atm.

1.4.4   The rig must be equipped with a system for preparing, processing, and cleaning mud, including a pump, mixer, shale shaker, trench system, valves, and fittings.

1.4.5   Control of operations must be concentrated at a special post, from which the following mechanisms are controlled:

a) drawworks
b) rotary
c) pump
d) gear box

The location of the post must ensure good visibility of the work area around the rotary and the space in the pulley system's path of movement.

1.4.6   For night work, the rig must have lighting around the derrick, rotary, and pumping-unit area.

1.4.7   Instrumentation must be concentrated at the control post and provide monitoring of the hook load, rotary torque and rpm's, pressure on the riser, and number of double strokes of the mud-pump pistons.

1.4.8   The design of the rig must include a system for total flaring of production during well testing, with a 24-hour capacity of up to 1,200 mm³ of gas and 500 t of gas condensate.

1.5   Technological requirements

1.5.1   The rig must ensure reliable operation of its mechanisms at an ambient air temperature from +50° to −30° C.

1.5.2   Environmental characteristics: Clayey mud, oil, gas, condensate, formation water with mechanical admixture, and other corrosive fluids.

1.6   Requirements for safety, industrial sanitation and hygiene, and fire protection

1.6.1   Equipment must meet the requirements, norms, and rules for safety, fire protection, and industrial sanitation in the oil and gas industry.

1.7   Requirements for rig repair

1.7.1   Rig design must ensure the possibility of its repair in field conditions.

Along with the rig there must be supplied five sets of drawings and the manufacturing technology for rapidly wearing parts (in Russian), as well as recommendations for materials from which they are manufactured.

1.8   Equipment complement

1.8.1   The rig should be supplied with the following:

—Tools for mechanizing the processes of screwing and unscrewing pipes and rods
—Rotary
—Work area
—Pipe ramp
—System for vertical pipe installation and suspension of rods
—Pipe and rod tools
—Blowout prevention equipment
—Equipment for well testing and total production flaring
—System for mud preparation and cleaning
—Tools for tripping of tubing with diameter of 60.3-114.5mm and rods
—10 copies of instructions for assembly and operation of the rig in Russian and two copies in English

1.9   Transportation requirements

1.9.1   Rig weight must not exceed 40 t.
Overall dimensions in operating position should not exceed:

length: 10,000 mm
width: 8,000 mm
height: unlimited

ANSWERS TO ENQUIRIES

A. It often happens that the Seller is not in a position to send a quotation immediately upon receipt of the Buyer's enquiry. For instance, in the case of an enquiry for machinery the Seller sometimes wants to get in touch with the manufacturing plant in order to find out whether the machines are still available for sale or whether they can be manufactured in conformity with the Buyer's specification within the time required by him. In such cases the Seller uses the following or similar expressions in his answers to the Buyers' enquiries:

1. The matter (*or* Your enquiry) is having (*or* is receiving) our careful attention and we hope to send you our quotation (*or* proposal) at an early date.

2. We are contacting the manufacturers with the view of (*or* with a view to) finding out whether the machine is available for sale and will advise you immediately upon receipt of their reply.

3. We have forwarded (*or* We have passed) your enquiry to our works and asked them to inform us whether this model can be altered to meet your specification within the time required by you.

B. When the Seller is not able for some reason to offer the goods for sale, he uses, according to the circumstances, one of the following or similar expressions:

1. We thank you for your enquiry dated ... but regret to inform you that at the present time we are not in a position to make you an offer for the goods required by you.

2. As our plant is fully engaged with orders, we find it impossible to put forward a quotation for delivery this year.

3. We very much regret that we are unable to accept new orders for delivery within the time specified by you.

4. We are sorry that at the present time our machines Type AB12 are not available for sale and must ask you to excuse us from sending you a quotation.

5. We should prefer not to put forward an offer for this machine as it is under re-designing now.

6. We will revert to the matter at the end of next week.

MANUFACTURERS PROMISE TO SEND A QUOTATION

Birmingham, 24th October, 19...

Dear Sirs,

Many thanks for your kind enquiry of the 20th October concerning two sets of Machinery for Coagulating, Extracting and Drying Synthetic Rubber according to the specification enclosed with the enquiry. The matter is receiving our careful attention and we hope to send you our quotation at an early date.

Yours faithfully,

. . . .

ENQUIRY PASSED TO ANOTHER ORGANIZATION

Moscow, 15th November, 19...

Dear Sirs,

We acknowledge with thanks receipt of your enquiry of the 12th November for Rails and Switches. As our organization does not export such goods, we have taken the liberty of passing your enquiry to V/O "Promsyrioimport", Smolenskaya-Sennaya 32/34, Moscow-200 who are the sole exporters of such kind of equipment from the U. S. S. R. and who will communicate with you direct.

Yours faithfully,

. . . .

DIFFERENT QUALITY OFFERED

Moscow, 19th February, 19...

Dear Sirs,

Peroxide of Manganese Ore

We thank you for your enquiry dated the 15th February concerning Peroxide of Manganese Ore. We regret to inform you that at the present time we cannot offer you any ore containing minimum 89% of MnO_2 for prompt shipment.

We could send you a quotation for ore containing 85% of MnO_2 if such quality should be of interest to you.

We look forward with interest to your answer.

Yours faithfully,

. . . .

MACHINE UNDERGOING FINAL TESTS

Moscow, 20th October, 19...

Dear Sirs,

We acknowledge with thanks receipt of your enquiry of the 16th October for Grinding Machines Model TM-100 shown to your representatives in Leningrad and are glad to learn that in your opinion there should be a good demand for such machines in the U. K.

We regret, however, to advise you that these machines are not yet available for sale. As you are aware, this model represents a new design and before being put on the market is undergoing final service tests at a number of engineering plants in this country. We believe that the results of the tests will have been summarized by the end of this year. As soon as the machine is available for sale, we shall not fail to revert to your enquiry.

Meantime we remain,
Yours faithfully,

. . . .

FACTORY FULLY ENGAGED WITH ORDERS

Moscow, 25th March, 19...

Dear Sirs,

We thank you for your enquiry of the 21st May concerning Textiles for delivery in June. We very much regret to inform you that our factory which produces the type of textiles required by you is fully engaged with orders and we are unable to put forward an offer for these goods for delivery before October.

We hope that you will send us your enquiries should you need such textiles later on.

Yours faithfully,

. . . .

OFFERS

Offers made in writing usually state the nature and description of the goods offered, the quantity, the price, the terms of payment and the time and place of delivery. Offers may be firm (*or* binding) or without engagement.

A firm offer is made by the Seller to one potential Buyer only and usually indicates the time during which it will remain open for acceptance. If the Buyer accepts the offer in full within the stipulated time, the goods are considered to have been sold to him at the price and on the terms stated in the offer.

According to English and American law, a person making a firm offer has the right to revoke it at any time before it has been accepted. According to Soviet law, a person making an offer is bound by it until the expiration of the time stated in the offer.

When no time for acceptance is stipulated in the offer, the acceptance must be made within a reasonable time.

Some of the expressions used in firm offers are as follows:

1. We have pleasure in offering you, subject to your acceptance by cable, 1,000 tons of .... .

2. This offer is made subject to your acceptance by cable (*or* subject to an immediate reply).

3. We offer you the goods subject to receiving your confirmation within ... days of the date of this letter.

4. We hold (*or* We are holding) this offer open for your acceptance until the 15th May.

An offer without engagement does not bind the Seller and therefore may be made to several potential Buyers. If the Buyer accepts such an offer, the goods are considered to have been sold to him only when the Seller, after receipt of the Buyer's acceptance, confirms having sold him the goods at the price and on the terms indicated in the offer.

OFFER OF PARAFFIN WAX

Moscow, 16th June, 19...

Dear Sirs,

Paraffin Wax

We thank you for your enquiry of the 12th June concerning Paraffin Wax.

We are pleased to inform you that today we have sent you, by parcel post, the following samples of Paraffin Wax:

Grade A — Melting point 52°—54° C.
Grade B — Melting point 51°—52° C.

We can offer you 100 tons of Paraffin Wax Grade A at the price of £45/10/0d per English ton and 100 tons of Grade B at £43/10/0d per English ton. Both prices include delivery c. i. f. London. Shipment can be made from Leningrad within three weeks after receipt of your order. The terms of payment and other conditions are stated in the enclosed copy of our General Conditions forming an integral part of our Sales Contract.

This offer is subject to the goods being unsold on receipt of your reply.

Please let us hear from you as soon as possible.

Yours faithfully,

· · · · · · · · · · · ·

Enclosure.

OFFER OF PEROXIDE OF MANGANESE ORE

Moscow, 24th Feb., 19...

Dear Sirs,

Peroxide of Manganese Ore

We thank you for your telegram of the 23rd February reading as follows:

"YOURLET 19TH FEBRUARY PLEASE SEND OFFER ONETHOUSAND TONS 85 PERCENT PEROXIDE MANGANESE ORE".

In reply we have pleasure in offering you, subject to receiving your confirmation within 8 days from today:

1,000 tons (10 per cent more or less at our option) of Manganese Ore containing minimum 85 per cent MnO_2 in the dry, at the price of £36—12—6 per English ton of 2,240 lbs in bulk c. i. f. London for March shipment. Three per cent will be deducted by us from the weight as compensation for moisture. Payment is to be effected in cash against shipping documents in London. You are to submit, within 5 days of the date of signing the agreement, a letter of guarantee of a first-class British bank for the full contract value of the goods as a security of the fulfilment of the contract.

Sampling and analysis will be carried out by our laboratory at the port of loading, and the result of the analysis shall be considered final and binding upon both parties.

Our General Conditions are stated in the enclosed Form of Contract.

We look forward with Interest to your answer.

Yours faithfully,

. . . .

Enclosure: Contract Form.

OFFER OF CAVIAR

Moscow, 27th January, 19 ...

Dear Sirs,

Caviar of 19... Preparation

We are obliged for your enquiry of the 23rd January and have pleasure in offering you as follows:

1. DESCRIPTION AND QUANTITY: Barrelled Caviar in bulk of 19... preparation, viz.:

Beluga Caviar	5,000 lbs.
Osetrova Caviar	4,000 lbs.
Pressed Caviar	3,000 lbs.
Total	12,000 lbs. net weight.

We reserve the right to increase or decrease each of these quantities by 15 per cent.

2. QUALITY: First quality in accordance with Government Standards of the U. S. S. R. and/or Sojuzexport's standards. We undertake to submit, as final proof of quality, certificates of the State Inspection of the U. S. S. R. for Quality.

3. PRICES:

... per pound	net	for Beluga Caviar.
...	ditto	for Osetrova Caviar.
...	ditto	for Pressed Caviar.

These prices are strictly net f. a. s. Leningrad.

4. TERMS OF PAYMENT: In pounds sterling net cash against shipping documents by an irrevocable and confirmed Letter of Credit to be opened by you by cable in our favour with the Bank for Foreign Trade of the U. S. S. R., Moscow, for the full value of each lot to be shipped under the contract. Each Letter of Credit is to be established within 3 days of receipt of our telegraphic advice of the readiness of the respective lot for shipment and is to be valid for 30 days.

5. SHIPMENT: We could ship the goods from Leningrad in separate lots, when ready for shipment, and in assortment at our option, in the following approximate periods:

In June — August, 19 . . ., about 4,500 lbs.
In September — December, 19 . . ., about 7,500 lbs.

All other terms are stated in the enclosed Form of Contract. This offer is subject to your acceptance within 6 days of this date.

We look forward with interest to your reply.

Yours faithfully,

. . . .

Enclosure.

QUOTATION FOR A HEAVY-OIL ENGINE

Air-Mail

Birmingham, 20th July, 19 . . .

Dear Sirs,

We thank you for your telex of the 18th July running as follows:

"PLEASE SEND QUOTATION ONE HEAVY-OIL ENGINE MODEL 8C-9 COMPLETE WITH ALL ACCESSORIES".

We are pleased to offer you our 8 Cylinder Heavy-Oil Engine of 800 H. P., Model 8C-9, as per enclosed specification. The net price of the engine complete with all the necessary accessories enumerated in the specification is £4,250 f. o. b. Hull. The cost of delivering the engine from our works on board vessel in Hull is estimated by us at £65.

The engine can be supplied without the engine bed, and in that case the above price would be reduced by £42. Should you prefer to order the engine without the engine bed and manufacture the latter at your own works, we shall supply you with the necessary working drawings. We would like, however, to draw your attention to the comparatively low price of the engine bed and would advise you to order the engine with the engine bed.

The cost of packing the engine for sea transportation in 12 strong cases is £75 extra.

Payment is to be made by you in cash within 45 days of the dispatch to you of the Bill of Lading together with all the necessary documents.

The machine can be dispatched in the second half of September, provided that we receive your formal order not later than July 31st.

We enclose a list of spare parts and their prices. The parts marked S are kept in stock and are ready for immediate delivery. Those that are not kept in stock can be made at short notice.

We are sending you, under separate cover, descriptive literature relating to this type of engine, photographs, drawings, etc.

We hope to receive your order which will be carefully executed by us.

Yours faithfully,

Enclosures: Specification. · · · · · · · · · · ·
　　　　　List of Spare Parts

QUOTATION FOR A PORTABLE COMPRESSOR STATION

Moscow, 25th May, 19 ...

Dear Sirs,

We thank you for your enquiry of the 19th May and have pleasure in offering you the equipment specified below on the terms and conditions stated herein including those printed on the reverse side of this tender.

SPECIFICATION: One Portable Compressor Station Type КСЭ-5, coupled with an electric motor mounted on a welded frame, designed for supplying various pneumatic tools with compressed air:

　　　　Capacity — 5 cu. m./min. (= 175 cu. ft./min.)
　　　　Pressure — 7 atm.
　　　　Speed　　 — 730 r. p. m.
　　　　Weight　 — 1,500 kg. (= abt. 3,300 lbs)

Overall dimensions:

　　　　　Length — 2,130 mm. (= 6.98 ^{1} ft.)
　　　　　Width　 — 1,030 mm. (= 3.38 ft.)
　　　　　Height — 1, 258 mm. (= 4.12 ft.)

The Compressor is delivered with a Slipring Electric Motor A. C. 3 Phase, 50 cycles, 400/440 volts, a Starting Rheostat and a standard set of spare parts and accessories.

PRICE: The total price of the Compressor with the electric motor, spare parts and accessories is ... c. i. f. Bombay including packing in three strong boxes.

PAYMENT: By an irrevocable, confirmed and divisible Letter of Credit to be valid for 90 days.

SHIPMENT: Within 12 weeks of the date of signing the contract.

VALIDITY of TENDER: The Tender is open for acceptance within 30 days of the date of its issue.

Should you find the above data insufficient in any respect, we shall be glad to send you any further information you may desire.

Yours faithfully,

· · · · · · · · · · · · ·

QUOTATION FOR RUBBER PROCESSING EQUIPMENT

London, 20th December, 1960

Dear Sirs,

With reference to your enquiry of the 10th November last and to the recent discussions with your experts in Moscow, we are prepared to supply you with complete equipment for a Synthetic Rubber Crumb Processing Plant in accordance with the enclosed detailed specification showing three groups of machinery and spares (A, B and C) required for the normal running of the plant and indicating prices for each item separately.

PRICES: Packed and f. o. b. British port:

	Machines	Spares	Total
Group A	£ 150,000	£ 20,000	£ 170,000
Group B	£ 120,000	£ 10,000	£ 130,000
Group C	£ 80,000	£ 5,000	£ 85,000

Total price for the complete equipment — £385,000 (three hundred and eighty-five thousand pounds sterling).

Subject to: Our Conditions of Sale enclosed herewith.

Note: This quotation is subject to your immediate acceptance.

TERMS: Net cash in effective pounds sterling in the U. K. as follows:

10% (thirty per cent) of the total amount of the order to be paid in advance in London through the Moscow Narodny Bank, Limited, London, within 15 days of the receipt by yourselves in Moscow of our confirmation of the order.

90% (seventy per cent) of the total amount of each part delivery to be paid in London through the Moscow Narodny Bank, Limited, London, within 45 days of the date of dispatch to you of the following documents:

Full set of clean "on board" Bills of Lading made out to order of V/O "Sojuzimport".

Invoice in triplicate.

Packing lists in triplicate.

Our letter of guarantee as to the quality of the equipment delivered.

Test certificate of the equipment delivered.

Photostatic copy of the corresponding export licence, if required.

Delivery to commence in six to eight months and to be completed in twelve to sixteen months from the date of your final instructions enabling us to proceed to the execution of the order.

Note: This offer does not include the erection of the equipment or any electrical wiring.

GUARANTEE: The equipment is guaranteed for a period of 12 months after despatch against defective material and bad workmanship.

We look forward with interest to your reply.

Yours faithfully,

. . . .

Enclosures: Specification
(24 pages).
Conditions of Sale.

15

ORDERS IN IMPORT TRADE
AND THEIR EXECUTION

FORM OF ORDER

Moscow, ... 19 . . .

Messrs. . . . .
. . . .
Dear Sirs,

Order No. . . . Trans. No. . . .

Please supply and deliver the goods described below on the terms and conditions specified herein and on the reverse of this order as well as those attached to the order,

TYPE OF EQUIPMENT: . . . .
. . . .

TOTAL AMOUNT OF ORDER: . . . .

DELIVERY: Free on board . . . .

DELIVERY TIME: . . . .

TERMS OF PAYMENT: . . . .
. . . .

CONSIGNEE: Postal Address — . . . .
Destination — . . . .

MARKING: In English — . . . .
In Russian — . . . .

Quantities, description, prices and technical conditions — see following pages.

This order contains ... pages.

ITEM	QUANTITY	DESCRIPTION	PRICE PER UNIT	AMOUNT

V/O "Sojuzimport"

. . . . . . President

. . . . . . Manager of . . Department

General Conditions of the Order

1. Only the following conditions of the order together with those contained in the order shall be binding upon the parties.

2. Any amendment and/or alteration to this order shall be issued in writing only and in order to be binding must be duly signed by the parties.

3. PRICE: The prices for the goods specified in this order are fixed and not subject to any alterations.

The prices are understood to include packing for overseas shipment and delivery f. o. b. any British port, i. e. the Suppliers are to place the goods on board steamer at their expense including quay porterage, port and dock dues on the cargo, attendance to customs formalities, cranage, stevedoring, etc.

4. TERMS OF PAYMENT: Payment will be effected in cash in London through the Moscow Narodny Bank Ltd. within forty-five (45) days of the date of despatch to V/O "Sojuzimport" 32/34, Smolenskaja-Sennaja, Moscow G-200, of the original and one copy of Bills of Lading provided that all other documents such as:

Invoices (one original and one copy);

Release Note for Shipment — one copy;

Certificates of Works' Test for the goods — two copies;

Packing Lists — three copies,

etc. have already been delivered to the Buyers in due time.

Payment will be effected only after complete shipment of the goods.

5. DELIVERY DATE: The delivery date is understood to be the date on which the Suppliers apply to the Buyers' Shipping Agents notifying them that the goods have been inspected and passed for shipment by the Buyers' Inspectors and are packed ready for shipment.

The Suppliers shall dispatch the goods by the date indicated by the Shipping Agents; any delay in doing so shall be counted as delay in delivery on the part of the Suppliers.

Should the Suppliers fail to deliver the goods or part thereof by the delivery date specified in the order, they shall pay the Buyers agreed and liquidated damages for delay in delivery at the rate of ... per cent. per week of the value of the undelivered goods.

In addition Sojuzimport reserves the right to reject any goods delayed over ... weeks, and such rejection of the goods shall not free the Suppliers from their liability to pay the Buyers agreed and liquidated damages calculated up to the date of rejection but not more than ... per cent. of the value of the rejected goods.

Sojuzimport has the right to deduct the amount of agreed and liquidated damages, calculated on the basis stipulated in this contract, from the amounts due to the Suppliers.

6. INSPECTION AND TEST: The Suppliers must notify the Buyers' Representatives in the Trade Delegation of the U. S. S. R. in the U. K., 32 Highgate West Hill, London N. 6, at least ten (10) days in advance of the readiness of the manufactured goods for inspection and/or test.

The Suppliers are to accord the Buyers' Inspectors all assistance in obtaining information concerning the goods ordered and supply them with all necessary testing equipment, labour, services, etc., free of charge. If the Buyers'. Representatives inform the Suppliers that they will not participate in the tests, the tests are to be carried out in the absence of the Buyers' Representatives.

The Buyers shall have the right to inspect and test the goods at any time during their manufacture.

Besides the Buyers' inspection, the Suppliers shall make the usual inspection and/or test at their works during and at the completion of manufacture and shall supply the Buyers' Representatives with the certificates of such tests immediately after the completion of the said tests.

The inspection and/or tests shall not free the Suppliers from their liabilities and shall not prejudice the rights of the Buyers under the conditions contained in clause 9 "Guarantee".

The final inspection and test of the goods shall take place in the U. S. S. R. at the works of Sojuzimport's Clients after erection and/or installation. Such inspection and test shall not free the Suppliers from any of their guarantees and undertakings under their Letter of Guarantee or from any other guarantees given by the Sellers in this contract.

7. RELEASE NOTE FOR SHIPMENT: If the goods are passed by the Buyers' Inspector for shipment, the Inspector will furnish the Suppliers with 4 copies of a Release Note for Shipment stating that the goods are passed for shipment. The Release Note for Shipment is to be signed by the Suppliers and by the Buyers' Inspector. If the Buyers' Representatives do not participate in the test, the Release Note for Shipment will be marked "Buyers' Inspector not present".

The 4 copies of the Release Note for Shipment are to be used by the Suppliers in the following way:

a) the pink copy to be sent to the Buyers' Shipping Agents, Messrs. . . . ;

b) the blue copy to be retained by the Sellers;

c) the white copy together with the documents enumerated in clause 12, item "b" to be sent to V/O "Sojuzimport";

d) the yellow copy to be returned to the Trade Delegation of the U. S. S. R. in the U. K.

8. DRAWINGS AND TECHNICAL DOCUMENTS: The Suppliers are to furnish for each machine two (2) sets of drawings, technical materials and documents as listed below:

Foundation drawings.

General arrangement drawings with list of parts.

Detailed working drawings of parts subject to rapid wear.

Packing Lists.

Certificates of Works' Test of the goods.

Letter of Guarantee.

Complete instructions for the erection, operation, maintenance and repair of the machines.

The listed drawings and technical documents are to be marked with the serial number of the machine, order number and transport number. They are to be wrapped in waterproof paper and packed together with the machine in case No. 1.

9. GUARANTEE: The Suppliers guarantee that the goods are in all respects in accordance with the description, technical conditions and specifications of the order, that they are free from defects in material, design and workmanship and that they conform to the Suppliers highest standards. Should the goods prove defective during the period of 12 months from the date of putting the machine, equipment or instruments into operation but not more than 18 months from the date of shipment, the Suppliers undertake to remedy the defects or to replace the faulty goods delivering them c. i. f. Baltic or Black Sea port at Buyers' option, free of charge, or to refund the value of the goods paid by the Buyers.

10. PACKING: The Suppliers shall take all measures to have the goods securely and properly packed to withstand overseas and overland transport to and in the U. S. S. R. The Suppliers shall be held responsible for all losses and/or damage to the goods owing to inadequate or unsuitable packing or greasing the goods that are liable to rust.

All goods must have marks showing the two parts of the case under which the slings may be inserted in order to keep the balance in lifting.

A detailed packing note is to be inserted in each case.

11. MARKING: Each case should bear the following marking both in English and in Russian:

WITH CARE	ОСТОРОЖНО
TOP	ВЕРХ
DO NOT TURN OVER	НЕ КАНТОВАТЬ
V/O "SOJUZIMPORT"	В/О „СОЮЗИМПОРТ"
ORDER No. ...	ЗАКАЗ № ...
TRANSPORT No. ...	ТРАНС. № ...
CASE No. ...	ЯЩИК № ...
CASE DIMENSIONS ...	РАЗМЕРЫ ЯЩИКА ...
GROSS WEIGHT ... kgs	ВЕС БРУТТО ... кг
NET WEIGHT ... kgs	ВЕС НЕТТО ... кг

The Case No. is to be a fraction of which the numerator refers to the consecutive number of the case and the denominator shows the total quantity of cases in which the whole consignment (set, unit) under the indicated transport number is packed.

The marking is to be done in indelible ink on three sides: on the cover, on the front side and on the left hand side of the cases.

12. SHIPPING INSTRUCTIONS: The Suppliers shall apply to the Buyers' Shipping Agents for instructions regarding the shipment of the goods and send:

a) to the Shipping Agents, Messrs. ... : Advice Note of the readiness of the goods for shipment together with three copies of the invoices, Release Note for Shipment (pink copy) and ony copy of Packing List;

b) to V/O "Sojuzimport", 32/34, Smolenskaja-Sennaja, Moscow G-200: one copy of Advice Note of the readiness of the goods for shipment, two copies of the invoices, one copy of Release Note for Shipment (white copy), two copies of Works' Test Certificates of the goods, three copies of Packing Lists;

c) to the Trade Delegation of the U. S. S. R. in the U. K.: One copy of Advice Note of the readiness of the goods for shipment.

The Advice Note is to include, among others, the following data:

Description and quantity of the goods.
Number of packages and kind of packing.
Gross weight and net weight in kilos.
Total value of the goods.

13. EXPORT LICENCE: The goods specified in this contract are ordered for export from the United Kingdom to the U. S. S. R. The Suppliers are to obtain from the appropriate Authorities a licence for export of the ordered goods, where such licence is necessary. Expenses incurred in this connection shall be borne by the Suppliers. The original or a copy of the export licence shall be handed over to the Buyers' Shipping Agents together with the advice that the goods are ready for despatch. The Buyers have the right to cancel the order without any obligation on their part in the event of the Suppliers being unable to obtain the necessary export licence to fulfil this order, or if the issued licence is revoked.

14. ARBITRATION: All disputes and differences arising out of or in connection with this contract shall be settled in Moscow by the Foreign Trade Arbitration Commission of the U. S. S. R. Chamber of Commerce in accordance with the Rules for Procedure of this Commission and by the law of the U. S. S. R.

15. Should the order not be confirmed by the Suppliers within ... days of its receipt, Sojuzimport reserves the right to cancel it.

EXTRACT FROM A FORM OF CONTRACT FOR THE PURCHASE OF GOODS BY AN IMPORTING ORGANIZATION

Contract No. ...

. . . . 19 ...

Messrs. ... hereinafter called the "Sellers", on the one part, and V/O "Sojuzimport" hereinafter called the "Buyers", on the other part, have concluded the present contract as follows:

1. SUBJECT OF THE CONTRACT

The Sellers have sold and the Buyers have bought the equipment shown in the specification enclosed with the contract (Appendix 1), and indicating the name and description of each item, quantities, weights and prices. The equipment is to conform to the Technical Conditions enclosed with the contract (Appendix 2).

2. PRICES AND TOTAL AMOUNT OF THE CONTRACT

Total amount of the contract . . . .
The prices are firm, and not subject to any alterations. The prices are understood f. o. b. ... including packing for overseas shipment, marking, dock and port dues on the goods, attendance to customs formalities, cranage and stevedoring.

3. DELIVERY TIME

The equipment against the present contract is to be delivered as follows: . . . .
By the time stipulated above the equipment is to be manufactured in accordance with the conditions of the contract, tested, packed and delivered to ... .
All the questions connected with the shipment of the goods are to be settled in accordance with the instructions given to the Sellers by the Buyers or by their Forwarding Agents, Messrs. ... .
... days before the date of delivery the Sellers are to notify the Buyers by cable about the readiness of the goods for shipment from ... and to advise the Buyers of the weights and the volumes of the goods. The same notification is to be sent to the Buyers' Forwarding Agents.

Within 24 hours of shipment of the goods the Sellers are to cable the Buyers the date of shipment, contract and transport numbers, the number of the Bill of Lading, the denomination of the equipment, the quantity of the cases, their weight, the name of the vessel and the port of destination.

The delivery date is understood to be the date of the Bill of Lading.

If during ... days from the date of the readiness of the goods for shipment the equipment cannot be loaded on board ship owing to circumstances beyond the Sellers' control (no shipping facilities available) the Sellers have the right to hand over the goods to the Buyers' Forwarding Agents. In this case the date of the Forwarding Agents' receipt is to be considered the delivery date.

After the handing over of the goods to the Buyers' Forwarding Agents all the expenses connnected with the storage of the goods up to the moment of loading them on board ship are to be borne by the Buyers. But in such case the Sellers are to defray cranage and stevedoring expenses in accordance with clause 2 of the present contract.

If the goods are not ready for shipment by the date of arrival of the vessel, the Sellers are to compensate the Buyers for the losses they may sustain in connection with the underloading of the ship (dead freight).

4. AGREED AND LIQUIDATED DAMAGES

If the Sellers fail to deliver the equipment by the dates indicated in clause 3, they are to pay the Buyers agreed and liquidated damages at the rate of ... per cent. of the value of the delayed equipment for each week during the first four weeks of delay, and of ... per cent. for each following week. But the total amount of the agreed and liquidated damages is not to exceed ... per cent. of the total value of the goods delayed.

In case of delay in delivery exceeding 3 months the Buyers have the right to cancel the order in whole or in part.

The agreed and liquidated damages are to be deducted from the Sellers' invoices at the time the Buyers effect payment.

5. PAYMENT

Payment for the equipment delivered is to be effected in ... in the following way:

A. 90 per cent. of the value of the goods delivered is to be paid by acceptances of Sellers' drafts payable in London at ... months from the date of Bill of Lading against documents, viz.:

Original and 2 copies of a detailed invoice.

2 original "clean on board" Bills of Lading issued in the name of V/O "Sojuzimport" to any Soviet Port.

Packing Lists in triplicate.

Copy of the Buyers' Inspector's Release Note for Shipment issued in accordance with the Test Report or any other document as to the quality of the goods.

Sellers' letter about the despatch of the technical documentation in accordance with clause 6 of the present contract.

Copy of the Export Licence, if required.

B. The remaining 10 per cent. of the value of the equipment delivered is to be paid after putting the equipment into operation on condition that it reaches the capacity and quality of operation guaranteed by the Sellers. Payment of the 10 per cent. is to be effected within 45 days upon receipt of the Sellers' invoice and the Report of putting the equipment into operation at the factory of the Buyers.

6. DRAWINGS AND TECHNICAL DOCUMENTS

Within ... days of the date of the signing of the present contract the Sellers are to send the Buyers two copies of the following drawings and technical documents for each complete machine:

General view and assembly drawings with main sizes of the equipment as well as a detailed specification of all parts and assemblies of the machine.

Detailed technical description of the machine.

Technical conditions for testing the equipment; erection, maintenance and operation instructions, lubrication schemes, etc.

Foundation and installation drawings.

Working drawings of the rapidly wearing-out parts of the machine.

Certificates of the Boiler Supervising Board for the apparatuses operating under pressure.

All printed materials as well as inscriptions on the drawings are to be made in the Russian language.

In addition two copies of the above drawings and technical documents as well as the Certificate of the Quality of the equipment or the Test Report stating that the equipment is manufactured in accordance with the conditions of the contract, are to be wrapped in waterproof paper and packed in case No. 1 together with the equipment.

If the drawings and technical documentation are not placed in the case or not sent to the Buyers beforehand, the delivery is considered non-complete, and in this case the guarantee period is to begin on the date of receipt of the complete set of drawings and technical documents by the Buyers.

7. WEIGHT OF THE EQUIPMENT

The weight of the equipment delivered is to correspond to the weight indicated in the specification enclosed with the present contract (Appendix 1).

If the weight of any of the machines is 5 per cent. lower than that stipulated in the specification, the price of such machine is to be reduced in proportion to the shortage in the weight on the basis of the average price of the machine per kilogramme.

No extra payment is to be effected for any excess weight of the equipment. The excess weight of one machine is not to be taken into consideration in case of shortage in the weight of another machine.

If the shortage in the weight of any machine or its excess weight is more than 10 per cent. of the weight indicated in the specification, the Buyers have the right to reject such a machine and the Sellers are to replace it by another one.

8. INSPECTION AND TEST

The Buyers have the right to send their Inspectors to the Sellers' factories to check the process of manufacture of the equipment and the quality of the material and parts and to take part in the tests of the equipment. The Sellers shall place at the disposal of the Buyers' Inspectors, free of charge, all facilities necessary for carrying out the inspection.

Before shipment the Sellers are to test the equipment in accordance with the conditions of the contract. If no such conditions are given in the contract, the machines are to be tested in accordance with the conditions existing in the corresponding branch of industry in the Sellers' country. The results of the test are to be stated in the Test Report which is to be issued after the test.

10 days before the test the Sellers are to inform the Buyers and the Trade Representation of the U. S. S. R. in ... of the readiness of the goods for the test.

If the test is carried out in the presence of the Buyers' Inspector and no defects have been found, the Inspector will issue a Release Note for Shipment. If the test is carried out in the absence of the Buyers' Inspector, and the tests show that the equipment is manufactured in accordance with the conditions of the contract, the Buyers or the Trade Representation of the U. S. S. R. in ... will permit the shipment of the equipment upon receipt of the Test Report or other certificates as to the quality of the goods.

The Release Note for Shipment as well as the Test Certificates do not free the Sellers from their obligations stipulated by the Guarantee clause.

The final inspection and test of the equipment are to take place at the Buyers' plant in the U. S. S. R. after erection.

9. GUARANTEE

The quality of the delivered equipment is to correspond to the technical conditions stipulated in the contract or in the Appendix to it.

The Sellers guarantee that:

a) the delivered equipment corresponds to the highest technical level and the highest standards existing in the Sellers' country for the equipment in question at the moment of the fulfilment of the contract;

b) proper material and first-rate workmanship have been used in the manufacture of the goods;

c) the capacity of the delivered equipment and the quality of its operation are in all respects in conformity with the Technical Conditions of the contract;

d) the delivered equipment is complete in accordance with the conditions of the contract which provides for its normal and uninterrupted operation;

e) the technical documents and drawings are complete, accurate and sufficient for the erection and operation of the equipment.

The guarantee period is ... months from the date of putting the equipment into operation, but not more than ... months from the date of shipment of the last lot of the equipment. The date of the Report issued after the test of the equipment at the Buyers' factory is considered to be the date of putting the equipment into operation.

Should the equipment prove to be defective during the period of guarantee, or should it not correspond to the conditions of the contract, or not reach the ordered capacity, the Sellers undertake at the Buyers' option either to remedy the defects or to replace the defective equipment by new equipment to be delivered without any delay c. i. f. .... All the expenses incurred in this connection are to be borne by the Sellers.

If the elimination of the defects is effected by the Buyers by mutual agreement between the parties, the Sellers are to compensate the Buyers for all the expenses incurred by them in connection with this elimination.

In case the elimination of defects or the replacement of faulty equipment or parts takes place, the guarantee period is to be prolonged for the period used for such elimination or replacement.

If neither party can eliminate the defects, the Buyers have the right either to demand from the Sellers a proportionate decrease in the price of the equipment delivered or to cancel the contract and in this case the Sellers are to compensate the Buyers for the losses sustained by them.

. . . .
. . . .

   SELLERS: BUYERS:

SELLERS REQUEST BUYERS TO REVISE DELIVERY TIME AND GUARANTEE CLAUSE OF THE CONTRACT

1.   London, 3rd May, 19 ...

Dear Sirs,

One 900 H. P. Diesel Engine

We refer to your valued order of 30th April and before finally accepting it we wish to draw your attention to the following points:

1. If you will kindly refer to our quotation, you will find that the delivery time given for the Engine is quoted in working weeks. In calculating the estimated despatch date, you do not appear to have taken into account the annual summer works' shut-down which takes place in July. Taking the shut-down of the works into account, we estimate that the Engine will be ready for final inspection at our works in September, 19 . . . .

2. The Spare Parts which form part of your order are subject to export licence control, but we anticipate no difficulty in securing the necessary export licence.

3. Under paragraph 9 of your General Conditions of the order you stipulate that in the event of the Supplier replacing faulty goods, the new goods should be delivered c. i. f. Baltic or Black Sea port at the Buyers' option free of charge. We agree to this only on the understanding that the rate of freight does not exceed that which would be charged by a British Steamship Company.

We have already agreed on these points with your London representative Mr. A. B. Petrov, and for order's sake would appreciate your confirmation that they are acceptable to you, after which we will send you our formal confirmation of the order.

Yours faithfully,

. . . .

2.   Birmingham, 10th October, 19 . . .

Dear Sirs,

Order for One Gasifier Model DM69

We thank you for your Order No. 15/1225 dated the 5th October, 19 . . ., for the supply of one Gasifier Model DM69.

We confirm our acceptance of your order subject to your agreeing to the following:

1. As was stated in our tender dated the 15th September, 1961, Model DM69 Gasifier is practically of a new design and only a limited number of units have so far been manufactured. Although we have received highly satisfactory reports about their performance and are confident that the Gasifier will give excellent service, we are unable to formally guarantee the reliability of the machine for 12 months of operation. The unit is manufactured of the best materials available and with the highest standard of workmanship, and we are willing to guarantee that any component which proves defective owing to faulty material or workmanship during the first eight months of operation will be replaced free of charge.

2. We must insist that our original delivery estimate of 10/12 weeks from date of order should be indicated in the order. At the same time we promise to do our best to supply the machine by the date required by you, viz. December 15, 19 . . .

Apart from the foregoing, on which we should be pleased to receive your early confirmation, we are prepared to accept your General Conditions of the order.

Yours faithfully,

. . . .

CONFIRMATION OF ORDER BY SELLERS

. . . . 19 . . .

Dear Sirs,

Order No. ... dated ... for .... Trans. No. ...

We acknowledge receipt of the above-mentioned order and agree to execute it in strict accordance with its terms, conditions and General Conditions which we hereby accept and confirm in all respects.

Yours faithfully,

. . . .

EXCHANGE OF LETTERS CONCERNING THE TIME OF DELIVERY OF A TURBINE PLANT

1.

Moscow, 15th March, 19 ...

Dear Sirs,

Contract No. 50/16525. Trans. No. 14154

The time of delivery of the Turbine Plant against the above contract expires on the 1st July.

Please inform us by return of post of the progress of manufacture of the Turbine.

Yours faithfully,

. . . .

2. Air-Mail

Sheffield, 20th March, 19 ...

Dear Sirs,

Contract No. 50/16525

With reference to your letter of the 15th March we very much regret to advise you that there have been unexpected delays in the development of the air starting for the turbine which we are manufacturing against your order and in consequence there may be a two months' delay in delivery over and above the promised delivery date of the 1st July.

However, we can maintain the contract delivery time, namely 1st July, 19 ..., if electric starting equipment is fitted to the turbine, which, as you will recall, was included in our original quotation to you.

Yours faithfully,

. . . .

3. Air-Mail

Moscow, 22nd March, 19 ...

Dear Sirs,

Contract No. 50/16525

We have received your letter of the 20th March from which we learn with regret that you are unable to deliver the Turbine Plant by the 1st July, 19 ..., because of delay in development of the air starting for the turbine.

We have contacted our Clients of this question, and as the Turbine Plant is urgently required by them they agree to your fitting electric starting equipment to the turbine instead of the air starting.

In this connection we have cabled you today as follows:

"YOURLET 20TH MARCH PLEASE DELIVER TURBINE PLANT FIRST JULY 19 ... WITH ELECTRIC STARTING EQUIPMENT CONFIRM SOJUZIMPORT".

Yours faithfully,

. . . .

GOODS DELAYED. BUYERS REMIND SELLERS OF THE DAMAGES CLAUSE OF THE CONTRACT

Air-Mail

Moscow, ... 19 ...

Dear Sirs,

Contract No. . . . . Trans. No. ...

Up to the present time we have not received from you any advice of the readiness for shipment of the goods against the above contract.

While we have to draw your attention to § ... of the contract which provides for payment by you of agreed and liquidated damages for delay in delivery, we request you to take all the necessary measures for the speediest delivery of the goods and inform us by air-mail when delivery will be effected.

Yours faithfully,

. . . .

NOTICE OF READINESS OF GOODS FOR INSPECTION

Sheffield, 15th June, 19 ...

The Trade Delegation of the U.S.S.R. in the U.K.
32, Highgate West Hill.
London, N. 6

Dear Sirs,

Grinding Machines. Order No. 51230/125

We have pleasure in informing you that the fourth Grinding Machine against the above order is ready for your inspection at our works at 12 City Road, Sheffield.

We shall be glad to learn when we may expect the visit of your Inspector.

The performance of the machine has been tested at our works and we enclose a copy of the Certificate of Works Test.

Yours faithfully,

. . . .

Encl.: Copy to V/O "Sojuzimport", Moscow.

LETTER WAIVING INSPECTION

London, 16th June, 19 ...

Dear Sirs,

Grinding Machines. Order No. 51230/125

In reply to your letter of yesterday's date, we wish to inform you that V/O "Sojuzimport", Moscow, have decided to waive the inspection of the fourth Grinding Machine against the above order and have requested us to release the machine for shipment on the basis of the test performed at your works.

It is self understood that the final inspection and test of the machine will take place in the U. S. S. R. at the works of the Clients of Sojuzimport in accordance with the terms of the order.

We are sending you our Release Note for Shipment in triplicate; shipping instructions will be sent to you in due course by the Shipping Agents of Sojuzimport, Messrs. . . . .

Yours faithfully,

. . . .

Encl.

LETTER OF GUARANTEE

November 15, 19 ...

Dear Sirs,

Order No. 50/77235

We hereby certify that the equipment supplied against this order is in accordance with the description,

F. O. B. INVOICE USED IN THE OIL EXPORT TRADE
OF THE U.S.S.R.

Bought of V/O "Sojuzexport"

Moscow, 16th Apr., 19...

Messrs———————

Invoice No. ...
  Terms: As per contract dated 12th Feb., 19 ...

To shipment of Gasoil

per m/t "Ashkhabad" (Voyage 118-6) B/L d/d Batumi 14th April, 19...
8500.10.0.0 at $ 31.1266 per ton F.O.B. Batumi

$264, 591.66
E.&O.E.

Price of Gasoil (Specific Gravity at 15° C — 0.86475):

10¢ × 311.266 = $31.1266

Quotation as per contract dated 12th Feb., 19...

CONSULAR INVOICE

No.. . . .

Invoice of merchandise produced in ——————————
(place and date)

shipped by——————— of—————— to——————
(Consignor)   (city, country)   (Consignee)

of———————————— to be carried per——————
(vessel or other carrier)

destined for——————————
(port of entry)

Marks and numbers	Quantities	Description of goods	Invoice value per unit	Total	Consular corrections or remarks

$\frac{I}{We}$ declare that all statements contained herein and in the attached
sheet or sheets are true and correct.

(Signature of Consignor or authorised Agent)

CONSULAR CERTIFICATE

  I certify that the present invoice composed of ... sheet (s) per copy in
triplicate has been presented to me by the signor of the preceding declaration
and that a fee of ... has been paid.

| Seal |

(Signature of Consul)

CERTIFICATE OF ORIGIN

This is to certify that the goods described below:

Name of merchandise	Number of parcels	Packing	Marking	Weight	Notes

Shipped the _____ by _____ from _____
(date)   (Consignor)   (city and

_____ to _____ of _____ to the
country)   (Consignee)   (city and country)

address of _____ are actually of U.S.S.R. origin.

_____   (Signature)
(date)

Seal of the organisation by which the Certificate is issued

MASHPRIBORINTORG

Address Moscow G-200, Smolenskaja-Sennaja, 32/34
Cable address Moscow "Mashpribor" Telex 235,236

Date   1964

PROFORMA - INVOICE N:o 69/ 16-

Consignee	Buyer					
Departure Moscow USSR				10		
Destination						

Steamer	Collection No
Railway Bill No date Bill of Lading No date	Contract N:o 69
Order N:o 69 Post receipt No date	Addendum to Contract

Number of cases	Weight	kgs	Marking

Description of goods		Quantity pcs	Price US.Doll.	Amount US.Doll.
I.Registration set				
1.Signalling unit "VISTI-EA-01"		1	755,00	755,00
2.Cable reel /pair/		1	295,00	295,00
3.Power supply		1	45,00	45,00
4.Cables /set/		1	52,00	52,00
5.Packing bag		1	120,00	120,00
			total	1267,00

Prices are understood FOB Soviet port
Estimated cost of freight to Buyer port : sea
                                         air
Delivery - three months after firm order
Payment - 100% L/C or by cheque or by bank transfer through
          the Bank for Foreign Trade of the USSR , Moscow within
          15 days after notification of goods readiness for shipment

Payment
Discount - depends on quantity ordered
Validity - 90 days   Total amount

16

REVISION OF PRICES AND TERMS: ACCEPTING OR DECLINING OFFERS

CORRESPONDENCE RELATING TO THE SALE OF PARAFFIN WAX

1. Request to reduce prices:
Air-Mail

London, 20th June, 19 ...

Dear Sirs,

Paraffin Wax

We have received your letter of the 16th June as well as the samples of Paraffin Wax sent by you by parcel post.

We are satisfied with the quality of the material, but we must point out that your prices are considerably higher than those of your competitors. We should be prepared to buy 50 tons of Grade A and 50 tons of Grade B on the terms proposed by you if you could reduce your prices by 10 per cent.

We look forward with interest to your reply.

Yours faithfully,

. . . .

2. Reply to request to reduce prices:

Air-Mail

Moscow, 22nd June, 19 ...

Dear Sirs,

Paraffin Wax

We thank you for your letter of the 20th June concerning Paraffin Wax.

We are pleased that the quality of the goods meets your requirements, but we are surprised to hear that you consider our prices to be higher than those of our competitors. If you will refer to the last issue of the "National Petroleum News", you will find that our prices are not above the quotations for Paraffin Wax of similar quality.

Wishing, however, to establish business relations with your company, we should be prepared to allow you 5 per cent. discount from the prices quoted by us, reducing the price of Grade A to £43/4/6 and that of Grade B to £41/6/6 per long ton c. i. f. London provided that you ordered at least 75 tons of each Grade. All other terms remain as stated in our letter of the 16th June and in our General Conditions enclosed with it.

This offer is subject to your immediate acceptance.

Yours faithfully,

. . . .

3. Accepting price and terms:

Air-Mail

London, 25th June, 19 ...

Dear Sirs,

We are obliged for your letter of the 22nd June in which you agree to reduce your prices c. i. f. London for Paraffin Wax, Grade A and Grade B, to £43/4/6 and £41/6/6 per long ton respectively, if we order minimum 75 tons of each grade.

We accept your prices as well as the terms stated in your letter of the 16th June including your General Conditions and shall be glad to receive your contract for the sale of 75 tons of Grade A and 75 tons of Grade B of Paraffin Wax. Please advise us by cable of the despatch of the contract.

Yours faithfully,

. . . .

4. Sending contract for signature:

Air-Mail

Moscow, 28th June, 19 ...

Dear Sirs,

150 tons of Paraffin Wax. Contract No. 250

We thank you for your letter of the 25th June and confirm our telegram of today running as follows:

"CONTRACT ONEHUNDRED AND FIFTY TONS PARAFFIN WAX SENT TODAY".

We have pleasure in sending you herewith two copies of our Contract No. 250 for the sale to you of 150 tons of Paraffin Wax. We shall be obliged if you will return us one copy of the contract duly signed by you.

Yours faithfully,

. . . .

2 Enclosures.

REQUEST TO REVISE QUOTATION

Moscow, 8th June, 19 ...

Dear Sirs,

During the visit of your representative Mr. A. B. Smith to Moscow in April last we handed him our enquiry for a Steam Turbine Plant of 5,000 kW capacity.

Mr. Smith assured us that your company had a wide experience in designing and manufacturing turbines of the type required by us and that you, therefore, could offer us a plant with better working characteristics as compared with those of turbines produced by other makers and, of course, at a quite competitive price.

We have now received your tender of the 28th May and regret to state that after its careful examination we have come to the conclusion that the turbine plant offered by you does not reflect the latest achievements in turbine building. Its efficiency is low, and some other important characteristics are inferior to those of other turbines offered us. An English translation of our experts' report on the matter is enclosed herewith.

As to the price quoted by you, we think that a mistake has probably occurred in your calculation as your price is very high. In the circumstances you will realize that your chances to secure this order are very slight.

Taking, however, into consideration the conversation we had on the telephone with Mr. Smith who informed us that your company was very much interested in the supply of this equipment, we suggest that you should revise your offer and send us as soon as possible. but by the 5th July at the latest, a new tender for a turbine conforming in all respects to the latest achievements in turbine building. The price of the turbine must certainly be much lower than that stated in your tender of the 28th of May.

We should be obliged if you would let us know immediately whether you agree to revise your offer as stated above.

Yours faithfully,

. . . .

Enclosure.

INFORMING MANUFACTURERS THAT QUOTATION HAS BEEN SENT TO CLIENTS FOR CONSIDERATION

Moscow, 3rd October, 19 ...

Dear Sirs,

We confirm our telephone conversation today with your Director Mr. A. D. Brown in the course of which we informed him that your quotation for a Hydraulic Press had been sent to our clients for consideration.

Immediately upon receipt of their reply we shall not fail to get in touch with you.

Yours faithfully,

. . . .

SPECIMEN LETTERS FOR ACCEPTING OR DECLINING OFFERS

1. Declining an unsolicited offer:

We thank you for your letter of ... offering us ..., but regret to inform you that at the present time we cannot make use of your offer.

We have, however, noted your address and, should need arise, will communicate with you again.

2. Declining offer and suggesting that Sellers should reduce prices and improve terms:

In reply to your letter dated ... we regret not being able to accept your offer as other firms have offered us better prices and more favourable terms.

If you are in a position to quote us lower prices and improve your terms, we may revert to the matter again.

3. Accepting offer:

We thank you for your letter of ... offering us ... at the price of ... per .... . We accept your price and the terms stated in your letter, subject to our General Conditions sent you with our letter of ·... .

Our contract will be sent you tomorrow.

REDUCING PREVIOUS ADVANCE IN PRICE

London, 15th Nov., 19 ...

Dear Sirs,

On the 15th September last we found it necessary to apply a 10 per cent. advance to our list prices. This advance was due to the rise in prices of raw materials and other increased charges.

As we find now that the increase in production costs has not been so high as we had at first expected, we are pleased to advise you that the 10% advance will be reduced to $2^1/_2$% forthwith.

In connection with the above, we refer to our tender of the 1st November for Gas Analysers and hope that you will be able to give us your order which will have our most careful attention.

Yours faithfully,

. . . .

CORRESPONDENCE RELATING TO AN ORDER FOR A TURBO-ALTERNATOR SET

1. Quoting prices and terms:

Air-Mail

Sheffield, 25th Sept., 19 ...

Dear Sirs,

6,000 kW Turbo-Alternator Set

We confirm the exchange of cables between us as follows: Yours 15th September:

"YOURS 5TH SEPTEMBER A153/54 PLEASE CABLE TOTAL PRICE TURBOALTERNATOR SET SEPARATE PRICE ALTERNATOR ALSO SHORTEST DELIVERY TIME WHOLE SET WITH OR WITHOUT ALTERNATOR".

Ours 25th September:

"YOUR CABLE 15TH SEPTEMBER PRICE COMPLETE SET ONEHUNDRED AND TENTHOUSAND EIGHTHUNDRED AND EIGHTY POUNDS STERLING WHICH INCLUDES ALTERNATOR AT THIRTYTHOUSAND TWOHUNDRED AND SIXTY POUNDS STOP SPARES EXTRA SIXTHOUSAND EIGHTHUNDRED AND FORTY POUNDS STOP BEST DESPATCH TWENTYONE MONTHS WITH OR WITHOUT ALTERNATOR".

It will be seen from our telegram that the total price for the Turbo-Alternator Set with Feed Heater and Condenser to be delivered f. o. b. British port in accordance with the specifications sent with our letter of the 5th September is £110,880. 0. 0.

The price of the Alternator which would be supplied by our sub-contractors the Brown and White Electrical Company, Ltd., is £30,260. 0. 0. Thus, the price of the Turbine with Feed Heating Equipment and Condensing Plant amounts to £80,620. 0. 0.

The extra charge for spare parts as per enclosed list showing the price of each item separately is:

For the Turbine	£ 2,300.0.0
For the Alternator	£ 4,220.0.0
For the Condensing Plant	£ 320.0.0
Total for Spare Parts . . .	£ 6,840.0.0

As regards delivery time, taking into account our present commitments we hope to have the whole set ready for despatch in twenty-one months from receipt of your order with full instructions enabling us to proceed to the work. This time will apply for the whole set or for the set exclusive of the Alternator.

Concerning the terms of payment, we suggest that they should remain as they are in our last contract, viz. in cash in London through the Moscow Narodny Bank, Ltd., within 45 days after despatch of the documents to Moscow.

We are sorry we could not reply to your cablegram earlier as it has been necessary to obtain the price of the Alternator from our sub-contractors.

We hope that we shall have the pleasure of supplying you with this set.

Yours faithfully,

. . . .

2. Request to reduce prices and shorten delivery time:
Air-Mail

Moscow, 3rd October, 19 ...

Dear Sirs,

6,000 kW Turbo-Alternator Set

We thank you for your telegram of the 25th September and for your letter of the same date quoting us prices and indicating the delivery time for a complete 6,000 kW Turbo-Alternator Set to be delivered in conformity with the specifications enclosed in your letter of the 5th September.

We have carefully compared your offer with the quotations received from other manufacturers and find that your prices are higher than those offered by your competitors. We consider that the prices quoted by you for the Turbo-Alternator with Feed Heater and Condenser as well as for the Spare Parts should be reduced by 10 per cent. Thus the total firm price which we should be prepared to pay is £105,948.0.0. including the price of the Spare Parts.

Concerning the time for delivery, we would ask you to shorten it at least by three months in order to meet the requirements of our clients.

As to the terms of payment suggested by you, considering the more favourable terms offered by other manufacturers, we propose that 50% of the amount of the invoice should be paid in cash within 45 days after despatch of the documents to Moscow and the balance by draft at 18 months from the date of the Bill of Lading with interest at 4% p. a.

We also suggest that the contract for this equipment should embody our General Conditions which are identical with the conditions included in our last contract with Messrs. Brown and White Electrical Company, Ltd., who are your subcontractors for the Alternator. A copy of these General Conditions is enclosed herewith.

We look forward with interest to your reply.

Yours faithfully,

. . . .

Enclosure.

3. Reducing total price and shortening time of delivery:
Air-Mail

Sheffield, 8th October, 19 ...

Dear Sirs,

6,000 kW Turbo-Alternator Set

We have received your letter of the 3rd October for which we thank you.

We have given careful attention to your counter-offer and discussed the matter with our sub-contractors the Brown and White Electrical Company, Ltd. The result of this is that we are prepared to allow you 5% discount from the prices quoted in our letter of the 25th September and accept the order for the total firm price of £111,834.0.0.d. We regret that we cannot reduce the price further.

As to the time for delivery, we have asked our subcontractors to look into the time required for the delivery of the Alternator to our works, and they have agreed to reduce their time down to eighteen months.

In a similar manner we have also examined the time required to manufacture and erect the turbine, carry out running tests and prepare and pack the whole set for shipment. We offer now a reduced delivery time of 19½ months, and this time would date from receipt of your order with instructions to enable us to proceed to the work.

We have also considered the terms of payment suggested by you as well as your General Conditions and, wishing to develop our business relations, we agree to accept them.

We await your decision with interest.

Yours faithfully,

. . . .

4. Agreement on price and delivery time:

Sheffield, 11th October, 19...

Dear Sirs,

6,000 kW Turbo-Alternator Set

We have pleasure in confirming the telephone conversation of today between your Vice-President Mr. A. B. Ivanov and our Managing Director Mr. C. D. Harris during which it was agreed that the total price of the Turbo-Alternator Set with Feed Heater, Condenser and Spare Parts should be £ 109,000.0.0 (one hundred and nine thousand pounds sterling). It was further agreed that the whole equipment should be delivered in nineteen months from the date of the contract.

We thank you for order which will have our most careful attention and shall be obliged if you will send us your contract as early as possible to enable us to proceed immediately to the execution of the order.

Yours faithfully,

. . . .

17

SALE OF GOODS THROUGH AGENTS

PROPOSAL TO ACT AS AGENTS

Delhi, 15th Sept., 19...

V/O "Sojuzexport",
Moscow, U. S. S. R.

Dear Sirs,

Our object in writing to you is to enquire whether you would be willing to appoint us as your Agents for the sale of Compressors, Pumps and Blowers in India.

We have for some years past been representing the well-known British manufacturing concern of A. B. Brown & Co., Ltd., who have now established their own branch in Delhi.

We have considerable experience in the sale of different types of machinery and are sure that we could sell a large number of your machines annually.

We have large show-rooms in Delhi, Bombay and Calcutta where the machines could be shown to advantage.

If you should appoint us as your Agents, we should charge a commission of 5 per cent. on the net amount of all invoices for the goods sold through us. We should also be prepared to accept the del credere, if you should so desire , for which we should charge a commission of $\frac{3}{4}$ per cent.

For references you may apply to the City Bank of New Delhi, who would provide you with all information you might desire concerning our status.

We should be glad to hear whether our proposal is acceptable to you. If so, we should be pleased to receive the terms upon which you would be willing to entrust us with the sale of the machines in question as well as your prospectuses and illustrated catalogues with prices.

Yours faithfully,

. . . .

POSSIBILITIES OF RECIPROCAL TRADING IN MACHINE-TOOLS BETWEEN A BRITISH COMPANY AND V/O "SOJUZIMPORT"

1.

Sheffield, 20th October, 19...

Dear Sirs,

We refer to the recent discussions we had with Mr. A. B. Petrov of the Trade Delegation of the U.S.S.R. in London on the possibility of our supplying you with machine-tools manufactured by our company and in return distributing in Great Britain, as your exclusive Agents, specified Soviet machines to an equal value.

We enclose catalogues of our range of machine-tools with complete technical information as well as a list of our today's prices.

On the other hand, we have carefully examined the catalogues and specifications given to us by Mr. Petrov and are attaching to this letter a list of Soviet machines which, in our opinion, would be in demand in this country and which it would be advisable for you to send us on consignment.

To further the matter , the writer and our Export Manager, Mr. Arnold Jackson, are prepared to travel to Moscow and have personal discussions with members of Sojuzimport so that our proposal can be discussed in detail and an agreement reached to our mutual benefit.

During our discussions with Mr. Petrov he suggested that we should list the points which we would like to be clarified in Moscow and we enclose herewith an enumeration of such questions.

We look forward with much pleasure to your reply.

Yours faithfully,

. . . .

Enclosures.

2.

Moscow, 25th October, 19 ...

Dear Sirs,

We thank you for your letter of the 20th October. We have carefully considered your proposal and are pleased to advise you that we agree in principle that you should act as our Consignment Agents in Great Britain for the sale of machine-tools manufactured in the U.S.S.R. We should also agree to purchase from you machines of your manufacture equal in value to the sales of our machines from consignment stock.

We shall be glad to meet here Mr. James Moore and Mr. Arnold Jackson and discuss with them the points listed by you as well as other problems connected with the sale of our machines in Great Britain, such as advertising, show-rooms, technical service, del credere etc. with the view of working out a detailed consignment agreement. We suggest that the visit of your representatives shuld take place about the 10th November next. If this time is convenient for you, kindly let us know the date of their arrival in Moscow.

Yours faithfully,

. . . .

SALE OF WHEAT THROUGH BROKERS

1. On the 14th of Oct., 19 ..., Mr. Donaldson of Messrs. Donaldson & Son, Grain Brokers, called on Messrs. Simpson and Jones, Brokers of Sojuzexport, and enquired on behalf of Messrs. Frank & Sons, Ltd., Millers, about two cargoes of 6,000 tons each of Winter Wheat for shipment in November and November/December 19 .... The negotiations which took place at that meeting are seen from the following letter sent on October 15th by the Brokers to Sojuzexport, Moscow:

London, 15th October, 19 ...

Dear Sirs,

Mr. Donaldson of Messrs. Donaldson & Son, Grain Brokers, paid us a visit yesterday and enquired whether we were in a position to supply their Principals, Messrs. Frank & Sons, Ltd., Millers, with two cargoes of about 6,000 tons each of South Russian Winter Wheat for shipment in November and November-December, 19 ...

We acquainted Mr. Donaldson with samples Nos. 421 and 441 received by us last week, and must say that he was favourably impressed by sample No. 421, intimating he was sure it would meet the requirements of his Principals.

However, he desired to receive their approval before definitely settling any business.

We agreed to this arrangement, subject to his reply reaching us by Thursday, 18th October, and gave him our idea of the price at 32 pounds per English ton.

We will keep you informed of any further developments.

Yours faithfully,

. . . .

2. Messrs. Frank & Sons, Ltd., approved the samples submitted to them by their Brokers, but desired the shipment of the first cargo to be made during the second half of November or the first half of December, and that of the second cargo during the second half of December or the first half of January. The Brokers of Sojuzexport accordingly informed Sojuzexport by air-mail asking their confirmation by cable:

Air-Mail

London, 17th October, 19 ...

Dear Sirs,

Further to our letter of October 15th, we are pleased to inform you that Messrs. Frank & Sons, Ltd., Millers, have approved sample No. 421 of South Russian Winter Wheat presented to them by their Broker Mr. Donaldson.

It appears, however, that the Buyers desire the first cargo to be shipped during the second half of November or the first half of December. The shipment of the second cargo must take place during the second half of December or the first half of January.

Kindly let us know by cable whether you agree to this postponement of the shipping dates.

We presume that we shall be able to fix the price mentioned in our letter of the 15th October.

Yours faithfully,

. . . .

3. Telegram sent on 20th Oct. by Sojuzexport to their Brokers, confirming postponement of shipping dates:

"GRAINBROKERS LONDON — YOURS SEVENTEENTH OCTOBER AGREE SHIPMENT ONE CARGO SECOND HALF NOVEMBER FIRST HALF DECEMBER SECOND CARGO SECOND HALF DECEMBER FIRST HALF JANUARY SOJUZEXPORT".

4. Telegram sent by the Brokers on the 21st Oct., advising Sojuzexport of the sale of two cargoes of Wheat on sample 421:

"SOJUZEXPORT MOSCOW—SOLD TWO CARGOES WHEAT SAMPLE 421 ABOUT SIX THOUSAND TONS TEN PER CENT EACH PRICE THIRTYTWO POUNDS PER ENGLISH TON CIF HULL SHIPMENT FIRST CARGO SECOND HALF NOVEMBER FIRST HALF DECEMBER SECOND CARGO SECOND HALF DECEMBER FIRST HALF JANUARY GRAINBROKERS".

5. The above telegram was confirmed on the same day by a letter of the Brokers, in which they also informed Sojuzexport of favourable prospects of further business with the same Buyers:

London, October 21, 19 ...

Dear Sirs,

We confirm our telegram sent you today concerning the sale of two cargoes of Winter Wheat on sample No. 421, reading decoded as follows:

"SOLD TWO CARGOES WHEAT SAMPLE 421
ABOUT SIX THOUSAND TONS TEN PERCENT
EACH PRICE THIRTYTWO POUNDS PER ENGLISH
TON CIF HULL SHIPMENT FIRST CARGO SE-
COND HALF NOVEMBER FIRST HALF DECEMBER
SECOND CARGO SECOND HALF DECEMBER
FIRST HALF JANUARY".

Our Buyers, Messrs. Frank & Sons, Ltd., have assured us that
if the quality of these two cargoes suits their requirements as a
component part of a mixture of flour which they intend to introduce on the local market, they will be interested in further quantities of this wheat, provided you could guarantee a regular
supply at definite intervals, approximately of one cargo of about
6,000 tons each month.

We wish to draw your attention to the fact that Messrs. Frank
& Sons, Ltd., have been buying wheat for the past few years and
that business with them has been done to the satisfaction of all
concerned.

As soon as the contract is drawn up, we shall send you a copy
of it.

Yours faithfully,

. . . .

ENCL.: Advice of Sale.

6. Letter enclosing contract forms for two cargoes of wheat
sold:

London, 25th October, 19 ...

Dear Sirs,

We enclose two copies of contracts Nos. 65 and 66 dated 24th
October, covering the sale of two cargoes of 6,000 tons each of
Winter Wheat, sample No. 421, to Messrs. Frank & Sons, Ltd.,
Hull.

Yours faithfully,

. . . .

ENCL.: 2 Contract Forms.

7. Sojuzexport chartered for the execution of these contracts
two steamers of 6,000 tons, 10 per cent more or less, each.

About 10 days before the expected arrival of the first vessel
intended for the first cargo, the Owners informed the Charterers
that the s. s. "Fairfield" had been in collision with another vessel
during a dense fog in the Mediterranean and was towed to Genoa
disabled. The vessel was therefore unable to arrive at the loading
port before the 15th of December.

Upon receipt of the information of the Owners, Sojuzexport
took urgent steps to replace the "Fairfield" by another prompt
vessel, but without success.

Having at their disposal another vessel ready to load about
the 6th December, but of a larger size, Sojuzexport requested the
Buyers to accept, instead of 6,000 tons, 10 per cent more or less,

a larger cargo of 6,500 tons, 10 per cent more or less, and accordingly wrote to their Brokers asking them to communicate with Messrs. Frank & Sons, Ltd.:

Air-Mail

Moscow, 25th November, 19 ...

Dear Sirs,

<u>Contract No. 65</u>

We have received from Messrs. Gardigan & Laurence, Owners of the s. s. "Fairfield", the following telegram dated London, 24th November, reading decoded as follows:

> "S. S. FAIRFIELD CHARTER PARTY 28TH OCTOBER REGRET TO INFORM UNABLE ARRIVE LOADING PORT BEFORE DECEMBER FIFTEENTH OWING TO COLLISION MEDITERRANEAN DURING DENSE FOG STEAMER TOWED GENOA REPAIRS STOP SHALL COMMUNICATE UPON RECEIPT DETAILS".

This vessel, placed by us against Contract No. 65, was to arrive in the Black Sea about the 6th December.

Owing to the collision, however, it is quite evident that the vessel will not be able to arrive at the loading port in time for shipping the cargo in question.

We have done all we could to secure another boat of this size, but there is practically no chance of finding a vessel which could guarantee the required position.

In view of the above, we have carefully investigated the position of all tonnage chartered by us and, after considerable changes in our loading program, find we could arrange shipment by another vessel at the time required, the only obstacle being the size of the vessel which is of 6,500 tons, 10 per cent.

We greatly regret this unforeseen complication, but in the circumstances, the only thing that remains for us to do is to request the Buyers to accept against Contract No. 65 a cargo of 6,500 tons, 10 per cent more or less, instead of 6,000 tons, 10 per cent more or less, as stipulated in the contract.

We ask you therefore to communicate urgently with the Buyers and to use your best endeavours to settle the matter.

Yours faithfully,
V/O "Sojuzexport"

8. Brokers request the Buyers to increase the cargo:

URGENT

London, 27th November, 19 ...

Dear Sirs,

<u>Contract No. 65. Winter Wheat</u>

We confirm our telephone conversation of today with Mr. Brown and enclose a copy of a letter received by us from V/O "Sojuzexport", Moscow, regarding the shipment of the above cargo.

The letter being self-explanatory , we would only add that the difficulties which have arisen in this case through no fault of our friends have already caused them much trouble, and they would greatly appreciate it if you saw your way to meet their request to increase the cargo up to 6,500 tons in view of the absence of other suitable tonnage.

Hoping to receive your early reply,

We are,

Yours faithfully,

. . . .

ENCL. 1.

9. Having considered the above communication, the Buyers informed the Brokers of Sojuzexport of their agreement to increase the contract quantity, provided Sojuzexport agreed to ship the goods not before 12th December:

Hull, 28th November. 19 ...

Dear Sirs,

Contract No. 65

We acknowledge receipt of your letter of the 27th inst. together with a copy of a letter of V/O "Sojuzexport", Moscow, and have noted their contents.

We wish to inform you that the increase of the cargo by 500 tons as requested by the Sellers would practically mean to us storage expenses on the above quantity for a period of at least two weeks, as the requirements of our mills for the coming month are fully covered by the quantity originally stipulated in the contract.

Nevertheless we are willing to increase the cargo up to 6,500 tons, 10 per cent more or less, provided V/O "Sojuzexport" agree to ship the cargo not before the 12th December.

Yours faithfully,

. . . .

10. Telegram from the Brokers advising Sojuzexport of the Buyers' consent (sent on November 29):

"SOJUZEXPORT MOSCOW — YOUR LETTER 25 NOVEMBER CONTRACT 65 BUYERS AGREE INCREASE CARGO SIXTHOUSAND FIVEHUNDRED TONS TEN PER CENT PROVIDED SHIPMENT NOT BEFORE TWELFTH DECEMBER CABLE URGENTLY GRAINBROKERS"

11. Sujuzexport's confirmation:

"GRAINBROKERS LONDON — YOUR TELEGRAM
29 NOVEMBER CONTRACT 65 CONFIRM SIXTHOU-
SAND FIVEHUNDRED TONS TEN PER CENT
SHIPMENT NOT BEFORE TWELFTH DECEMBER
SOJUZEXPORT"

18

CONTRACTS IN EXPORT TRADE AND THEIR PERFORMANCE

LETTER OF INTENT

Of the negotiations between the delegation from the Ministry of the Chemical Industry of the USSR, headed by L. A. Kostandov, minister (the Soviet party), and TTR Industries, Inc., a United States corporation (the American party), which took place during the period from March 6, 1985, to March 8, 1985, in the United States.

1. During the negotiations, the Soviet party included L. A. Kostandov, minister of the Chemical Industry of the USSR; A. Y. Riabenko, vice-chairman, Gosplan; V. I. Bessmertniy, president, Amtorg Trading Corporation; L. K. Lukianov, president, V/O Techmashimport; Y. V. Koumlev, assistant to Minister Kostandov; S. E. Dorokhin, chief of compensation, Ministry of the Chemical Industry of the USSR; V. E. Allaverdov, representative of Amtorg Trading Corporation.

2. The American party included John S. Davidson, chairman of the board and chief executive officer; Peter R. Richardson, president and chief operating officer; Neal A. Smith, vice-president, corporate marketing; James K. Reiter, vice-president, corporate development; Ronald B. Gold, vice-president,

general manager, Chemical Division; Richard C. Ruxteron, director of planning and development, Chemical Division; Robert T. Johnson, vice-president, general manager, Fiberglass Division; Gerald N. Frieman, director, International Operations Fiberglass Division; Charles M. Woodman, president, general manager, Coatings and Resins Division; Lindon R. Ruder, vice-president, Industrial Coatings, Coatings and Resins Division; Louis A. Fricks, director, International Operations Coatings and Resins Division; Erwin Z. Cook president, American International, Inc.; and Michael I. Reed, vice-president, American International, Inc.

3. The Soviet and American parties expressed a desire to cooperate on the construction of a vinyl chloride monomer (VCM) complex in the USSR, which would have a production capacity of 1 million tons per year and, in accordance with paragraph 7 of the "Basic Principles of Relations between the USSR and USA" signed by General Secretary L. I. Brezhnev and President Richard M. Nixon on 29 May 1972 as well as Article II of the "Agreement between the Government of the USA and the Government of the USSR Regarding Trade" dated 18 October 1972, the Soviet and American parties agreed in principle on such cooperation. The VCM complex would include:

a. Natural gas separation unit

b. Ethylene unit

c. Chlorine and caustic soda plant

d. Liquid-phase ethylene dichloride unit

e. Oxychlorination ethylene dichloride unit

f. Vinyl chloride monomer unit (this VCM unit will include two installations of not less than 500,000 tons per year production capacity each)

g. Ethylene glycol unit

h. Oxygen plant

i. Steam-producing facilities

j. Product-storage facilities

k. General plant facilities, pipeline, and cooling systems (water and utility distribution)

It was decided that the VCM complex should be constructed in a manner that will allow expansion.

4. The Soviet and American parties agreed that the cooperation for the construction of the VCM complex should include:

a. The sale of technology, licenses, machinery, and equipment to the proper Soviet foreign trade organization on a competitive basis either by the American party directly or by the American party to an engineering company acceptable to the Soviet party and to the proper Soviet foreign trade organization and which would be responsible for the construction of the entire complex. Appropriate guarantees will be included by the American party in the agreement for the sale of technology, licenses, machinery, and equipment to the proper Soviet foreign trade organization.

b. The American party would work cooperatively with the proper Soviet foreign trade organization in arranging the purchase of at least 200,000 tons per year of VCM or an equivalent quantity of other products produced by the complex such as Energy Development Complex (EDC) on a long-term basis and based upon world market prices. The exact quantity of such products would be agreed upon by the American party and the proper Soviet foreign trade organization. However, such purchases should cover the cost of the technology, licenses, machinery, and equipment necessary for the construction of the entire complex noted in Section 4a above as well as the cost of financing the complex.

c. Within a reasonable time, the proper Soviet foreign trade organization should provide the American party with an inquiry with specifications necessary for the preparation of a proposal for the construction of the above-mentioned complex.

d. Contracts for the purchase of VCM, EDC, or other products from the complex should be signed at the same time that the contracts for the delivery of the complete technology and equipment for the complex are signed with the proper Soviet foreign trade organization.

5. The Soviet and American parties agreed to continue discussions on other projects of mutual interest, including the construction of a 20,000-ton-per-year fiberglass-manufacturing facility in the USSR, solution mining for potash, and the use of polyurethane and other coating and resin technology.

This Letter of Intent was agreed to, and signed on 8 March 1985 in New York, in the English and Russian languages, both copies having equal validity.

Either party may announce or publish the fact that this Letter of Intent has been signed, but the parties agree not to publish the contents of this Letter of Intent unless and until final agreements are concluded with the proper Soviet foreign trade organizations.

For and on Behalf of the
Soviet Party:

For and on Behalf of the
American Party:

_____

_____

L. A. Kostandov, Minister

Peter R. Richardson, President

PROTOCOL

On negotiations between representatives of the USSR Ministry of Iron and Steel Industry and officers of American Corporation.

1. The negotiations between representatives of the USSR Ministry of Iron and Steel Industry and officers of American Corporation took place from 3 to 17 December 1985 in Moscow.

The Ministry of Iron and Steel Industry was represented by Messrs V. V. Lempitsky, B. N. Malinin, S. N. Belorusov, A. A. Dello, B. V. Molotilov, D. I. Aleksieev, and L. A. Lobov.

American Corporation was represented by Messrs H. C. Smith, M. H. Gold, R. L. Johnson, A. B. Pretsler, and T. D. Shultz.

2. As a result of an exchange of opinions, the parties have agreed that scientific and technical cooperation may be established in the areas of:

[*Specify areas.*]

3. The USSR Ministry of Iron and Steel Industry has transferred a list of possible subjects for scientific and technical cooperation in various areas of ferrous metallurgy to American Corporation enabling it to determine details of such subjects.

[*Application*]

American Corporation will study these proposals and will submit to the USSR Ministry of Iron and Steel Industry within the shortest period possible its outline of subjects for joint scientific and technical cooperation.

4. The parties have exchanged the lists of licenses covering iron and steel-making technologies, which may represent mutual interest for both parties. The parties agreed to investigate the proposals exchanged.

Drawn up and signed the _____ day of December 1985, in duplicate, one copy in Russian and one in English, both texts being equally authentic.

For the USSR Ministry
of Iron and Steel   For American
Industry: Corporation:

_____   _____

AIDE-MEMOIRE

From October 15 to 17, 1985, negotiations took place at the Ministry of Foreign Trade of the USSR, with a delegation from American Steel Corporation (United States), headed by the chairman of the board of the corporation, Richard S. Richardson.

On October 16, 1985, N. S. Patolichev, minister of foreign trade of the USSR, received Mr. Richardson.

During the discussions, the parties confirmed their desire to expand mutually advantageous trade and economic cooperation in various branches of commerce including cooperation in commercial ventures on a compensation basis.

During the discussions the following projects were considered:

1. The design and delivery of the technical equipment for a factory for the manufacture of deep-water stationary platforms for a sea depth of 200 meters with a general production capacity of 70,000 tons of steel structures per year as well as the license for their production.

The possible delivery to the USSR of:

—A ship-shape vessel for drilling exploratory wells to a depth of 6,000 meters in a sea depth of up to 300 meters with complete underwater well-head equipment and testing instruments

—Three deep-water vessels for offshore drilling maintenance

—Two stationary deep-water platforms with complete equipment for exploratory drilling and production of offshore gas and gas-condensate sites having 50-60 wells and placed in a sea depth of 100-200 meters

—Two semisubmersible drilling vessels for drilling oil and gas exploratory wells to a depth of 6,000 meters in a sea depth of up to 200 meters with complete underwater well-head equipment and testing instruments

—Two diving capsules with equipment for underwater technical work, inspection, and maintenance of underwater well-heads, drilling and operation of wells, stationary platforms, and underwater pipelines at a sea depth of up to 300 meters

—Pipe-laying vessel for installing offshore pipelines at a sea depth of up to 60 meters

—Two vessels for cementing casing columns of offshore wells

—An automatic floating crane with a lift capacity of 1,000-2,000 tons

—Nine lifesaving capsules designed for 28 persons

The specific inquiries with specifications for preparation of a proposal on the above-listed items were submitted by the Soviet party (V/O Sudoimport).

American Steel Corporation promised to prepare detailed proposals (with indications of all necessary technical and commercial conditions) and to send it in the near future to V/O Sudoimport, with whom discussions will continue on this subject.

2. On October 9, 1985, American International, Inc., gave to V/O Techmashimport a proposal for the delivery of complete equipment for a factory to manufacture 20,000 tons of fiberglass per year. The Soviet party stated that

the proposal has been directed to the concerned organization for examination, and V/O Techmashimport will advise the results of the examination in order to continue discussions. The Soviet party noted that the purchase of the indicated equipment will be carried out on the basis of credit and that the transaction will be a compensation transaction and that fiberglass or other chemical products will be purchased. American International, Inc., promised to consider these questions and to inform V/O Techmashimport of additional suggestions for possible purchases.

3. American International, Inc., presented the initial proposal for cooperation on the construction in the USSR of a chemical complex for the production of polyvinyl chloride, vinyl chloride, and many other chemical products.

The parties agreed that this project will be consummated on a compensation basis, keeping in mind, that chemical products produced at the complex will be delivered from the USSR in the form of compensation, including VCM, caustic soda, trichlorethylene, ethylene glycol, polyvinyl chloride, and propylene.

The Soviet party stated that the proposal would be considered and the results communicated by the foreign trade organization V/O Techmashimport. It was also agreed that the amounts and period of compensation of the listed types of products will be defined, and the firms will advise on the possibility of financing the delivery of equipment and technical documentation, as well as financing such purchases through bank credits.

4. V/O Techmashimport submitted a specific inquiry and technical specifications for the preparation of proposals for the delivery of complete equipment for helium production. American International stated that proposals would be prepared and directed to V/O Techmashimport.

5. American International submitted to V/O Techmashimport a proposal for the delivery of equipment for the production of electronic watches. This proposal will be studied by the Soviet organizations. Discussions on this subject will continue with the indicated organization.

6. American Steel Corporation received specific inquiries from V/O Metallurgimport for the preparation of a proposal on the delivery of equipment for the production of steel with aluminum and zinc coatings and electric steels. The firm stated that its proposals on this equipment would be submitted in the near future.

AGREEMENT

On Scientific and Technical Cooperation between the State Committee of the Council of Ministers of the USSR for Science and Technology and the American Corporation (United States).

The State Committee of the Council of Ministers of the USSR for Science and Technology (GKNT) and American Corporation (United States), hereinafter called "Parties,"

Considering that favorable conditions have been created for extensive development of a long-term scientific and tehcnical cooperation;

Taking into account the mutual interest of both Parties in the development of scientific and technical cooperation and recognizing the mutual benefit thereof;

In accordance with Paragraph 8 of the "Basic Principles of Relations between the Union of Soviet Socialist Republics and the United States of America," signed on 29 May 1972, and Article 4 of the "Agreement between the Government of the USSR and the Government of the USA on Cooperation in the Fields of Science and Technology," concluded on 24 May 1972;

Have agreed as follows:

ARTICLE 1

Scientific and technical cooperation between the parties shall be implemented first and foremost in the fields of

a) Ferrous metallurgy, specifically in areas such as production of electrical stainless steels and direct reduction

b) Joint development of technical means for offshore drilling

This agreement does not prevent either Party from entering into similar cooperation in the said fields with a third party.

The scope of this Agreement may at any time be extended to include other fields or specific subjects of cooperation by agreement of the Parties.

ARTICLE 2

Scientific and technical cooperation between the Parties can be implemented in the following forms with specific arrangements being exclusively subject to mutual agreement between appropriate Soviet organizations and the firm of American Corporation (or its corresponding division):

a) Exchange of scientific and technical information, documentation, and production samples

b) Exchange of delegations of specialists and trainees

c) Organization of lectures, symposia, and demonstrations of the production samples on problems that are of interest to both Parties

d) Mutual consultations for the purpose of discussing and analyzing scientific and technical problems, technical principles, ideas, and concepts in the appropriate fields of technology

e) Joint research, development, and testing and exchange of research results and experience

f) Joint development and implementation of programs and projects

g) Other forms of cooperation including exchange, acquisition or transfer of methods, processes as of "know-how" and of licenses for the manufacture of products.

ARTICLE 3

For the practical implementation of the present Agreement the Parties shall establish special groups of experts whose task it will be to develop specific programs of cooperation on agreed-upon problems, to draw up plans of work, as well as to draft proposals for further cooperation. The results of the discussions of these groups of experts will be presented in the form of protocols, which may be used as the basis for preparations of special agreements or contracts provided for in Article 4 of the present Agreement.

Groups of experts shall meet, as necessary, alternatively in the USSR and the USA, unless otherwise agreed upon.

The Parties will define organization and/or persons responsible for the practical implementation of the cooperation programs and other specific arrangements.

ARTICLE 4

The Parties have established that commercial, financial, and legal questions that may arise in the course of their cooperation are to be the subject of special agreements and contracts between appropriate and competent Soviet organizations and the firm American Corporation (or its corresponding divisions). The foregoing is meant to include:

a) Renumeration for sharing of scientific and technological knowledge, sale of patents, or assignation of licenses

b) Exchange of experience, protection of patents or inventions, joint requests for patents, and also conditions governing issuance of licenses

c) Conditions governing use of patents, introduction of new production methods, and sale of finished goods

d) Other terms and conditions necessary or appropriate for implementing a specific activity or program

The Parties adhere to the opinion that in carrying this Agreement it is necessary to take into consideration existing contractual relations between either of the agreeing Parties and/or a third party.

ARTICLE 5

Scientific and technical information furnished by one Party to the other under this Agreement may be used freely for its own research, development, and production, as well as for the sale of finished products unless the Party supplying such information stipulates at the time of its transfer that the information may be used only on the basis of special agreement reached in accordance with Article 4 of the present Agreement. This information can be transmitted to a third party only with the approval of the Party that has furnished it.

Information received from a third party that cannot be disposed of at will by one of the contracting Parties is not subject to transmittal to the other Party unless mutually satisfactory arrangement can be made with the third party for communication of such information.

It is contemplated in the foregoing that both organizations or institutions of the USSR and subsidiary firms of whose capital the firm of American Corporation owns directly or indirectly more than 50% shall be not regarded as a third party.

ARTICLE 6

Expenses of traveling back and forth of specialists of both Parties under the programs related to this Agreement as a rule will be defrayed as follows:

—The Party sending the specialists pays the round-trip fare to and from the principal port of entry.
—The host Party bears all costs connected with their sojourn while in its own country.

The duration of the above visits and the number of specialists in each group shall be mutually agreed to by the Parties in advance of the visits.

ARTICLE 7

The present Agreement shall continue for a period of five (5) years and shall enter into force immediately upon its signature. It can be canceled by either Party upon six (6) months' notice in writing to the other Party.

The cancelation of the present Agreement shall not affect the validity of any agreements and contracts entered into in accordance with Article 4.

On expiration of the present Agreement it can be renewed for a further period if both Parties are interested.

Drawn and signed 17 December 1985, in Moscow and in duplicate, one copy in Russian and one in English, both texts being equally authentic.

For the State Committee
of the Council of Ministers
of the USSR for Science
and Technology:

For the American
Corporation (United States).

_____   _____

December 8, 1985

V/O Metallurgimport
Ul. Arkhitektora Vlasova, 13
Moscow, USSR

We hereby confirm that the Sellers and the Buyers have come to the following agreements in addition to the said below clauses of Contract No. 29-04/26167-422 of 17 December 1985.

I. Under Clause 4.6.3.6.3 of Appendix No. 1 it is agreed upon that Sellers will continue to study modern hearth-roll technology and development. If Sellers determine that any alternative appears equally desirable or preferable to Masrock sleeved hearth rolls, Sellers will advise Buyers. Sellers and Buyers will attempt to negotiate a mutually agreeable modification to the Contract in the event that such alternate hearth rolls are desired by the Buyers. The Sellers are willing also to consider the recommendations of the Buyers under the condition that such recommendations are submitted within five (5) months from the date of signing the above Contract.

II. Under the general terms and conditions of the Contract it is agreed that "direct damages" mentioned in various clauses of the present Contract is understood to be the following expenses to the Buyers:

—The Buyer's expenses connected with repair of the defects of the equipment delivered by the Sellers and/or defects preventing the equipment delivered by the Sellers from reaching the level stated in the Contract.

—The Buyers' expenditures connected with supervision at Sellers' request of installation and the Sellers' control of the repair or replacement of the defective equipment or its portion.

—The Buyers' expenses connected with disassembly and reinstallation of the defective equipment or its portion.

—The Buyers' transport expenses incurred at Sellers' request connected with delivery of the replacement equipment or its portion from the Sellers' country frontier to the Buyers' plant and/or shipment of items that exceed dimensions listed in Section 5.23.

—The Buyers' expenses connected with consumption of all types of power and the Buyers' materials to eliminate the defects.

—The Buyers' expenses connected with the payment of wages of the Buyers' personnel used at Sellers' request for the elimination of defects.

—Value of the additional engineering made by the Buyers at Seller's request to eliminate the defects.

III. Under Clause 2.6 of the general terms and conditions it is agreed that the $45 million budget price for out-of-furnace equipment for silicon steel processing contained in Appendix 4 to the Contract is shown for the purpose of financing. The Sellers and the Buyers have agreed to work together to reduce this amount to the lowest possible level consistent with providing delivery of the suitable equipment.

In the opinion of the Sellers, the cost can be reduced more if the recommendations of the Sellers are acceptable.

In any case, the Buyers and Sellers will work together to reduce this amount to the minimum possible level.

1. After final agreement of the price of out-of-furnace equipment, the price specified in Section 4.2 of the Contract ($340,036,872) will be corrected by deducting the budget price from it ($45 million) and by adding to it the above said final agreed-upon price for out-of-furnace processing equipment. Thus the amounts specified in Clauses 4.2, 4.2.2.1, 4.2.3, 4.2.4, and 4.2.5 shall be altered.

2. In the event that the Sellers and the Buyers do not come to agreement on the commercial and/or technical points and reject the mutual work on the purchase of out-of-furnace processing equipment, correction of the price per Clause 4.2 and the corresponding portions will be effected by deducting budget price equal to $45 million from the price under Clause 4.2 and from corresponding portions specified in Clauses 4.2.1.1, 4.2.2.1, 4.2.3, 4.2.4, and 4.2.5. As a result, the price under Clause 4.2 of the Contract will amount to $295,036,872.

   a) By "working together" Sellers mean the joint preparation of an inquiry and mutual study of offers or proposals received and technical and mutual commercial negotiations on the Contract with potential suppliers of AOD and DH vacuum degasser equipment in a manner that will allow the Buyers to be fully informed of all necessary technical and commercial points.

   Sellers, on our behalf, will supply V/O Metallurgimport with the necessary competitive materials and at the same time Sellers also will use competitive materials supplied by the Buyers. If for any reason the Buyers and the Sellers do not come to agreement regarding the commercial and/or technical points, either Party shall have the right to reject the purchase of the AOD converter and DH vacuum degassers. In the event of any such rejection:

1. Sellers shall provide Buyers with specifications for the purchase of AOD converter and vacuum degassing equipment suitable for production of dynamo steel meeting the quality guarantees set forth in Section 13 of this Contract when American International's technology is used.
2. Buyer's obligation under the present Contract to purchase any other items shall be unaffected.

b) In accordance with 0.5.2 of Appendix 4 to the present Contract, it is agreed that the Sellers will supply the initial data necessary to the Buyers to design and complete construction work for the buildings and foundations at NLMP (Novo-Lipetsk Metallurgical Project) to install AOD- and DH-type vacuum degassing equipment in the time periods listed in points 1, 3, and 4 of schedule 1 and point 1.2 of schedule 2 of Appendix 4, however, calculating such periods to begin from the date of signing of the main Contract.

IV. Under Clause 15 of the general terms and conditions it is agreed that if in connection with performance of the above-mentioned Contract an occasion arises whereby V/O Metallurgimport has the right to cancel the contract, V/O Metallurgimport, before exercising such cancellation right, will take into consideration events causing the improper performance of the Contract if they are beyond the Sellers' control.

V. Under Clause 4 of the general terms and conditions it is agreed that if as a result of depreciation of Japanese yen against U.S. dollars the cumulative amount of payments in Japanese yen to be made pursuant to Section 4.2.4.1 of the Contract should reach the limit of the amount in Japanese yen financed under the Loan Agreement specified in Section 4.2.4 of the Contract to be made thereafter shall be, notwithstanding the provisions of the Section 4.1.4.1 of the Contract, effected in U.S. dollars in cash by telegraphic transfer at Sellers' expense to the bank account designated by Soponn Steel within 30 days of the date(s) of receipt by the Bank for Foreign Trade of the USSR in Moscow of the invoice stated below and the documents specified in Section 4.2.3 of the Contract.

—Soponn's invoice in one original and four (4) copies indicating invoiced amount, number of the Contract, transaction number, and basis for calculating the invoiced amount.

VI. Under Section 4 of the present Contract it is agreed that upon successful completion of the guarantee tests for the full processing circuit or if the commencement of such tests has been delayed beyond the 58th month after the signing of the present Contract because of Buyers' fault, Buyers will pay to the Sellers at the rate of 5 percent of the price of each item of equipment and spare parts for each line and each unit of auxiliary equipment for which a load test (or first-stage acceptance test in the case of the PITS system) has been successfully completed by the time of said successful completion of the guarantee tests and thereafter will pay to the Sellers at the rate of 5 percent of the price of each item of equipment and spare parts for each line and each unit of auxiliary equipment upon completion of the load test of such line or unit.

Payment of the said guarantee sums shall be effected in cash by telegraphic transfer at Sellers' expense to the bank account within thirty (30) days from the date of receipt by the Foreign Trade Bank of the USSR of the following documents:

—Sellers' invoice in one original and four copies.

—Two copies of Protocol stipulated in Section 13.7.14 for the full processing circuit, or if 58 months have elapsed from the date of the Contract, the Buyers will issue to the Sellers a Release Protocol by the 59th month from the date of the Contract if the guarantee tests for the full circuit have been delayed beyond the 58th month due to the fault of the Buyers. Such Release Protocol will authorize payment of 5 percent of the price of each item of equipment and spare parts for each line and each unit of auxiliary equipment for which a load test has been successfully completed.

—Two copies of Protocol for each line or unit stipulated in Item 1.3.4 of Appendix No. 3 or Section 13.7.5 of the Contract.

—Original letter of guarantee of the first-class Japanese bank for the amount equal to the invoiced sum, according to the specimen attached hereto.

VII. Under Clause 14 of the general terms and conditions it is agreed upon that if the Sellers fail to pay the penalty in accordance with Section 14.2 of the Contract the Buyers may deduct the amount of such penalty due and receivable by the Buyers under the Contract from the payment(s) due and payable to the Sellers under the Contract.

This letter is confidential and only for the present transaction.

Respectfully yours,

AMERICAN INTERNATIONAL, INC.   SOPONN STEEL CORPORATION

H. C. Smith   M. N. Gold   A. Tanada   T. Futava

Accepted and agreed to for
V/O Metallurgimport by:

_____

N. P. Maximov

_____

O. P. Eliseev

FORM OF CONTRACT FOR THE SALE OF OIL PRODUCTS

Contract No ...
For Oil Products in Bulk, c. i. f. Terms

Moscow   Date
. . . .

This contract is made between Vsesojuznoje Objedinenije "Sojuzexport", Moscow, hereinafter called "Sellers" and . . . .
hereinafter called "Buyers" , whereby it is agreed as follows:

1. SUBJECT OF THE CONTRACT

Sellers have sold and Buyers have bought c. i. f. . . . . . .
. . . .

2. QUALITY

The goods sold under the present contract shall be of the
following specification: . . . .

3. PRICE

. . . .

4. TIME OF DELIVERY

The goods sold under the present contract are to be delivered
by Sellers and accepted by Buyers . . . .
. . . .
 The date of the Bill of Lading to be considered as the date
of delivery.

5. PAYMENT

Payment for the goods sold under the present contract is to be
effected out of an irrevocable confirmed Letter of Credit to be
opened by Buyers in ... with the Bank for Foreign Trade of the

U. S. S. R, Moscow, or with ... in favour of Sellers for the value of each lot of the goods to be shipped plus 10%. The Letter of Credit to be valid 45 days.

The Letter of Credit to be opened not later than 15 days before the agreed time of shipment of each lot of the goods. Expenses in connection with the opening, amendment and utilization of the Letter of Credit to be paid by Buyers.

Should Buyers fail to open the Letter of Credit in time, they are to pay Sellers a fine for each day of the delay, but not more than for 20 days, at the rate of 0.1 per cent. of the amount of the Letter of Credit and in that case Sellers shall have the right not to load the tanker until the Letter of Credit has been opened. Should the delay in the opening of the Letter of Credit exceed 20 days, Sellers shall have the right to refuse to deliver the goods which were to be paid for out of this Letter of Credit. And in all the above cases demurrage and dead freight paid by Sellers in connection with the delay in the opening of the Letter of Credit are to be repaid by Buyers. Payment out of the Letter of Credit is to be made against presentation by Sellers to the Bank for Foreign Trade of the U. S. S. R. in Moscow of the following documents:

Commercial invoice.

Insurance Policy or Certificate of Ingosstrakh of the U. S. S. R.

. . . .

In case of the opening of the Letter of Credit with another Bank, payment is to be made against a telegram of the Bank for Foreign Trade of the U. S. S. R., Moscow, acknowledging the receipt of the above documents.

The rate of exchange of U. S. dollars into . . . .

. . . .

6. DELIVERY AND ACCEPTANCE

The goods are considered to be delivered by Sellers and accepted by Buyers in respect to quantity: as per weight indicated in the Bill of Lading in conformity with the measurements of the shore tanks at the port of loading, and in respect to quality: as per certificate· of quality issued by a laboratory at the port of loading. The weight stated in the Bill of Lading is to be considered final and binding upon both parties.

Previous to the loading of the goods, 4 arbitration samples are to be taken from each of the shore tanks from which the goods are to be loaded in the carrying tanker. These samples to be sealed by Sellers as well as by the Captain of the tanker; 2 samples to be handed over through the Captain of the tanker at the port of unloading to Buyers or to another person according to Buyers' instructions and the other 2 samples to be retained by Sellers. Both parties shall keep these samples for 2 months from the date of delivery. Should, however, a claim be presented by

Buyers, the parties shall keep these samples longer until final settlement of the claim.

In case of a dispute on the quality of the goods in connection with divergencies in the analyses of the arbitration samples made by the Sellers' and Buyers' laboratories, an analysis which is to be final and binding upon both parties is to be made by a neutral laboratory agreed upon by the parties.

7. INSURANCE

Sellers are to insure the goods for their account against usual marine risks including risks of leakage exceeding 1% with Ingosstrakh of the U. S. S. R. in accordance with the Transport Insurance Rules of Ingosstrakh for the amount of the invoice value of the goods plus 10 per cent. The goods may be insured against war and other risks upon special request of Buyers and for Buyers' account. The Insurance Policy or Certificate of Ingosstrakh of the U. S. S. R. is to be made out in the name of Buyers or another person according to their instructions and is to be sent together with the other shipping documents.

8. TERMS OF TRANSPORTATION

(1) Sellers are to inform Buyers by telegraph or by telex not later than 5 days before the starting of loading of the name and capacity of the tanker, the date and port of shipment of the goods.

Furthermore, the Captain is to advise Buyers or their agent by cable of the forthcoming arrival of the tanker at the port of discharge 4 days before her arrival.

Sellers have the right to substitute one tanker for another informing Buyers thereof by cable or telex.

(2) On arrival of the tanker at the port of discharge, the Captain is to give Buyers' representative at this port a written notice of readiness of the tanker for discharging. The Captain is entitled to hand in the above notice at any time of the day or the night.

(3) Lay time to commence 6 hours after such notice of readiness is handed in by the Captain, berth or no berth. Sundays, holidays, time of stormy weather preventing discharging as well as time during which discharging operations could not be carried out owing to technical and other conditions depending on the tanker are not to be included in the lay time.

(4) Time allowed for tanker's discharging is fixed at 50 per cent. of the time stipulated in the Charter Party for loading and unloading.

The time allowed for unloading, however, is not to be less than:

for tankers of 1,000 tons deadweight and less — 18 running hours
for tankers from 1,001 up to 2,000 tons deadweight — 24 — » —
» » » 4,001 » » 8,000 » » — 60 — » —
» » of 8,001 tons deadweight and over — 72 — » —

(5) Demurrage is to be paid at the rate stipulated in the Charter Party per day and pro rata for any part of the running day but not more than:

for tankers	of	1,000 tons d. w. and less	— £ 175.0.0
»	»	from 1,001 up to 2,000 tons d. w.	— £ 200.0.0
»	»	» 2,001 » » 3,000 » » » »	— £ 225.0.0
»	»	» 18,001 » » 21,000 » » » »	— £ 725.0.0

9. CLAIMS

In case of non-conformity of the quality of the goods actually delivered by Sellers with the contract specification, any claim concerning the quality of the goods may be presented within two months of the date of delivery.

No claim shall be considered by Sellers after expiration of the above period.

No claim presented for one lot of the goods shall be regarded by Buyers as a reason for rejecting any other lot or lots of the goods to be delivered under the present contract.

10. CONTINGENCIES

Should any circumstances arise which prevent the complete or partial fulfilment by any of the parties of their respective obligations under this contract, namely: fire, ice conditions or any other acts of the elements, war, military operations of any character, blockade, prohibition of export or import or any other circumstances beyond the control of the parties, the time stipulated for the fulfilment of the obligations shall be extended for a period equal to that during which such circumstances last.

If the above circumstances last for more than 20 days, any delivery or deliveries which are to be made under the contract within that period may be cancelled on the declaration of any of the parties, and if the above circumstances last more than 40 days, each party shall have the right to discontinue any further fulfilment of their obligations under the contract in whole and in such cases neither of the parties shall have the right to make a demand upon the other party for compensation for any possible losses.

The party for whom it became impossible to meet its obligations under the contract shall immediately advise the other party as regards the beginning and the termination of the circumstances preventing the fulfilment of its obligations.

Certificates issued by the respective chamber of commerce of Sellers' or Buyers' country shall be sufficient proof of such circumstances and their duration.

11. ARBITRATION

Any dispute or difference which may arise out of or in connection with the present contract shall be settled, without recourse to courts of law, by the Foreign Trade Arbitration Commission of the U. S. S. R. Chamber of Commerce in Moscow in accordance with the Rules for Procedure of the said Commission.

The awards of this Arbitration shall be considered final and binding upon both parties.

12. OTHER CONDITIONS

(1) Neither party is entitled to transfer its rights and obligations under the present contract to a third party without the other party's previous written consent.

Besides, Buyers are not entitled to resell or in any other way alienate the goods bought under this contract to any third country without Sellers' previous written consent.

(2) After the signing of the present contract all previous negotiations and correspondence between the parties in connection with it shall be considered null and void.

(3) All amendments and additions to the present contract are valid only if they are made in writing and signed by both parties.

(4) All taxes, customs and other dues connected with the conclusion and fulfilment of the present contract, levied within the U. S. S. R., except those connected with the Letter of Credit, to be paid by Sellers, and those levied outside the U. S. S. R. to be paid by Buyers.

(5) The U. S. S. R. is regarded as the place of conclusion and fulfilment of the contract.

13. JURIDICAL ADDRESSES

Sellers: . . . .
Buyers: . . . .

SELLERS   BUYERS
(Signatures)   (Signatures)

FORM OF CONTRACT FOR THE SALE OF GRAIN

Contract No. ...
C. I. F.

. . . . 19 . . .

Vsesojuznoje Exportno-Importnoje Objedinenije "Sojuzexport", Moscow, hereinafter referred to as the "Sellers", and Messrs. ..., hereinafter referred to as the "Buyers", have concluded this contract to the effect that the Sellers have sold and the Buyers have bought on the terms and conditions set forth and subject to General Conditions of Sale endorsed hereon, the following goods:

1. DESCRIPTION OF THE GOODS AND QUANTITY: ....
. . . .
metric tons, 10 (ten) per cent more or less, at the Sellers' option, in bulk.

2. QUALITY: The grain intended for shipment must be in sound condition and free from any foreign smell. Natural weight

.... kilos per hectolitre. Admixture of foreign substances ....
per cent, including dirt up to .... per cent.

3. PRICE ... (...) per metric ton c. i. f. ... in bulk.

4. DELIVERY TIME: Shipment is to be effected during...
19... from the port/s of the Black Sea and/or Baltic Sea at the
Sellers' option. The Sellers have the right to effect partial shipments.

5. TERMS OF DISCHARGE: A. Discharge of the goods out
of vessel's holds at the port of destination to be effected by the
Buyers at their own expense, free of risk and expenses to the
vessel, at the average rate of ... metric tons per hatch per weather day, Sundays, official general and local holidays are excepted
unless used. For detention of the vessel over the time allowed
for discharge the Buyers to pay to the Sellers demurrage at the
rate of ... per GRT of the vessel per day and pro rata for any
part of a day, and for all lay time saved in discharge the Sellers
to pay to the Buyers dispatch money at the rate of ... per GRT
of the vessel per day and pro rata for any part of a day.

B. Discharge of the goods shall be at the Buyers' expense,
once they have passed the ship's rail. The Buyers must accept the
goods from the vessel as quickly as the vessel can deliver them
and are responsible for any detention of the vessel being through
their fault (particularly for not placing lighters in due time when
discharge is being effected into lighters) paying as compensation
for detention of vessel in unloading ... per GRT of the vessel
per day.

As a compensation for expenses connected with discharge of
the goods from ship's rail the Buyers to pay to the Sellers ...
per each metric ton of the goods discharged.

6. PAYMENT: A. Payment to be effected in ... at the rate of
exchange .... The Buyers to establish by cable an irrevocable
confirmed Letter of Credit with the Bank for Foreign Trade of
the U. S. S. R., Moscow, in favour of the Sellers covering the
full value of the goods sold under this contract plus 10% margin.
The Letter of Credit to be established by the Buyers not later than
three days after receipt of the Sellers' cable advice of the readiness of the goods for shipment. The Letter of Credit to be valid
... days. Payment from the Letter of Credit to be effected against
the presentation of the following documents:

Invoice/s in ....

Bill/s of Lading.

Certificate/s of Quality issued by the State Grain Inspection
of the U. S. S. R.

Insurance Policy/ies or Certificate/s of Ingosstrakh.

All expenses connected with the establishment and extension,
if any, of the Letter of Credit and any other Bank charges as
well as Bank's commission to be for the Buyers' account.

B. Payment to be effected in ... at the rate of exchange ...

through ... by cash against cable advice of the Bank for Foreign Trade of the U. S. S. R., Moscow, stating that the Bank has received from the Sellers the following documents:

Invoice/s in ....

Bill/s of Lading.

Certificate/s of Quality issued by the State Grain Inspection of the U. S. S. R.

Insurance Policy/ies or Certificate/s of Ingosstrakh.

As soon as payment is effected the Bank for Foreign Trade of the U. S. S. R. will forward the documents to the Buyers' Bank.

The Sellers' Invoices shall be paid in full. Claims, if any, to be settled separately. The Buyers shall not make any deductions from invoice amounts without the Sellers' consent.

Should payment not be effected within 24 hours upon receipt by the Buyers' Bank of the cable from the Bank for Foreign Trade of the U. S. S. R. confirming receipt of Invoices, shipping and other documents, the Buyers shall pay the Sellers 0.05% of invoice amount for each day of the delay. All Bank expenses for collecting payments as well as Bank's commission to be for the Buyers' account.

7. OTHER CONDITIONS: . . . .

8. LEGAL ADDRESSES OF THE PARTIES: The Sellers — Vsesojuznoje Exportno-Importnoje Objedinenije "Sojuzexport", Moscow G-200, Smolenskaja-Sennaja 32/34. The Buyers — . . .

. . . .

The SELLERS　　　　　　　　The BUYERS
(Signatures)　　　　　　　　(Signatures)

Some of the General Conditions of Sale

1. Everything which in a shipment of cereals is mixed with grains of the cereal contracted for is considered as foreign admixture.

Admixture of wheat grains in rye up to 5 (five) per cent, admixture of wheat and rye grains in barley up to 5 (five) per cent. and admixture of wheat, rye and barley grains in oats up to 5 (five) per cent. shall not be considered as foreign admixture.

2. The Sellers shall be entitled to ship cereals with natural weight and foreign admixture superior or inferior to those stipulated in clause "Quality" of the present contract. Should the natural weight be superior or the contents of foreign admixture inferior, the Buyers pay to the Sellers a bonus to the contract price at the rate of 1 per cent. per each kilogram or each per cent. of difference respectively; should the natural weight be inferior or the contents of foreign admixture superior, the Sellers grant the Buyers an allowance at the rate of 1 per cent. of the contract price per each kilogram or each per cent. of difference respectively. Fractions to be counted pro rata.

Where the natural weight is guaranteed by two figures (i. e. 78/79 kg per hectolitre), the computation will be made on the basis of the average of the two figures (78.5 kg per hectolitre).

Bonuses and allowances shall be computed according to the data given in the Certificates of Quality of the State Grain Inspection of the U. S. S. R.

3. The date of the Bill of Lading shall be sufficient evidence of the date of shipment.

A. The goods shall be considered as delivered by the Sellers and accepted by the Buyers with regard to the quantity according to weight stated in the Bill of Lading. The Bill of Lading weight shall be final and binding upon both parties.

B. The weight of the goods shall be ascertained at time of discharge. Both the Buyers and the Sellers have the right of supervision of the weighing. The weight ascertained at time of discharge of the goods, including goods damaged by water, oil or other liquids or by any other means whatsoever, to be final. If the weight ascertained at discharge exceeds the weight indicated in the Bill/s of Lading, the surplus is to be paid for by the Buyers, whereas shortweight, if any, is to be refunded by the Sellers. Surpluses or shortweights to be settled on the basis of final invoices issued by the party in favour of which the final balance is to be paid.

GENERAL CONDITIONS OF SALE
(Reverse Side of the Offer)

1. ACCEPTANCE: The acceptance of this tender includes the acceptance of the following terms and conditions unless there is a special agreement to the contrary in respect of any of them.

2. VALIDITY: No order shall be binding on the Sellers until confirmed by them in writing. The tender may be withdrawn or the price and/or the terms quoted may be altered in any respect before the order has been received and accepted by the Sellers.

3. QUALITY: Unless otherwise specified, the quality of the goods shall be in conformity with the corresponding U.S.S.R. Standards or in the absence of such standards with the technical specifications adopted by the manufacturing plant and confirmed by Certificates of Quality. The Sellers reserve the right without special consent of the Buyers to introduce alterations of minor importance which do not affect materially the quality and the price of the goods.

4. PRICE: The price includes the cost of a standard set of spare parts if such parts are required. Erection costs or technical service, if any, are not included in the price and will be charged extra.

5. DELIVERY: The tender is made subject to prior sale. The time indicated for shipment shall be reckoned from the date of

the contract or of the Sellers' confirmation of the order. The date of delivery shall be 'considered for land transport — the date on which the goods pass the U.S.S.R. border and for sea transport — the date of the Bill of Lading.

6. PAYMENT: Unless some other arrangement is made, payment shall be effected by an irrevocable, confirmed and divisible Letter of Credit to be established by the Buyers in favour of the Sellers with the Bank for Foreign Trade of the U.S.S.R., Moscow, within 15 days of receipt of the Sellers' notification of the readiness of the goods for shipment.

Unless otherwise specified, the Letter of Credit is to be valid for 90 days, all Bank charges being at the expense of the Buyers.

7. GUARANTEE: The technical data given by the Sellers and the high quality and normal operation of the equipment are guaranteed for the period stated in the contract or in Sellers' confirmation of the order. Should the equipment prove to be defective during the guarantee period, the Sellers undertake to replace or repair any defective part free of charge. The guarantee shall not apply to normal wear or damage caused by improper storage, inadequate or careless maintenance.

CONDITIONS OF SALE

The acceptance of this tender includes the acceptance of the following terms and conditions:

1. This tender is subject to written or cabled confirmation of the order.

2. We undertake that the machinery manufactured by us shall be of good material and of sound workmanship and that we will eliminate any defects or replace any defective parts therein, particulars of which are given to us in writing, within six months of delivery and which are proved to be due solely to the use of defective materials or bad workmanship, any defective parts replaced to be our property. Any machinery not of our own manufacture included in this tender is sold under such warranty only as the makers give us, but is not guaranteed by us in any way.

3. In the case of machinery for export, we do not accept any responsibility for damage during transit.

4. This tender is based upon the cost of labour, material and services ruling at the date hereof and, if by reason of any increase or decrease therein before delivery the actual cost to us shall increase or decrease, the price shall be adjusted accordingly.

5. All descriptive and forwarding specifications, drawings and particulars of weights and dimensions submitted with this tender are approximate only, and the descriptions and illustrations contained in our catalogues, price lists and other advertising matter, are intended merely to give a general idea of the goods described therein and none of these shall form part of the contract.

6. In the case of machinery for export, packing cases are not returnable and no allowance will be made in respect of them.

7. The time for delivery stated in this tender is an estimate only.

8. Notwithstanding any agreed terms of payment, the machinery is not sold and delivered on credit, but on condition that the ownership therein shall not pass to the Purchaser until it is fully paid for.

9. All machinery included in this tender, after delivery by us, is at the Purchaser's risk, notwithstanding our property therein, and should be insured by the Purchaser.

EXTRACT FROM A CONTRACT FORM FOR THE SUPPLY OF GOODS TO AGENTS ON CONSIGNMENT BASIS

Contract No. ...

Moscow . . . . 19 . . .

Vsesojuznoje Objedinenije "Sojuzexport", Moscow, hereinafter referred to as "Sojuzexport" on the one part, and Messrs. ... hereinafter referred to as the "Agents" on the other part, have concluded the present contract whereby it is agreed as follows:

1. SUBJECT OF THE CONTRACT

Sojuzexport shall supply to the Agents on consignment basis goods in accordance with the enclosed specification as well as with any further specifications that may be agreed upon between the parties during the period of validity of the present contract for demonstration and sale, the above specifications constituting an integral part of the contract.

The Agents undertake to sell on the territory of ... the goods delivered by Sojuzexport on consignment in their own name and for their own account.

The period for which the goods are sent on consignment shall not exceed ... months from the date of delivery of the goods.

In case the goods are not sold within the period of consignment the Agents undertake to purchase the goods for their own account and pay Sojuzexport the full value of same.

The period of consignment can be extended in particular cases only, upon agreement of both parties.

Sojuzexport have the right to recall the goods prior to the expiration of the stipulated period but not before ... months from the date of delivery of the goods on consignment.

The Agents undertake to procure the necessary licences for the import of the goods to ... and if required for the export of the goods from ... , all expenses connected therewith being borne by ....

2. ORGANIZATION OF WORK

In connection with the present contract the Agents undertake:

a) to make arrangements to have the goods demonstrated and shown in operation in special show-rooms or on other premises suitable for that purpose;

b) to organize shows of the goods:

c) to set up warehouses adapted for the storage of the goods;

d) to provide advisory services and render technical assistance to purchasers of the goods:

e) to arrange for regular advertising of the goods on show making use of the most efficient forms of publicity and also to issue catalogues, leaflets and other advertising matter, the form and contents of the advertisements being agreed upon with Sojuzexport;

f) to give quarterly reports to Sojuzexport regarding the state of the market in respect of goods supplied on consignment under the present contract;

g) to submit reports to Sojuzexport on the first day of each month regarding both the goods sold and the balance of goods unsold as indicated in the proforma-invoices.

The representatives of Sojuzexport shall have the right to visit the consignment warehouse and show-rooms with the view of investigating the maintenance of the goods delivered by Sojuzexport and the arrangements made for their demonstration.

Each item of goods delivered by Sojuzexport on consignment basis shall bear a plate indicating its name and type and stating that it is exported by V/O "Sojuzexport", Moscow, U. S. S. R.

3. PRICE

The goods will be delivered at prices agreed upon by the parties and indicated in the specifications, packing being either included or excluded, depending upon the nature of the goods supplied.

The prices are . . . .

The Agents will fix the selling prices for the goods upon agreement with Sojuzexport, taking into consideration that the difference between the selling price and the contract price is to constitute the commission fee of the Agents and is to cover all expenses connected with the demonstration and sale of the goods as provided for by the present contract.

4. DELIVERY TIME

The goods shall be delivered within the period stipulated in the specifications agreed upon between the parties.

The date shown on the Bill of Lading or on the Railway Bill shall be considered as the date of delivery.

Sojuzexport have the right to deliver the goods prior to the stipulated dates, notifying the Agents beforehand.

5. NOTIFICATION OF SHIPMENT

Sojuzexport undertake to advise the Agents by cable of the shipment of the goods, indicating the date of shipment, port of shipment or station of despatch, name of ship, number of the Bill of Lading when shipment is effected by sea, or of the Railway Bill when the goods are dispatched by rail, as well as gross and net weight.

Simultaneously with the shipment of the goods Sojuzexport shall send to the Agents a specified proforma-invoice in ... copies giving the value of the goods shipped in accordance with clause 3 of the present contract.

When shipment is effected by sea Sojuzexport shall send along with the goods a copy of the Bill of Lading and ... copies of specification by Captain's mail.

6. TRANSHIPMENT AND RETURN OF GOODS

In case the goods are recalled by Sojuzexport, the Agents undertake:

a) to pack and mark the goods to be returned in conformity with the instructions forwarded by Sojuzexport and in accordance with the conditions of this contract, applying all the necessary means of preservation to fully protect the goods from corrosion;

b) to ship the goods not later than within one month of receipt of Sojuzexport's shipping instructions;

c) the date shown on the Bill of Lading or on the Railway Bill shall be considered as the date of transhipment or return of the goods to Sojuzexport.

All expenses connected with the return of the goods to be borne by .... .

7. EXPENSES CONNECTED WITH THE DEMONSTRATION AND ADVERTISING OF THE GOODS

The Agents shall bear all transport expenses from ... to the place of destination as well as all expenses connected with the organization and maintenance of the consignment warehouse and show-rooms, installation and demonstration of goods also expenses connected with showing the goods in operation, with advertising and insurance of goods kept at the consignment warehouse and in show-rooms and with the sale of the goods to third parties.

8. TERMS OF PAYMENT

Within two days after the sale of the goods the Agents shall notify Sojuzexport accordingly.

Payment of the full value of the goods sold shall be made by the Agents within 7 days from the date of sale.

The Agents shall inform Sojuzexport of the prices at which the goods have been sold to third parties.

The Agents are not entitled to make any deductions from the sums due to Sojuzexport as a security for claims which might have been made on Sojuzexport or on third parties.

9. RESPONSIBILITY OF THE AGENTS FOR THE GOODS DELIVERED BY SOJUZEXPORT

The Agents bear full liability for the safe and sound condition of the goods delivered by Sojuzexport on consignment to the full value of same in accordance with clause 3 of the present contract beginning on the date of arrival at the port of destination and ending on the date of payment or on the date of transhipment or return of the goods to Sojuzexport according to the instructions received from Sojuzexport.

The Agents shall insure the goods for the above mentioned period for the full value of the goods for their account and send the Insurance Policy to Sojuzexport within ... days upon receipt of same.

During the above mentioned consignment period beginning on the date of delivery and ending on the date of payment or on the date of return of the goods to Sojuzexport, the delivered goods shall be considered the property of Sojuzexport that cannot be mortgaged, pledged or otherwise encumbered.

As a security of fulfilment of their obligations under the present Contract the Agents shall submit to Sojuzexport a Letter of Guarantee of a first-class bank, the wording of which is to be agreed upon with Sojuzexport.

The Letter of Guarantee shall cover the full value of the goods to be supplied on consignment and shall be presented not later than within 20 days of the date of signing of the present contract.

In case further specifications of goods are agreed upon, the Agents shall submit to Sojuzexport additional Letters of Guarantee covering these goods not later than within 20 days of the date of signing of the said specifications.

All expenses connected with the Bank guarantees shall be borne by the Agents.

In case the Bank guarantee is not submitted within the stipulated time, Sojuzexport will be entitled to delay shipment of the goods or to extend the delivery dates shown in the specifications accordingly.

10. GUARANTEE OF SOJUZEXPORT

Sojuzexport guarantee the quality as well as the normal operation and capacity of the goods for the period of ... months from the date of putting the goods into operation, but not more than ... months from the date of delivery.

If the goods or any part thereof prove defective within the guarantee period, Sojuzexport shall eliminate the defects for their own account, or replace the defective part and/or defective goods.

The guarantee of Sojuzexport does not apply to rapidly wearing parts or natural wear, or to damage which has occurred as a result of improper or careless storage, irregular or careless maintenance or overloading, incorrect installation and/or assembly and putting into operation, and/or non-fulfilment by the Buyer of the technical instructions on installation and/or assembly, on putting into operation and on operation of the goods.

The claims should contain a detailed and well grounded description of the case indicating the types of goods not conforming to the conditions of the contract as well as the actual demands of the claimants.

The claims should be forwarded by a registered letter enclosing the respective survey reports, drawn up in the presence of a neutral expert, and other documents justifying the claim.

Sojuzexport have the right to inspect the goods found defective as well as to verify the correctness of the claim.

In case the claim is satisfied, Sojuzexport shall have the right to ask the Agents for the return of the defective goods after the shipment of the replacement goods has been effected.

All expenses connected with the return of the defective goods including freight, insurance, etc. to be borne by Sojuzexport.

The presentation of claims does not entitle the Agents to refuse acceptance of other consignments delivered under the present contract.

EXCHANGE OF CORRESPONDENCE BETWEEN THE BRITISH STEEL CO., LTD., MANCHESTER, AND V/O "SOJUZEXPORT", MOSCOW, RELATING TO THE SALE OF MANGANESE ORE

1. Air-Mail

Manchester, 5th May, 19...

Dear Sirs,

Washed Poti Manganese Ore

We are indebted for your address to the Trade Delegation of the U. S. S. R. in London from whom we learn that you are exporters from the U. S. S. R. of Washed Poti Manganese Ore.

We shall be obliged if you will quote us your lowest price c. i. f. Manchester for 11,000—12,000 tons of Washed Poti Manganese Ore for delivery in lots of about 4,000 tons, commencing from the middle of June at the rate of one cargo every month.

As we should like to cover our requirements at the earliest possible moment, we request your reply by cable.

We would also ask you to send us a full analysis of the ore by air-mail.

Yours faithfully,

. . . .

2. Air-Mail

Moscow, 8th May, 19...

Dear Sirs,

Washed Poti Manganese Ore

We thank you for your enquiry of the 5th May for 11,000—12,000 tons of Washed Poti Manganese Ore and confirm our cable to you of today reading:

"REGRET CANNOT OFFER FOURTHOUSAND TON LOTS MANGANESE ORE CIF MANCHESTER OWING TO DIFFICULTY CHARTERING SUITABLE TONNAGE STOP PLEASE CABLE WHETHER YOU CAN ACCEPT TWO LOTS ABOUT FIVETHOUSAND TONS EACH IF SO WILL CABLE QUOTATION STOP FULL ANALYSIS CONTRACT FORM AIR-MAILED TODAY 1225 SOJUZEXPORT".

We regret to advise you that at present it is very difficult to obtain vessels of small tonnage from the Black Sea to U. K. ports, the minimum tonnage being 5,000 tons.

If you can take the quantity you require in two lots of about 5,000 tons each, we shall be pleased to cable you our quotation.

We enclose a detailed analysis of Washed Poti Manganese Ore as well as our contract form.

We look forward with interest to your reply.

Yours faithfully,

. . . .

2 Enclosures.

3. Telegram dated 10th May, 19...:

"SOJUZEXPORT MOSCOW — YOURLET MAY 8 CABLE QUOTATION TWO CARGOES FIVETHOU-SAND TONS EACH WASHED MANGANESE ORE CIF MANCHESTER SHIPMENT JUNE JULY STEELCO".

4. Air-Mail

Moscow, 11th May, 19...

Dear Sirs,

Washed Poti Manganese Ore

We have received your telegram of the 10th May asking us to send you a quotation for two cargoes of 5,000 tons each of Washed Poti Manganese Ore and have pleasure in quoting you as follows, subject to your immediate acceptance:

DESCRIPTION AND QUANTITY: Two cargoes of about 5,000 tons each, 10 per cent. more or less at our option, of Washed Poti Manganese Ore as per specification enclosed with our letter of the 8th May.

PRICE: Sixty-two pence per unit of metallic manganese per English ton c. i. f. Manchester.

SHIPMENT: One cargo in June and the other in July 19...

PAYMENT: In pounds sterling net cash against documents by an irrevocable and confirmed Letter of Credit to be established by you with the Bank for Foreign Trade of the U. S. S. R., Moscow, within 15 days after the contract is signed. The Letter of Credit is to be valid for 60 days. Payment is to be made on the basis of 50 per cent. of manganese in the ore with final adjustment after the analysis is known.

SAMPLING, ANALYSIS AND OTHER TERMS: As per contract form sent you with our letter of the 8th May.

In accordance with the above, we have sent you today the following cable:

"YOURTEL MAY TENTH WE OFFER SUBJECT IMMEDIATE ACCEPTANCE TWO CARGOES ABOUT FIVETHOUSAND TONS EACH TEN PERCENT MORE LESS OUR OPTION WASHED POTI MANGANESE PRICE SIXTYTWO PENCE PER UNIT MANGANESE PER ENGLISH TON CIF MANCHESTER SHIPMENT FIRST CARGO JUNE SECOND JULY PAYMENT BASIS FIFTY PERCENT MANGANESE CASH AGAINST DOCUMENTS BY IRREVOCABLE CONFIRMED CREDIT OPENED BANK FOR FOREIGN TRADE MOSCOW WITHIN FIFTEEN DAYS AFTER SIGNING CONTRACT FINAL ADJUSTMENT BASED ON ANALYSIS STOP OTHER TERMS ASPER CONTRACT FORM SOJUZEXPORT"

We hope that this offer will prove acceptable to you.

Yours faithfully,

. . . .

5.   Manchester, 14th May, 19...

Dear Sirs,

Abt. 10,000 Tons Washed Poti Manganese Ore

We thank you for your cable of the 11th May and for your letter of the same date and confirm the following interchange of telegrams:

Ours May 12:

"YOURTEL AND LETTER ELEVENTH MAY ACCEPT YOUR PRICE TIME OF SHIPMENT CONTRACT FORM SUGGEST PAYMENT EACH CARGO NINETY PERCENT BY L/C AGAINST DOCUMENTS BASIS FIFTY PERCENT MANGANESE BALANCE AGAINST FINAL INVOICE BASED ON ANALYSIS CABLE IF YOU AGREE".

Yours May 13:

"YOURTEL TWELFTH MAY ARGEE PAYMENT NI-
NETY PERCENT BY IRREVOCABLE CONFIRMED
L/C AGAINST DOCUMENTS BALANCE AGAINST
FINAL INVOICE SENDING CONTRACT FOR SIG-
NATURE".

Awaiting your contract,
                We remain
                        Yours faithfully,
. . . .

6.   Moscow, 14th May, 19...

Dear Sirs,

Abt. 10,000 Tons Washed Poti Manganese Ore

In confirmation of our cable sent to you yesterday as per copy
enclosed, we have pleasure in sending you herewith 2 copies of
our contract relating to the sale to you of about 10,000 tons of
Washed Poti Manganese Ore.

We shall be obliged if you will return us one copy of the
contract duly signed by you.

                        Yours faithfully,
. . . .

3 Enclosures.

EXPRESSIONS USED IN OFFERS AND CONTRACTS IN CONNECTION WITH TERMS OF PAYMENT

1. Cash on delivery (C. O. D.).
2. Cash with order (C. W. O.).
3. Spot cash.
4. Cash (or In cash) against first presentation of documents.
5. Terms: Net by (or against) a three months' draft from date
of invoice.
6. Terms: 1.5% discount for cash in 14 days or net within
60 days with interest at 5 per cent. p. a.
7. 3 d/s D/P.
8. 60 d/s D/A.
9. Terms: 10 per cent with order, 20% within 3 days against
shipping documents, and the balance against a 90 days' draft
with interest at 5% p. a.
10. Payment is to be made by the Buyers in instalments suc-
cessively as the machine is being completed at the Sellers' works,
as follows: ...

EXAMPLE OF A CLAUSE PROVIDING FOR PAYMENT IN A CURRENCY DIFFERENT FROM THE CURRENCY OF THE PRICE

The price of the goods is ... USA dollars per English ton. Payment to be made in pounds sterling and the amount to be paid is to be ascertained by converting the total amount of the invoice in USA dollars into pounds sterling at the London average close rate of telegraphic transfer on New York as published in the "Financial Times" on the day preceding the day of handing over the documents by the Bank to the Buyers.

EXAMPLE OF A CLAUSE PROVIDING FOR THE ACCEPTANCE BY BUYERS OF SELLERS' DRAFTS AGAINST DOCUMENTS

Payment to be made in pounds sterling by Bills of Exchange drawn by the Sellers on the Buyers for the value of each delivery at ... months from the date of the Bill of Lading. These Bills of Exchange to include interest at ... per cent per annum and are to be accepted by the Buyers on delivery to them of the Bill of Lading, invoice, check sheets and Letter of Guarantee. Stamp duty on the Bills of Exchange to be at the expense of ...

EXAMPLE OF A CLAUSE PROVIDING FOR PAYMENT IN INSTALMENTS BY ACCEPTANCES

Payment will be made in effective pounds sterling in London through the Moscow Narodny Bank, Ltd., London, as follows:

1. The Buyers shall pay in advance 10% of the total contract value against Sellers' invoice within thirty-five days of the date thereof. The Sellers will arrange for a first-class British bank to guarantee the refund of this initial payment proportionately to the value remaining unexecuted in the event of cancellation of the contract by the Buyers in accordance with the terms of the contract. The bank guarantee, together with a photo-copy of the licence, if required, will be forwarded with the invoice.

2. The balance of 90% in respect of each consignment shall be paid as follows:

10% in cash within thirty-five days of presentation to the Moscow Narodny Bank, Ltd., in London of a complete set of original Bills of Lading (or Certificate of Receipt issued by the Buyers' Forwarding Agent) accompanied by three copies of invoices, two copies of specification, one copy of a Release for Shipment issued by the Buyers' Inspectors and one copy of Guarantee.

80% in ten equal instalments plus interest at the rate of four percent per annum by drafts drawn (in 2 copies for each instalment) at 24, 30, 36, 42, 48, 54, 60, 66, 72 and 78 months from the date of the Bill of Lading or Certificate of Receipt by the Buyers' Forwarding Agent.

3. Drafts representing the ten instalments are to be drawn by the Sellers on the Buyers and accepted by them and domiciled for payment at the Moscow Narodny Bank, Ltd., London, the acceptances to be returned to the Sellers for presentation in London at maturity.

Within 60 days of signing the contract, the Buyers will furnish the Sellers with a guarantee of the Bank for Foreign Trade of the U. S. S. R. for the amount ot 80 per cent of the total value of the contract including interest charges. The amount of the guarantee will diminish automatically by the sums of the drafts paid by the Buyers.

19

EXPORT LICENSE PROCESS

EXPORT LICENSE PROCESS
Metallurg Original
11. Export License

11.1 The Sellers will take care of and bear all expenses connected with the obtaining of export licenses from respective officials for export to the USSR of the equipment (submission of technical documentation) in the volume provided for by the present Contract.
Copies of export licenses will be submitted to the Buyers before the signing of the Contract.

11.2 If the export licenses are not granted or are revoked by the appropriate authorities, the Buyers have the right to cancel the Contract entirely or partially and to demand reimbursement of losses and return of the effected payments.

11.3 In this case the Sellers will also pay a penalty in accordance with Clause 15 of the present Contract.

Solution
11.0 Export License

11.1 The Sellers shall take care and bear all expenses connected with obtaining the export license from the respective authorities for export to the USSR of the equipment (submission of technical documentation) in the scope stipulated in the present Contract. Copy of the export licenses or the letter of the respective competent authorities of the country of origin that any such is not required will be granted to the Buyers within 60 days after signing the Contract. If within six (6) months from the date of signing the Contract the export license for the computer hardware and associated peripherals and complete software including application programs, spare parts, and test equipment ("Computer System") is not granted or is revoked, then within two (2) months thereafter the Sellers and the Buyers will agree upon a suitable substitute, and the Sellers shall provide its delivery within the delivery dates specified below, and the cost of the Contract is not to be subject to any increase. In such case the delivery dates shall be extended accordingly by mutual agreement without issuance of penalties.

If within six (6) months from the date of agreement to the substitution the license for the above substitute is also not received, the Buyers and the Sellers will meet and find a mutually acceptable solution. In this case the Buyers will not use the right to cancel the Contract entirely.

11.2 If any other license is not granted or is revoked, the Buyers shall have the right to cancel the Contract entirely or partially. In this case the Sellers shall return all payments made on the canceled portion of the Contract plus accrued interest at the rate of 6 percent per annum.

SUDOIMPORT CONTRACT SOLUTION

XVI

Export License

SUDOIMPORT BIG CONTRACT

The Seller undertakes to obtain at its expense export licenses from competent authorities and to submit to the Buyer within three (3) months from the date of signing of this Contract the Seller's notification stating that any such licenses have been received or are not required.

If the Seller fails to submit to the Buyer within the period of time mentioned above a photocopy of any such export license or such official notification or if any such export license is canceled in the course of time, either party shall be entitled to cancel this Contract without any further liability or responsibility on its part. In such case the Seller shall refund to the Buyer all payments received by it from the Buyer, without interest. It is understood, however, that there shall be no cancelation privilege even if a license is not granted for the Honeywell* underwater-detection and location apparatus, but the parties shall meet to discuss an alternative solution, and Seller shall use its best efforts to find a supplier who can furnish a different system.

---

*Honeywell—not granted license; Simrad—Norwegian substitute.

GUARANTEE RE: RIGHT TO CANCEL
FOR DEFECTIVE EQUIPMENT

Metallurg Original

14.10 If both Parties state that the defects cannot be eliminated or it is required over four months for their elimination, the Buyers have the right to terminate the Contract. In this case the Sellers will return to the Buyers the cost of the delivered equipment and pay penalty at the rate of _____ percent of the price of the contract and reimburse to the Buyers the losses suffered by them.

14.11 In case the Buyers do not use their right to cancel the contract the Sellers are obliged without delay for their account to eliminate all defects and pay to the Buyers penalty at the rate of _____ percent of the value of the Contract.

Solution

13.14 If both parties admit that equipment and/or technology defects found cannot be eliminated or admit that more than six (6) months (not including transportation time) are required to eliminate the equipment defects and more than six (6) months are required to eliminate the technology defects in excess of a twelve (12) month period that is calculated from the moment of signing the Protocol by the Sellers and the Buyers under Section 13.8.9.6 of the present Contract, the Buyers will have the right to cancel the Contract as follows:
—In full in case that the mentioned defects substantially prevent achievement of the Contract guarantee figures for workshop production capacity and quality of the finished product according to Section No. 13 of the present Contract.
—In part for the defective part only (equipment and/or technology) in the case that defects prevent achievement of certain Contract-guarantee figures for production and quality of the finished product.
In case of the cancellation of the Contract in full or in part, the Buyers' complete remedy shall consist of the following:
—The Sellers will return to the Buyers the cost of the delivered equipment and/or the technology in the canceled portion with an interest of 6 percent per annum and reimburse to the Buyers the direct damages suffered by them.
—Parties will meet for the discussion of the situation before making final solution of the cancelation.
However, in the event that the mentioned defects are in equipment supplied from the United States the Sellers and the Buyers shall within two (2) months after it is established that the defective equipment has to be replaced agree upon a suitable substitute for the defective equipment and the Sellers shall deliver FOB vessel within twelve (12) months thereafter without any increase in the cost of the Contract. In the case of such defects the Buyers shall not use the right to cancel the Contract entirely, and the Sellers shall extend the warranty according to Sections 13.6.2 and 13.6.4 and shall extend the validity

of technical services rates to $250 per person per day until the defect is corrected.

If the exchange of the defective equipment cannot be accomplished within the stipulated period or if the Buyers would like to use the non-defective equipment during that period, the sides will meet to discuss the situation and will make a mutually satisfactory decision.

FORCE MAJEURE

Metallurg Original

16. Force Majeure

16.1 The Parties are released from responsibility for partial or complete non-fulfillment of their liabilities under the present Contract, if this non-fulfillment was caused by the circumstances of force majeure, namely: fire, flood, earthquake, provided these circumstances have directly affected the execution of the present Contract. In this case the time of fulfillment of the Contract obligations is extended for the period equal to that during which such circumstances last.

16.2 The Party, for which it became impossible to meet obligations under the Contract, is to notify in written form the other Party of the beginning and cessation of the above circumstances immediately but in any case not later than ten (10) days from the moment of their beginning. The notification of the force majeure circumstances not made within fifteen (15) days deprives the corresponding Party of the right to refer to such circumstances in future.

16.3 The certificates issued by the respective Chambers of Commerce will be sufficient proof of the existence and duration of the above-indicated circumstances.

16.4 If these circumstances last longer than six (6) months, each Party will be entitled to cancel the whole Contract or any part of it, and in this case neither Party shall have the right to demand any compensation of eventual losses from the other Party.

The Sellers undertake in this case immediately to reimburse the Buyers for all amounts paid by the latter under the present Contract.

Solution

15.0 Force Majeure

15.1 The Parties are released from responsibilty for partial and complete non-fulfillment of their liabilities under the present Contract, if this non-fulfillment was caused by circumstances of force majeure, namely: fire, flood, earthquake, and other acts of nature that cannot be overcome provided these circumstances have directly affected the execution of the present Contract. In such case the time of fulfillment of the Contract obligations is extended for a period equal to that during which such circumstances and their consequences last.

15.4 In case these circumstances last for more than six (6) months, each of the parties will have the right to cancel the Contract concerning the non-executed part. In this case neither party shall have the right to demand any compensation for the losses from the other party.

INSURANCE

Metallurg Original

13. Insurance

13.1 The Buyers are to take care of and to bear expenses for insurance with Upravlenic Inostrannogo Strakhovanija SSSR (Ingosstrakh) of the equipment to be delivered under the Contract from the moment of its dispatch from the Sellers' and/or their subcontractors' works up to the moment of its arrival at the Buyers' works.

13.2 The expenses for insurance from the Sellers' and/or their subcontractors' works up to the moment of loading the goods on board the ship at the port of shipment (or franco-railway car-border) at the rate of 0.075 percent of the insurance amount are to be charged to the Sellers' account and deducted by the Buyers from the Sellers' invoices when effecting payment for the equipment.

13.3 Insurance within the whole period of transportation and transshipment will be effected on conditions of "Responsibility for Particular Average" according to item 2, Clause 2, of the "Rules of Transport Insurance of Goods," Ingosstrakh of the USSR, including damage to the goods caused by cranes, oil, fresh water (excluding sweating), and other cargo, also including breakage, theft of whole packages or parts thereof, and non-delivery of whole packages in all of the cases mentioned above irrespective of the percentage of damage.

13.4 Within thirty (30) days of the signing of the Contract the Buyers are to send to the Sellers the Insurance Policy issued in the name of the Sellers covering insurance of the equipment from the moment of its dispatch from the Sellers' and/or their subcontractors' works up to the moment of loading on board the ship at the port of _____, with delivery by franco-railway car-border to _____.

Machinoimport Original

Clause 13. Insurance

The Buyers shall be responsible for insuring with Ingosstrakh USSR at their expense for all of the equipment delivered under this Contract from the time of its dispatch from the Sellers' and/or their subcontractors' works up to the moment when the equipment arrives at the Buyers' works.

The expenses connected with the insurance of the equipment from the Sellers' and/or their subcontractors' works up to the moment when the equipment is loaded on board the ship in the port of shipment at the rate of 0.075 percent of the sum insured shall be charged to the Sellers' account and deducted by the Sellers when issuing invoices for the equipment.

Solution

17.0 Insurance

17.1 The Sellers will bear the expenses for insurance of the equipment delivered according to the Contract from the moment of its dispatch from the Sellers' and/or their subcontractors' works up to the moment of loading the goods on board the ship in the port of shipment (Articles 3.3 and 3.3.1). Such insurance may be obtained from insurance companies according to the Sellers' choice, which may include Upravleniy Inostrannogo Strakhovaniya SSSR (Ingostrakh).

17.2 In the case that the Sellers choose Ingosstrakh as the insurance company, the Buyer will bear all of the arrangements and expenses for the insurance in accordance with the following procedures:

17.2.3 Within thirty (30) days of Buyers' reception of the Sellers' notice about the selection of Ingosstrakh as the insurance company the Buyers are to send to the Sellers the Insurance Policy issued in the name of the Sellers covering its dispatch from the Sellers' and/or their subcontractors' works up to the moment of loading on board the ship at the port of shipment in accordance with Section 1 of the present Contract.

SANCTIONS (DELAY IN DELIVERY)

Metallurg Original

15. Sanctions

15.1 In the event of any delay in delivery of the equipment and spare parts to it and technical documentation against the dates stipulated in Clause 3 of the Contract, the Sellers are to pay to the Buyers a penalty at the rate of 0.5 percent of the value of the equipment overdue for every started week within the first four weeks and 1.0 percent for every following started week thereafter.

However, the total amount of penalty for delay in delivery is not to exceed _____ percent of the value of each complete machine or unit not delivered in due time.

15.2 The above rates of penalty cannot be changed by arbitration. Although when calculating the penalty for delay, the amount of days that comprise less than half of a calendar week is not taken into account, the amount of days comprising over half a calendar week is considered to be a full week. The Buyers are also entitled to deduct the penalty charged while effecting payment against the Sellers' invoices.

In case the Buyers will not be able to deduct the amount of penalty due for payment of the Sellers, the Sellers undertake to pay penalty at the first request of the Buyers. Delay in delivery of technical documentation or the delivery of incomplete technical documentation and/or of that of inferior quality are considered as delay in delivery of the equipment to which this technical documentation applies.

15.3 Should the delay in delivery of the equipment or the technical documentation exceed six (6) months, the Buyers have the right to cancel the Contract entirely or partially. In this case the Sellers are to pay a penalty at the rate of _____ percent.

Solutions

14.0 Sanctions

14.1 In the case of delay, due to the fault of the Sellers, in delivery of the equipment or spare parts or technical documentation that is to be delivered together with the equipment in the cases according to Appendix No. 2 of the present Contract (except in the event that the Sellers are able to provide prompt delivery of the said documentation by other means without damage to the Buyers) from the dates stipulated in the Contract, the Sellers are to pay to the Buyers a penalty at the rate of 0.5 percent of the price of each complete transaction number overdue for every calendar week within the first four weeks of the delay and 1.0 percent of the price of each complete transaction number for every following calendar week thereafter. However, for each complete transaction number not delivered in due time, the total amount of the penalty for delay in delivery is not to exceed 8.0 percent of the price of such complete transaction number.

14.3 In case of delay in delivery of the equipment exceeds twelve (12) months, the Buyers have the right to cancel the Contract for the non-delivered part of the equipment only; however, if the delivered part of the equipment cannot be put into operation and cannot function without the equipment that cannot be delivered in due time, the Buyers have the right to cancel the Contract. In case of the cancelation of the Contract in full or in part, the Buyers' complete remedy shall consist of the following:
—The Sellers will return to the Buyers the cost of the delivered equipment and/or the technology in the canceled portion with an interest of 6 percent per annum and reimburse to the Buyers the direct damages suffered by them. Parties will meet for the discussions of the situation before making final solution of the cancelation. However, in the event that the mentioned non-delivery and/or delay is in equipment supplied from the United States, the Sellers and the Buyers shall within three (3) months after such U.S. equipment has been delayed meet in Moscow and shall agree within two (2) months upon a solution that will ensure the delivery of such U.S. equipment within twelve (12) months

from the original date of delivery without any increase in the cost of the Contract. In the case of any non-delivery and/or delay in U.S. equipment, the Buyers shall not use the right to cancel the Contract entirely and the Sellers shall extend the warranty according to Sections 13.6.2 and 13.6.4 and shall extend the validity of technical services rates equal to $250 per man per day until the delivery is completed. If the substitution for the non-delivered and/or delayed equipment cannot be accomplished within the stipulated period the sides will meet to discuss the situation and will make a mutually satisfactory decision.

SIDE-LETTER SOLUTION

IV. Under Clause 15 of the general terms and conditions it is agreed that if in connection with performance of the above-mentioned Contract an occasion arises whereby V/O Metallurgimport has the right to cancel the Contract, V/O Metallurgimport before exercising such cancelation right will take into consideration events causing the improper performance of the Contract if they are beyond the Sellers' control.

20

SEA TRANSPORTATION OF GOODS

EXTRACT FROM THE SOVIET COAL CHARTER 1962 FOR COAL, COKE AND COALTARPITCH FROM THE U.S.S.R.

CODE NAME: "SOVCOAL"

Agreed January, 1962, between
The Documentary Council of the Baltic and
International Maritime Conference,
The Scandinavian Coal Importers
Federation, Copenhagen, Helsinki —
Helsingfors, Oslo, Stockholm,
U. S. S. R. Chamber of Commerce, Moscow,
V/O "Sojuzpromexport", Moscow,
V/O "Sovfracht", Moscow.

. . . . 19 . . .

IT IS THIS DAY MUTUALLY AGREED between . . . . . .
Owners of the . . . .
of . . . tons net register . . . . tons or
thereabouts deadweight, exclusive of bunkers, classed . . . .
. . . . now . . . .
and expected ready to load on or about . . . .
and . . . . Charteres, as follows:

PORT OF LOADING. (*Note* : Delete the ports not agreed upon.) 1. The said vessel being in every way fitted for the voyage, shall with all possible despatch proceed to —
one Baltic port: Leningrad, Riga, Ventspils, Klaipeda;
Black Sea and Azov Sea ports:

Odessa, including Iljichevsk, Izmail, Reni, Jdanov,	one or two ports at Charterers' option; first port to be declared latest on vessel passing Istanbul

where she can safely lie always afloat, and there load, as may be ordered by Shippers' Agents, below deck, unless otherwise agreed, in the customary manner a full and complete cargo of

coal coke coaltarpitch	of about ... tons of 1000 kilos (5 per cent. more or less in Owners' option).

Should the cargo or part of the cargo consist of coke, the Owners shall have the liberty to load coke on deck at Charterers' risk, but no freight shall be paid on any deck cargo lost or jettisoned; deck cargo to be properly secured and winches to be kept free from cargo.

QUANTITY. When giving notice of the loading date under clause 3 the Owners shall state the approximate quantity and kind of cargo and bunkers required in tons of 1000 kilos and also the grain cubic capacity of each hold.

PORT OF DISCHARGE. Being so loaded, the vessel shall proceed with all possible despatch to . . . . and deliver the cargo alongside any wharf, floating depot or lighters as may be ordered by the Consignees, where she can safely lie always afloat.

FREIGHT. 2. A. The freight shall be paid at the rate of ... per ton of 1000 kilos intaken weight, provided the vessel arrives without having broken bulk, with option to the Consignees (which must be declared in writing latest before breaking bulk) to pay on delivered weight, in which event the cargo shall be weighed simultaneously with the discharging by official weighers, the Consignees paying all expenses incurred thereby, but the Owners or their Agents having liberty to provide check clerks at the Owners' expense.
B. The Owners shall put their Agents at the loading ports in funds, sufficient to cover the vessel's ordinary disbursements, including charges for bunkers and trimming, if any, prior to the vessel's sailing from the port of loading; if not, the total amount, not exceeding one third of the freight, shall be endorsed upon the Bill of Lading as a freight advance, increased by 2 per cent. to cover interest and commission (whereof 1 per cent. shall be for the Charterers) plus actual cost of insurance.

C. The total freight (less advance at port of loading, if any) shall be paid on unloading and right delivery of the cargo, unless the Consignees exercise their option to pay on delivered weight as provided for in § 2, A, in which case the freight shall be paid as follows: 90 per cent. on unloading and right delivery of the cargo and the balance upon receipt from the Owners of the certificate stating the quantity of cargo delivered and the timesheet covering the discharging.

D. The total freight (less advance at port of loading, if any) shall be paid on unloading and right delivery of the cargo in cash at the port of discharge at the official rate of exchange on the final day of discharge.

Note: Delete alternatives C or D not adopted.

LOADING LAYDAYS. OWNERS' DEFINITE NOTICE. 3. The loading date shall not be before 8 a. m. on the . . . but Charterers, ... and Sovfracht at the port of loading are to receive from the Owners at least 5 clear running days' written notice of the definite loading date (at 8 a. m.) also 24 hours' notice to be given to Sovfracht at the port of loading. The Master or the Owners or their Agents shall keep Sovfracht advised by telegram of any alterations regarding the vessel's position.

If the vessel be not ready to load within 48 hours after the definite loading date, 24 hours' extra loading time shall be allowed.

SAILING TELEGRAM. A sailing telegram shall be sent or communicated to Sovfracht at the port of loading when the vessel leaves her last port, or if bound to or lying at a local port to discharge 24 hours' written notice shall be given when the vessel is expected to be clear of cargo, or in default 24 hours more shall be allowed for the loading.

NOTICE OF READINESS. MASTER'S NOTICE. 4. Written notice of readiness (Master's Notice) to receive the entire cargo not to be given to Sovfracht before the vessel is actually ready to receive the entire cargo and provided the vessel is cleared at custom house whether in berth or not, and such notice thereafter to be handed in to Sovfracht within the office hours between 9 a. m. and 5 p. m. on a working day, or 1 p. m. on Saturdays and days before holidays.

TIME TO COUNT. Time for loading to count from 8 a. m. on the next working day after the receipt of Master's Notice.

HATCH BEAMS. The vessel shall not be considered ready to commence the loading until the holds intended for cargo are free of inward cargo and properly cleaned. All hatch beams shall be removed before the loading commences. If the hatch beams are not removed the vessel shall not be considered ready to receive the cargo until they have been actually removed.

LOADING TIME. The cargo shall be loaded at the average

rate of . . . metric tons per weather working day of 24 consecutive hours (2 p. m. Saturdays and days preceding holidays to 8 a. m. Mondays and days following holidays as well as Sundays and holidays excepted, unless used). If the loading be commenced earlier than the time stipulated, only effectively used time to count. The same applies when loading is effected during excepted periods as above. Shippers to have the right of working during excepted periods, they paying overtime expenses for shore operations only.

. . . .
. . . .
. . . .

COSTS. 12. A. The Consignees shall effect the discharge of the cargo, the vessel paying . . . per ton of 1000 kilos for all work in connection with unloading and providing winches, motive power and running gear customary at the port of discharge. All extra expenses in connection with discharging beyond ordinary working hours to be paid by the party at whose request such work is performed. The vessel shall also provide vessel's winchmen if requested and permitted, otherwise the Consignees shall provide and pay for winchmen, who shall nevertheless be regarded as servants of the Owners.

FIXED PRICE. B. The Consignees shall effect the discharge of the cargo, the vessel paying . . . per ton of 1000 kilos on the quantity for which freight is paid or payable, covering all costs and charges whatsoever in connection with the unloading, and providing winches, motive power and running gear customary at the port of discharge. All extra expenses in connection with discharging beyond ordinary working hours to be paid by the party at whose request such work is performed. The vessel shall also provide winchmen from the crew, if requested and permitted, otherwise the Consignees shall provide and pay for winchmen from shore, who shall be regarded as servants of the Consignees, but shall follow the instructions of the Master in connection with discharging.

FREE DISCHARGE. C. The Consignees shall effect the discharge of the cargo free of all risk and expense to the vessel. The vessel shall provide winches, motive power and running gear customary at the port of discharge. The vessel shall also provide winchmen from the crew, if requested and permitted, otherwise the Consignees shall provide and pay for winchmen from shore, who shall be regarded as servants of the Consignees, but shall follow the instructions of the Master in connection with the discharging.

Note: Delete alternatives A, B or C not adopted, but if the Owners shall effect the discharge delete the entire clause 12.

EXEMPTIONS. 13. In case of strikes, lock-outs, civil commotions, accidents, or any other causes beyond the control of the Consignees which prevent or delay the discharging, such time shall not count unless the vessel be already on demurrage.

DEVIATION. 14. The vessel shall have liberty to tow and to be towed and to assist vessels in distress and to deviate for the purpose of saving life or property, to sail without pilot and to call at any ports in any order, for bunkering or other purposes or to make trial trips after notice, or adjust compasses and/or radio equipment and reasonable exercise of any of these liberties shall not be deemed to be a departure from the contractual route.

DEMURRAGE. 15. Demurrage, if any, at the rate of ... per day of 24 hours or pro rata to be paid by the Charterers if the vessel be detained beyond her loading time or by the Consignees, payable day by day, if the vessel be detained beyond her discharging time.

DUES AND CHARGES. 16. The Charterers shall pay all dues and duties on the cargo at the port of loading. The Consignees shall pay all dues and duties on the cargo at the port of discharge, also the additional cost of discharging, if any, in consequence of separation of different parcels. The Owners shall pay port dues, pilotage, towage and other charges appertaining to the vessel.

CANCELLING. 17. Should the vessel not be ready to load at 4 p. m. ... or if any misrepresentation be made respecting the size, position or condition of the vessel, the Charterers shall have the option of cancelling the Charter, such option to be declared latest on notice of readiness (Master's Notice) being given under clause 4. If the Charter is cancelled the Charterers shall inform the Owners.

Should the vessel be fixed to load at port(s) of the Black Sea or Azov Sea, if when the vessel be ready to leave her last port of call (whether a discharging port or not), the Owners inform the Charterers by telegram that she cannot reach the loading port before the cancelling date, the Charterers shall have the option of cancelling this charter by telegram within 72 hours (Sundays and legal holidays excepted) from the receipt of such notice, unless a cancelling date has been agreed upon.

. . . .
. . . .
. . . .

ARBITRATION. 24. A. Should any dispute arise under the provisions applying to the loading port in the Charter, the same shall be referred to two Arbitrators, one to be appointed by each party, sitting in the country of the loading port, and in case the said Arbitrators cannot agree, then to an Umpire sitting in the same country, to be elected by the same Arbitrators.

B. Any such dispute under the provisions applying to the discharging port shall be settled in like manner, the Arbitrators and Umpire sitting in the country of the discharging port.

> *Memo*: Clause 24, A and 24, B are optional and either or both of them may be deleted on the signing of the Charter by the parties unless mutually agreed.

. . . .

FORM OF BILL OF LADING USED BY THE U.S.S.R. STATE BALTIC SHIPPING LINE

Bill of Lading No. . . . .

Shipped in apparent good order and condition by _____

_____

on board the $\frac{\text{steamship}}{\text{motor vessel}}$ called the _____

whereof Master is _____

trading under U. S. S. R. flag, Owners Baltic State Steamship Line, Carrier _____ and now lying in _____

the following goods, viz: _____

SUPPLIER: _____

Full address) _____

IMPORT INSTITUTION: _____

TERMS OF DELIVERY: _____ COUNTRY OF ORIGIN: ____

(If f. o. b. also

     state port) _____

Lic. No.	Transport Instruction No.	Order No.	Nariad No.	Calling Forward No.

CONSIGNEE: _____

(Address) _____

DETAILS OF GOODS:

Marks and numbers	Nos. of packages and kind of packing	Total cubic measurement	Description of goods

WEIGHT: Total Gross _____
(tons cwts. qrs. lbs.)

Total Net _____
(tons cwts. qrs. lbs.)

VALUE: _____

Rate of freight	Received on account of freight	To be paid by Consignee

Being marked and numbered as above but not guaranteed for the adequacy of marks and to be carried and delivered subject to all conditions, terms and clauses inserted into this Bill of Lading in the like apparent good order and condition from the ship's deck (either into lighters or on the quay at Master's option) where the responsibility of the Carrier for the carriage of aforesaid goods shall cease.

The goods to be delivered at the port of . . . . or as near there as the ship may safely get always afloat, to the Consignee or to his or their assigns, on payment of freight as per margin of this Bill of Lading and all other charges due under this contract of carriage.

Nothing of this Bill of Lading whether printed, or written, or stamped shall limit or affect the above-mentioned conditions. If the freight and all charges in connection with the contract of carriage payable on or before delivery of goods have not been paid, the Carrier, on delivery of the goods to warehouse (warehousemen), or into lighters (lighterman) or other custodian entrusted to hold the goods for their Owner, shall be entitled to stipulate that the said custodian shall not part with the possession thereof until payment has been made of full freight and any other charges due under this contract of carriage.

Neither the weight nor the measure of goods carried in bulk as well as the conformity of all kinds of goods with their description in this Bill of Lading are checked by the Carrier during loading.

The shipper, the receiver of goods and the holder of the Bill of Lading as well as any other person interested hereby expressly accept and agree to all printed, written or stamped provisions, terms and reserves of this Bill of Lading, including those on the back hereof.

In witness whereof the Master, Carrier or his Agent has affirmed to . . . . Bills of Lading, all of this tenor and date, one of which being accomplished the others to stand void. One Bill of Lading duly endorsed is to be given up in exchange for the goods, or for a delivery order for same.

Dated in . . . . . this . . . . day of . . . . 19 . . .

AGREEMENT

BETWEEN THE GOVERNMENT OF THE UNITED STATES OF AMERICA AND THE GOVERNMENT OF THE UNION OF SOVIET SOCIALIST REPUBLICS REGARDING CERTAIN MARITIME MATTERS

The Government of the United States of America and the Government of the Union of Soviet Socialist Republics;

Being desirous of improving maritime relations between the United States and the Soviet Union, particularly through arrangements regarding port access and cargo carriage by sea; and

Acting in accordance with Article Seven of the Basic Principles of Relations Between the United States of America and the Union of Soviet Socialist Republics, signed in Moscow on May 29, 1972,

Have agreed as follows:

Article 1

For purposes of this Agreement:

a. "Vessel" means a vessel sailing under the flag of a Party, registered in the territory of that Party, or which is an unregistered vessel belonging to the Government of such Party, and which is used for:

(i) Commercial maritime shipping, or

(ii) Merchant marine training purposes, or

(iii) Hydrographic, oceanographic, meteorological, or terrestrial magnetic field research for civil application.

b. "Vessel" does not include:

(i) Warships as defined in the 1958 Geneva Convention on the High Seas;

(ii) Vessels carrying out any form of state function except for those mentioned under paragraph a of this Article.

Article 2

This Agreement does not apply to or affect the rights of fishing vessels, fishery research vessels, or fishery support vessels. This Agreement does not affect existing arrangements with respect to such vessels.

Article 3

The ports on the attached list of ports of each Party (Annexes I and II, which are a part of this Agreement) are open to access by all vessels of the other Party.

Article 4

Entry of all vessels of one Party into such ports of the other Party shall be permitted subject to four days' advance notice of the planned entry to the appropriate authority.

Article 5

Entry of all vessels referred to in subparagraphs a(ii) and a(iii) of Article 1 into the ports referred to in Article 3 will be to replenish ships' stores or fresh water, obtain bunkers, provide rest for or make changes in the personnel of such vessels, and obtain minor repairs and other services normally provided in such ports, all in accordance with applicable rules and regulations.

Article 6

Each Party undertakes to ensure that tonnage duties upon vessels of the other Party will not exceed the charges imposed in like situations with respect to vessels of any other country.

Article 7

While recognizing the policy of each Party concerning participation of third flags in its trade, each Party also recognizes the interest of the other in carrying a substantial part of its foreign trade in vessels of its own registry, and thus both Parties intend that their national flag vessels will each carry equal and substantial shares of the trade between the two nations in accordance with Annex III which is a part of this Agreement.

Article 8

Each Party agrees that, where it controls the selection of the carrier of its export and import cargoes, it will provide to vessels under the flag of the other Party participation equal to that of vessels under its own flag in accordance with the agreement in Annex III.

Article 9

The Parties shall enter into consultations within fourteen days from the date a request for consultation is received from either Party regarding any matter involving the application, interpretation, implementation, amendment, or renewal of this Agreement.

Article 10

This Agreement shall enter into force on January 1, 1973; provided that this date may be accelerated by mutual agreement of the Parties. The Agreement will remain in force for the period ending December 31, 1975, provided that the Agreement may be terminated by either Party. The termination shall be effective ninety days after the date on which written notice of termination has been received.

IN WITNESS WHEREOF, the undersigned, being duly authorized by their respective Governments, have signed this Agreement.

DONE at Washington this 14th day of October 1972, in duplicate in the English and Russian languages, both equally authentic.

FOR THE GOVERNMENT OF THE
UNITED STATES OF AMERICA:

FOR THE GOVERNMENT OF THE UNION
OF SOVIET SOCIALIST REPUBLICS:

/s/
Peter G. Peterson
Secretary of Commerce

/s/
Timofey B. Guzhenko
Minister of Merchant Marine

ANNEX 1

*Ports of the United States of America
Open to Calls Upon Notice*

1. Skagway, Alaska
2. Seattle, Washington
3. Longview, Washington
4. Corpus Christi, Texas
5. Port Arthur, Texas
6. Bellingham, Washington
7. Everett, Washington
8. Olympia, Washington
9. Tacoma, Washington
10. Coos Bay (including North Bend), Oregon
11. Portland (including Vancouver, Washington), Oregon
12. Astoria, Oregon
13. Sacramento, California
14. San Francisco (including Alameda, Oakland, Berkeley, Richmond), California
15. Long Beach, California

16. Los Angeles (including San Pedro, Wilmington, Terminal Island), California
17. Eureka, California
18. Honolulu, Hawaii
19. Galveston/Texas City, Texas
20. Burnside, Louisiana
21. New Orleans, Louisiana
22. Baton Rouge, Louisiana
23. Mobile, Alabama
24. Tampa, Florida
25. Houston, Texas
26. Beaumont, Texas
27. Brownsville, Texas
28. Ponce, Puerto Rico
29. New York (New York and New Jersey parts of the Port of New York Authority), New York
30. Philadelphia, Pennsylvania (including Camden, New Jersey)
31. Baltimore, Maryland
32. Savannah, Georgia
33. Erie, Pennsylvania
34. Duluth, Minnesota/Superior, Wisconsin
35. Chicago, Illinois
36. Milwaukee, Wisconsin
37 Kenosha, Wisconsin
38. Cleveland, Ohio
39. Toledo, Ohio
40. Bay City, Michigan

ANNEX II

Ports of the Union of Soviet Socialist Republics Open to Calls Upon Notice

1. Murmansk
2. Onega
3. Arkhangel'sk
4. Mezen'
5. Nar'yan-Mar
6. Igarka
7. Leningrad
8. Vyborg
9. Pyarnu
10. Riga
11. Ventspils
12. Klaipeda
13. Tallinn
14. Vysotsk
15. Reni
16. Izmail
17. Kiliya
18. Belgorod-Dnestrovskiy
19. Il'ichevsk
20. Odessa
21. Kherson
22. Novorossiysk
23. Tuapse
24. Poti
25. Batumi
26. Sochi
27. Sukhumi
28. Yalta
29. Zhdanov
30. Berdyansk
31. Nakhodka
32. Aleksandrovsk-Sakhalinskiy
33. Makarevskiy Roadstead (Roadstead Doue)
34. Oktyabr'skiy
35. Shakhtersk
36. Uglegorsk
37. Kholmsk
38. Nevel'sk
39. Makarov Roadstead
40. Poronaysk

N. ZUEV, *President*
SOVFRACHT
MOSCOW G-200
SMOLENSKAJA SQ., 32/34

October 14, 1972

Honorable ROBERT J. BLACKWELL
Assistant Secretary for Maritime Affairs
U.S. Department of Commerce
Washington, D.C. 20230
U.S.A.

DEAR MR. BLACKWELL:

Enclosed is a copy of the letter which SOVFRACHT proposes to transmit to its chartering agents and which sets forth the charter party terms which we have agreed upon for fixtures made for the carriage of raw and processed agricultural commodities by American flag bulk cargo vessels under the Agreement Between the Government of the United States of America and the Government of the Union of Soviet Socialist Republics Regarding Certain Maritime Matters executed today.

Also enclosed is the schedule of rates we have agreed upon for practical purposes to be used under that Agreement in place of a precise calculation of the three year average rate for 1969, 1970, and 1971 for the carriage of specified categories of raw and processed agricultural commodities by American flag bulk cargo vessels on the routes specified, for fixtures made prior to July 1, 1973.

With respect to Item 5 of the charter party terms, relating to cargo insurance, we hereby confirm our verbal advice to you that we will enter into discussions with officials of INGOSSTRAKH for the purpose of directing the placement of a portion of the marine cargo insurance coverage for shipments of raw and processed agricultural commodities with United States underwriters.

Very truly yours,

/s/
N. ZUEV
President

Enclosures

MR. N. ZUEV, *President*
SOVFRACHT
MOSCOW G–200
SMOLENSKAJA SQ., 32/34

DEAR MR.

I wish to draw your attention to the following terms which have been agreed upon for the chartering of American flag tonnage for the carriage of grain to the Soviet Union:

1. The chartering of tankers is satisfactory to us.

2. The tonnage to be lifted by vessels will be limited only by draft limitations of the loading port since lightening down to the draft limitations of the discharge port is permitted.

3. Charters guarantee 32/33 feet salt water draft at discharge port. Lighterage, if any, down to 32/33 feet salt water draft to be at receiver's risk and expense and time used to count as lay time, owner contributing to receivers $3.50 per long ton of cargo lightened.

4. The rates for demurrage per day or prorata for part of a day are as follows:

for vessels loading less than
15,000 long tons $3,000 U.S. Ccy

for vessels loading between
15,000 and 30,000 long tons $4,000 U.S. Ccy

for vessels loading over
30,000 long tons $4,500 U.S. Ccy

with despatch rate being one-half of the demurrage rate.

5. Any extra cargo insurance due to vessel's age to be for owner's account. The amount will be at the actual cost of such insurance, net of discount, but shall not exceed the following scale:

Liberties/Ports/Parks/Ocean vessels and Empire of 7/8000 GRT built 1940/1945 inclusive—3 percent

Other dry cargo vessels built 1940/1945 inclusive in the countries which participated in the Second World War—1 percent.

All other vessels 16/20 years old   0.1875 percent
        "   "   21/25   "   "   0.375   "
        "   "   26/30   "   "   0.50   "
        "   "   31/35   "   "   0.75   "
        "   "   over 35   "   "   1.50   "

6. Receivers guarantee discharge at the rate of 2,000 metric tons alongside berth and 3,000 metric tons for lightening operations, per weather working day of twenty-four (24) consecutive hours, Sundays and official and local holidays and Saturdays after Noon (unless Saturday already a Holiday, in which case entire day not counting) excepted, whether used or not, provided vessel can deliver at such a rate. Days before holidays to count as three-quarters (3/4's) of a day. Discharge to be free of risk and expense to the Vessel and for account and risk of the Buyers or Receivers.

7. Cargo to be loaded, stowed, and trimmed by Charter's stevedores free of expense to the vessel within the following weather working days of twenty-four (24) consecutive hours, Sundays and Holidays excepted:

For vessels loading up to 25,000 long tons   —   5 days
   "   "   "   "   " 35,000   "   "   —   6 days
   "   "   "   "   " 55,000   "   "   —   7 days
   "   "   "   over 55,000   "   "   —   9 days

8. Ice clause to the effect that vessel is not required to force ice, but must follow ice-breaker.

9. Vacuvators employed for discharge of the vessel, including lightening, will be provided by receivers free of risk and expense to the vessel.

10. Form C Approved Baltimore Berth Grain Charter Party will be used with terms similar to those used for the charter of the Italian-flag MS DONATELLA, dated August 8, 1972, with Rider Clauses, subject to the following:

   a. modified as necessary to provide for tankers as follows:

(i) Clause 16—delete "holds" and insert "tanks"

(ii) Clause 19 to read "Separations, if any required, by tanks only"

(iii) Clause 25 to read "Owners guarantee tank top openings to be of sufficient size to permit unhindered loading as customary from elevator spouts and unhindered discharging as customary from suction pipes or vacuvators."

(iv) Add Clause to read: "Vessel to be inspected and passed by National Cargo Bureau Surveyor, U.S. Department of Agriculture Grain Inspector and/or Board of Trade Surveyor or Charterer's surveyor as free of odor and in all respects suitable for loading grain cargo in bulk."

b. the rate for second discharge port, if used, to be negotiated with owner; but not exceeding $.50 per long ton extra on the entire cargo. The owner's brokerage commission as agreed with owner.

c. modified to conform with the terms specified in items 1 through 9 above.

Sincerely,

/s/
N. ZUEV
President

ATTACHMENT II

MINIMUM FREIGHT RATES FOR THE CARRIAGE OF AGRICULTURAL BULK CARGO WITH RESPECT TO FIXTURES MADE PRIOR TO JULY 1, 1973

The following minimum freight rates have been agreed upon for the chartering of American-flag tonnage for the carriage of agricultural bulk cargo to the Soviet Union with respect to fixtures made prior to July 1, 1973:

For Heavy Grains—corn, wheat, sorghums, milo, rye, and soybeans

Trade Area	Base Rate Per L/T	Adjustment to Base Rate Per L/T	
U.S. Gulf Port/ Soviet Black Sea Port	$8.05 F.I.O.T.	....	
U.S. Gulf Port/ Soviet Baltic Port		−$ .30	Plus $1.00 per L/T F.I.O.T. if scheduled date of arrival is between Nov. 1 and Apr. 30
U.S. Gulf Port/ Soviet Pacific Port		+$2.00	
U.S.N.H. Port/ Soviet Black Sea Port		−$ .50	
U.S.N.H. Port/ Soviet Baltic Port		−$ .50	Plus $1.00 per L/T F.I.O.T. if scheduled date of arrival Baltic is between Nov. 1 and Apr. 30.
U.S. North Pacific Port/ Soviet Pacific Port		+$ .50	

For Barley

For the carriage of barley, the freight rates provided above will be increased by $.40 per long ton.

If vessel is directed by Charterers to trade outside of I.W.L. (Institute Warranty Limits) then any extra insurance premiums, if incurred, to be for Charterers' account.

Charter of American-flag ships for the carriage of raw and processed agricultural commodities involving trade areas or categories of cargo not provided for above will be established on the basis of the average market charter rates for the years 1969, 1970 and 1971. Where such market charter rates do not exist for a relevant route or category of cargo, agreed adjustments will be made to published current market charter rates for the most comparable route and category of cargo.

October 14, 1972

Honorable N. ZUEV
President
SOVFRACHT
Moscow G-200
SMOLENSKAJA SQ., 32/34

DEAR MR. ZUEV:

This will acknowledge receipt of your letter of today transmitting a copy of the letter which you informed me SOVFRACHT proposes to transmit to its chartering agents and which sets forth the charter party terms which we have agreed upon for fixtures made for the carriage of raw and processed agricultural commodities by American flag bulk cargo vessels under the Agreement Between the Government of the United States of America and the Government of the Union of Soviet Socialist Republics Regarding Certain Maritime Matters executed today.

Also enclosed with your letter was the schedule of rates we have agreed upon for practical purposes to be used under that Agreement in place of a precise calculation of the three year average rate for 1969, 1970, and 1971 for the carriage of specified categories of raw and processed agricultural commodities by American flag bulk cargo vessels on the routes specified, for fixtures made prior to July 1, 1973.

You also confirmed in your letter that with respect to Item 5 of the charter party terms, relating to cargo insurance, you will enter into discussions with officials of INGOSSTRAKH for the purpose of directing the placement of a portion of the marine cargo insurance coverage for shipments of raw and processed agricultural commodities with United States underwriters.

I am pleased to confirm that your letter and the enclosures reflect our agreement and understanding.

Very truly yours,

/s/
ROBERT J. BLACKWELL
Assistant Secretary
for Maritime Affairs

SPECIMENS OF TELEGRAMS IN CONNECTION WITH THE CHARTERING OF VESSELS *

1. Telegram to foreign Brokers inviting firm offer for tonnage to load 450 stds of Timber in Leningrad for Great Yarmouth:

"450 STDS GREAT YARMOUTH MAKE US FIRM OFFER".

2. Telegram from foreign Brokers offering a vessel for the transportation of Grain from Leningrad to Antwerp:

"S. S. ... UNDER OFFER ELSEWHERE OFFER YOU FIRM REPLY TOMORROW NOON, S. S. ... TWEENDECKER LENINGRAD ANTWERP 900—1,000 TONS MIN. MAX. ANY GRAIN NOT LIGHTER THAN BARLEY OPTION OF LENTILS L/C 12/17 MAY, 35/6 250 TONS LOADING PER WORKABLE HATCH PER WEATHER WORKING DAY CUSTOM OF PORT DISCHARGING ARBITRATION LONDON OWNERS LIBERTY COMPLETE WITH OTHER CARGO".

3. Firm offer of a vessel for loading 750 stds of Timber in Leningrad for Amsterdam:

"OFFER YOU FIRM WITH REPLY TOMORROW NOON S. S. ... 750 STDS 7½% L/C 29TH THIS MONTH — 8TH NEXT LENINGRAD AMSTERDAM 180 SHILLINGS ALL OTHER CONDITIONS AS PER LAST C/P S. S. ...".

4. Accepting offer with alterations:

"S. S. ... LENINGRAD ANTWERP ACCEPT YOUR OFFER WITH FOLLOWING ALTERATIONS WITH REPLY TOMORROW 10 A. M. L/C 1—12—NEXT MONTH 170 SHILLINGS ALL OTHER CONDITIONS AS PER LAST C/P SAME SHIP".

LETTERS IN CONNECTION WITH THE CHARTERING OF VESSELS

1. Confirming the fixture of a boat:

. . . . 19 ...

Dear Sirs,

S. S. " . . . . . . "

We refer to the telegrams exchanged and to your telephone call this morning and are pleased to confirm the fixture of the above vessel on the following terms as per our telegram this morning:

---

* Such telegrams are usually coded.

"S. S. . . . 850 STDS 7½% MORE OR LESS AT OWNERS' OPTION LENINGRAD S. C. D. LAYDAYS 20TH — 31ST JULY, BASIS RATE 200S. SOVIET-WOOD TERMS, 45 STDS. D. B. B. 30 STDS. BOARDS PER HATCH PER WEATHER WORKING DAY LOADING, £70 DEMURRAGE, HALF DES-PATCH AT LOADINGPORT, ARBITRATION AT HO-MEPORT OF CHARTERERS, OWNERS' AGENT AND STEVEDORES AT DISCHARGINGPORT".

We will send you tomorrow two originals and two copies of the Charter-Party.

Yours faithfully,

. . . .

2. Sending Charter-Parties for signature:

Dear Sirs,

I have sent you today under separate cover two originals and two copies of Charter-Parties for the following steamers: s. s. ". . . ." props Archangel Onega-Acton Grange, s. s. ". . . ." D. B. B. Leningrad — Antwerp, also two copies of Charter for the s. s. ". . . ." D. B. B. Belomorsk — Hull.

I shall be obliged if you will send us one original Charter for the s. s. ". . . ." and one original for the s. s. ". . . ." in return, duly signed.

Yours faithfully,

. . . .

21

MARINE INSURANCE OF GOODS

FORM OF INSURANCE POLICY ISSUED BY INGOSSTRAKH

UPRAVLENIE INOSTRANNOGO STRAKHOVANIJA SSSR
INGOSSTRAKH

Moscow, Ul. Kuibisheva, 11/10
Cable address: Moscow Ingosstrakh

Sum Insured   Cargo Insurance
POLICY No. ____

Upravlenie Inostrannogo Strakhovanija SSSR (Ingosstrakh).
pursuant to the Transport Insurance Rules insured _____

_____
(name of the insured)

for account of whom it may concern in the sum of_____

_____
(sum insured in words)

(whereof on deck_____)

on _____
(description of insured goods, number
of packages, weight etc.)

valued at_____
(insured value)

per _____
(name of vessel or description of means of transport)

B/L / Way Bill dated _____

at and from _____ to _____

with transhipment _____

sailing date _____

on the following conditions: _____

_____
_____

Premium _____

Issued at _____ the... day of _____ 19...

UPRAVLENIE INOSTRANNOGO STRAKHOVANIJA SSSR

(Signature)

Survey clause. In the event of a claim under this policy notice shall be given immediately to Ingosstrakh or its Agents, if any, at the port of arrival, previous to survey. List of Ingosstrakh's Agents see back hereof.

EXTRACT FROM THE TRANSPORT INSURANCE RULES OF INGOSSTRAKH

I. GENERAL STIPULATIONS

§ 1. Upravlenie Inostrannogo Strakhovanija SSSR (Ingosstrakh) accepts in accordance with these Rules for insurance cargoes and also anticipated profit and commission, freight and expenses connected with the carriage of cargo.

II. EXTENT OF LIABILITY

§ 2. Under insurance contracts concluded in accordance with these Rules are indemnified losses arising from fortuitous accidents and perils of the carriage.

The insurance contract may be concluded on the basis of one the following conditions:

A. "All risks".

Under an insurance contract concluded on this condition are indemnified irrespective of percentage:

a) losses due to damage to or total loss of the whole or part of the cargo arising from all perils except those specified in the items "a" — "i" of the § 6 of the Rules;

b) losses, expenses and contributions allowed in general average;

c) losses due to total loss of the whole or part of the cargo in consequence of accidents in loading, stowage and discharge of the cargo and in taking in fuel by the vessel;

d) losses due to damage to the cargo caused by stranding or collision of vessels, aircraft and other means of transport with each other or with any fixed or floating objects (including ice), grounding, fire or explosion on shipboard, aircraft or other means of transport;

e) losses, expenses and contributions allowed in general average;

f) any necessary and properly incurred expenses for the salvage of the cargo and also for minimizing the loss and ascertaining its extent if the loss is indemnified in accordance with insurance conditions.

§ 3. The liability under the insurance contract begins from the time when the cargo is taken from the warehouse at the place of shipment for transport and continues during the whole transport (including reloadings and transhipments as well as storage in warehouses at the places of reloadings and transhipments) until the cargo is delivered into warehouse of the Consignee or into another warehouse at the place of destination named in the policy, but not exceeding 60 days after discharge of the cargo from the oversea vessel at the final port of discharge.

§ 4. During the delivery of the cargo in lighters, barges and other delivering vessels Ingosstrakh bears liability only if the use of such vessels is common according to local conditions.

§ 5. Losses due to death or mortality of animals and fowls or accidents to them, due to leakage and strewing of cargo, breakage of glass, porcelain, pottery, ceramics, marble and articles made thereof, bricks of every kind, millstones, grindstones, and lithographic stones, graphite crucibles, electrodes and other objects liable to breakage under insurance on the conditions specified in the items 2 and 3 of the § 2 of the Rules are indemnified only when such losses have arisen in consequence of the wreck of the vessel or any other means of transport.·

§ 6. Losses arising in consequence of the following are not to be indemnified:

a) warlike operations or warlike measures of any nature and consequences thereof, damage or destruction by mines, torpedoes, bombs and other engines of war, actions of pirates and also in consequence of civil war, people's commotions and strikes, confiscation, requisition, arrest or destruction of cargoes by order of military or civil authorities;

b) direct or indirect effect of atomic explosion; radiation and radioactive contamination arising from any use of the atomic energy and utilization of fissile materials;

c) any necessary and properly incurred expenses for the salvage of the cargo and also for minimizing the loss and ascertaining its extent, if the loss is indemnified in accordance with insurance conditions.

B. "With particular average".

Under an insurance contract concluded on this condition are indemnified:

a) losses due to damage to or total loss of the whole or part of the cargo caused by fire, lightning, storm, whirlwind and other elemental disasters, stranding or collision of vessels, aircraft and other means of transport with each other or by contact with any fixed or floating objects, grounding, collapsing of bridges, explosion, damage to the vessel by ice, wetting by sea or river water and also owing to measures taken for salvage and extinction of fire;

b) losses in consequence of the vessel or aircraft being missing;

c) losses due to damage to or total loss of the whole or part of the cargo in consequence of accidents in loading, stowage and discharge of the cargo and in taking in fuel by the vessel;

d) losses, expenses and contributions allowed in general average;

e) any necessary and properly incurred expenses for the salvage of the cargo and also for minimizing the loss and ascertaining its extent, if the loss is indemnified in accordance with insurance conditions.

> R e m a r k. In the case of carriage of cargoes by sea, losses due to damage are not indemnified if they are under 3% (three per cent) of the insured amount of the whole cargo under one Bill of Lading, and when the cargo is in lighters, barges and other delivering vessels — of the insured amount of the cargo in each vessel. This limitation is not applied in case of general average or when the loss is due to stranding or collision of the vessel with another vessel or with any fixed or floating objects (including ice), grounding, fire or explosion on shipboard.

C. "Free from particular average".

Under the insurance contract concluded on this condition are indemnified:

a) losses due to total loss of the whole or part of the cargo caused by fire, lightning, storm, whirlwind and other elemental disasters, stranding or collision of vessels, aircraft and other means of transport with each other or by contact with any fixed or floating objects, grounding, collapsing of bridges, explosion, damage to the vessel by ice, wetting by sea or river water and also owing to measures taken for salvage and extinction of fire;

b) losses in consequence of the vessel or aircraft being missing;

c) malice or gross negligence of the insured or beneficiary or their representatives and also consequence of infringement by any one of them of the prescribed rules of carriage, sending and storage of cargoes;

d) effect of temperature, of the air in the hold or of specific properties of the cargo including drying up;

e) improper packing or corking of cargoes and the shipping of cargoes in damaged condition;

f) fire or explosion in consequence of the loading with the

knowledge of the insured or of the beneficiary or of their representatives, but without Ingosstrakh's knowledge, of substances and objects dangerous in respect of explosion or spontaneous combustion;

g) shortage of cargo while the outer packing is intact;

h) damage to cargo by worms, rodents and insects;

i) delay in the delivery of cargoes and falls in prices, neither are indemnified any other indirect losses of the insured except cases when, in accordance with the insurance conditions, such losses are subject to indemnification in general average.

Under the insurance contracts concluded on the conditions specified in items B and C of § 2 of the Rules, are not to be indemnified also losses arising from:

j) flood and earthquake;

k) sweating of the hold and wetting of cargoes by atmospheric precipitations;

l) depreciation of the cargo in consequence of contamination or damage to packing while the outer packing remains intact;

m) jettison and washing overboard of the deck cargo or of cargo carried by deckless vessels;

n) theft or non-delivery of cargo.

§ 7. By agreement between the parties the insurance conditions stated in § 2 of the Rules may be modified, amplified or replaced by other conditions generally used in insurance practice.

In particular, Ingosstrakh's liability for losses enumerated in Item "a" of § 6 of the Rules, liability during the storage of the cargo in warehouses at the place of shipment awaiting loading, and in the place of destination after discharge may be included; the terms of liability as provided in § 3 of the Rules may also be altered.

When insuring under conditions stated in items 2 and 3 of § 2 of the Rules the liability of Ingosstrakh for losses arising from causes enumerated in items "j", "k", "l", "m", "n" of § 6 of the Rules may be included and the liability for losses specified in § 5 of the Rules may be extended.

. . . .
. . . .
. . . .

22

COMPLAINTS AND CLAIMS: ARBITRATION

SETTLEMENT OF CLAIMS

1. It often happens that one of the parties to the contract considers that the other party has infringed the terms of the contract. In such cases the dissatisfied party may think it necessary to send the other party a letter of complaint which often contains a claim, i. e. a demand for something to which the sender of the letter, in his opinion, has a right as, for instance, a claim for damages or for a reduction in the price etc. Complaints and claims may arise in connection with inferior quality of the goods, late delivery or non-delivery of the goods; transportation, insurance and storage of the goods and in many other cases.

The Sellers, for example, may hold the Buyers responsible for omitting to give transport instructions in time, and the Buyers may make a claim on (against) the Sellers for damage to the goods caused by insufficient packing.

2. Very often the parties agree upon an amicable settlement of the claim in question. If, however, an amicable settlement is not arrived at, the dispute is decided either by a court of law or, which is more often the case, by arbitration. Contracts usually stipulate that in case of arbitration each party should appoint its arbitrator, and, if the two arbitrators cannot agree, they have to appoint an

umpire whose decision (award) is final and binding upon both parties.

Disputes between Soviet organizations and foreign firms arising out of foreign trade transactions are very often settled by the Foreign Trade Arbitration Commission at the U.S.S.R. Chamber of Commerce *. This Commission consists of fifteen members appointed by the Presidium of the U.S.S.R. Chamber of Commerce. When the parties refer their dispute to the Arbitration Commission, each party chooses its Arbitrator from among the members of the Commission. These two Arbitrators appoint an Umpire — another member of the same Commission. If the Arbitrators fail to agree on an Umpire, the Umpire is appointed from among the members of the Arbitration Commission by the President of the Foreign Trade Arbitration Commission.

3. Arbitration clauses in some contracts stipulate that all disputes and differences should be settled by arbitration in a third country, while some other contracts provide for arbitration in the country of the respondent party.

Contracts concluded in accordance with the Rules of different trade associations in the United Kingdom (the Coffee Trade Federation, the London Rubber Trade Association, the London Corn Trade Association, the London Cocoa Association) provide for arbitration to be held in conformity with these Rules.

In contracts for the sale of timber concluded on a standard form adopted by the Timber Trade Federation of the U.K. and V/O "Exportles", it is provided that certain kinds of disputes should be referred for settlement to arbitration in the U.K. and others — to the Foreign Trade Arbitration Commission at the U.S.S.R. Chamber of Commerce in Moscow.

COMPLAINT ABOUT INADEQUATE PACKING

1.

Stockholm, 15th May, 19...

Dear Sirs,

When unpacking your cases with "Moskvitch" cars we experience difficulties owing to the cases being too low. The space between the top of the cases and the top of the car is too small and as a result some cars are getting damaged on the top.

We suggest therefore that you should make the cases with one board of about 20 cm higher, which would enable us to unpack the cases without damaging the cars.

We are looking forward to your answer.

Yours faithfully,

. . . .

---

* Disputes arising out of Charter Parties, contracts of affreightment and marine insurance as well as those concerning salvage and collision liability are decided by the Maritime Arbitration Commission at the U.S.S.R. Chamber of Commerce.

2.

Moscow, 21st May, 19...

Dear Sirs,

We have received your letter of the 15th May and are sorry to hear you are experiencing difficulties in unpacking cases with "Moskvitch" cars owing to the insufficient height of the cases.

We have contacted the manufacturing plant and arranged for the cases to be made about 20 cm higher as suggested by you.

We thank you for bringing the matter to our attention and feel sure that in future the cases will not cause you any trouble.

Yours faithfully,

. . . .

COMPLAINT ABOUT THE BUYERS' FAILING TO ADVISE THE SELLERS OF THE EXPECTED ARRIVAL OF A VESSEL AT THE PORT OF LOADING

1.

Moscow, 11th August, 19...

Dear Sirs,

M. T. "Binta". Contract No. 525 dated Jan. 10, 19...

We have just received a telegram from Batumi informing us of the arrival of the M. T. "Binta" for lifting 10,000 tons of Gas-oil against our Contract No. 525. We would like to point out that up to present moment we have not had any advice from you about the chartering of this vessel. In this connection we refer to your letter of the 20th July, 19..., in which you informed us that you had not yet chartered a tanker and in which you promised to cable us immediately after chartering it. The unexpected arrival of the M. T. "Binta" at Batumi has put us in a difficult position so far as loading arrangements are concerned. Although in this case we have taken measures to ensure that the loading of the vessel should be effected without delay, we must insist, in accordance with § 6 of the contract, that in future you should inform us of the names of the vessels chartered by you as well as of their approximate loading dates at least two weeks before the expected arrival of each vessel at the port of loading.

Yours faithfully,

. . . .

2.

London, 14th August, 19...

Dear Sirs,

M. T. "Binta". Contract No. 525 dated Jan. 10, 19...

We are in receipt of your letter of the 11th August and have to apologize for failing to give you due notice of the chartering of the M. T. "Binta" and of the date of her expected arrival at Batumi.

As a matter of fact, the "Binta" was originally placed by us for loading oil products in the Persian Gulf, but when we subsequently decided to send her to Batumi, we omitted, through an oversight, to advise you of it.

We thank you for taking measures to start loading the tanker without delay and assure you that in future you will be notified in due time of the expected arrival of each tanker chartered by us against Contract No. 525.

Yours faithfully,

.   .   .   .

CLAIM IN CONNECTION WITH AN IMPORTED DRILLING MACHINE

1. Claiming cost of replacing broken parts of Drilling Machine:

Moscow, 2nd June, 19...

Dear Sirs,

Special Cluster Drilling Machine. Order No. 19086

We regret to inform you that our Clients have experienced serious trouble with the above machine.

After a short period of operation the teeth of two bevel gears and one wheel were crushed and the second wheel was broken.

We enclose 4 photos illustrating these defects. As the machine was brought to a standstill due to this damage, our Clients were compelled to manufacture replacement parts in order to prevent delay in production.

We enclose a statement showing the expenses incurred by our Clients in manufacturing one bevel gear with shaft, another bevel gear and two wheels as well as the cost of dismantling the machine, assembling and fitting the new parts. The expenses of our Clients amount to £ ... and we shall be glad to receive your remittance of this amount in due course.

Yours faithfully,

.   .   .   .

Enclosure.

2. Claim admitted. Manufacturers request to reconsider amount of claim:

Birmingham, 8th June, 19...

Dear Sirs,

Special Cluster Drilling Machine to Order No. 19086

In reply to your letter of the 2nd June we regret to see that there has been some trouble with the gears mentioned.

We are glad your Clients have effected the manufacture of replacement parts and quite appreciate their having to do this in order to prevent production delays.

We are also quite agreeable to recompense you for the cost

of this work, but we must say that your figures appear to be high.

In the circumstances, would you be good enough to review the costs again, and advise us what reduction you can make in the sum to be credited to your account.

Yours faithfully,

. . . .

3. Advising of inability to review amount of claim:

Moscow, 12th June, 19...

Dear Sirs,

Special Cluster Drilling Machine to Our Order No. 19086

We acknowledge with thanks receipt of your letter of the 8th instant.

Regarding the cost of replacing the damaged parts, which you find to be high, we wish to draw your attention to the fact that we have included in our claim only the cost of material and labour, all other expenses connected with the repair not having been taken into consideration. We really think that the sum indicated in our letter of the 2nd June is quite reasonable, and we request you to pay us the full amount claimed by our Clients.

Yours faithfully,

. . . .

4. Agreeing to pay the amount claimed. Information as to manner of payment requested:

Birmingham, 17th June, 19...

Dear Sirs,

Special Cluster Drilling Machine. Order No. 19086

We thank you for your letter of 12th June and note your remarks.

In the circumstances, we have decided to pay you the whole amount asked for, so will you be good enough to state how payment is to be effected, and to whom, and we will attend to the matter immediately.

Yours faithfully,

. . . .

5. Instructions as to payment sent:

Moscow, 22nd June, 19...

Dear Sirs,

Special Cluster Drilling Machine. Order No. 19086

We acknowledge receipt of your letter of the 17th June. Please remit the amount in question to Moscow to our account No. 100/1066 with the Bank for Foreign Trade of the U. S. S. R. advising us accordingly.

Yours faithfully,

. . . .

6. Payment effected:

Birmingham, 29th June, 19...

Dear Sirs,

With reference to your letter of the 22nd June we are pleased to inform you that we have today instructed the Midland Bank, Ltd., London, to remit £ ... to your Account No. 100/1066 with the Bank for Foreign Trade of the U. S. S. R., Moscow, as requested. Our instructions concerning the broken parts of the machine at the works of your Clients will follow in a few days.

Yours faithfully,

. . . .

CLAIM FOR INFERIOR QUALITY OF COFFEE

1. Provisional notice of claim:

London, 15th Oct., 19...

Dear Sirs,

Contract No. 232 dated 1st Sept., 19...

We have examined the consignment of Coffee shipped by the s. s. "Catrine" against Contract No. 232 and, in accordance with the terms of the contract, are hereby making a claim against you for inferior quality of the goods.

After a further examination of the Coffee we shall forward a claim to you with details.

Yours faithfully,

. . . .

2. Final notice of claim:

London, 18th Oct., 19...

Dear Sirs,

Contract No. 232 dated 1st Sept., 19...

Further to our letter of the 15th October, 19... ,regarding our claim for inferior quality of Coffee ex s. s. "Catrine" against Contract No. 232, we wish to advise you that as a result of a second examination of the Coffee we are making the following claim against you:

We find that 5,000 bags of Coffee ex s. s. "Catrine" sold to us as Santos Coffee New York Type No. 2 contain an excessive quantity of unripe, shelly, broken, weevilly and defective beans and correspond to Santos Coffee New York Type No. 3/4.

We are therefore claiming from you the amount of $ 7,200.00 being the difference in price between Santos N. Y. Type 2 and Santos N. Y. Type 3/4 of $ 1.20 per 50 kilos on 5,000 bags weighing 300 metric tons.

Please inform us if you agree to grant us this allowance.

Yours faithfully,

. . . .

3. Sellers' counter offer:

London, 23rd Oct., 19...

Dear Sirs,

5,000 Bags Santos Coffee ex s. s. "Catrine"

We acknowledge receipt of your letter of the 20th October, 19..., claiming an allowance of $ 1.20 per 50 kilos on 5,000 bags of Coffee ex s. s. "Catrine".

We have carefully examined the samples from this consignment and offer you, without prejudice, an allowance of 50 U. S. A. cents per 50 kilos in full settlement of your claim.

Failing your acceptance of this offer, the claim will be submitted to arbitration.

Yours faithfully,

. . . .

4. Buyers decline Sellers' counter offer:

London, 24th Oct., 19...

Dear Sirs,

Contract No. 232. 5,000 Bags Santos Coffee

We thank you for your letter of the 23rd October offering us an allowance of 50 U. S. A. cents per 50 kilos on the above consignment.

We regret to inform you that we do not see our way to accept your offer and are submitting the claim to arbitration.

Yours faithfully,

. . . .

5. Arbitration award:

The Coffee Trade Federation
Arbitration Award

Award No. A 151
London, 5th November, 19...

We, the undersigned Members of the Panel of Arbitrators, appointed to arbitrate on:

5,000 bags Santos Coffee CLF, AAI sold as Santos Coffee. N. Y. Type 2, good bean, greenish, strictly soft, cup tested.

Sold by: Messrs. A. White & Co.

Shippers: Messrs. B. Brown & Co., Santos ex s. s. "Catrine".

And, having carefully examined the samples, find them inferior to guarantee and award the Buyers an allowance of 80 U. S. A. cents per 50 kilos.

We further award that the arbitration fee of forty-eight guineas together with the Federation fee of 5 shillings be paid by Sellers and Buyers equally.

(Signatures)

ORGANIZATION AND A BRITISH FIRM PROVIDING FOR ARBITRATION IN A THIRD COUNTRY

Any disputes or differences arising out of or in connection with the present contract are to be settled, without recourse to Courts of Law, by an Arbitration Tribunal in Stockholm, Sweden. The Arbitration Tribunal shall consist of two Arbitrators and an Umpire.

The party giving notice of arbitration shall notify the other party by registered letter stating the question at issue and giving the name and address of its Arbitrator. Within ... days of receipt of such a letter, the other party shall inform the first party, also by registered letter, of the name and address of its Arbitrator, and if it does not do so, its Arbitrator shall be appointed by the President of the Chamber of Commerce in Stockholm at the request of the party giving notice of arbitration.

The two Arbitrators are to choose an Umpire within ... days of the appointment of the second Arbitrator. Should the Arbitrators fail to agree upon an Umpire, the Umpire shall be appointed by the President of the Chamber of Commerce in Stockholm, Sweden, within ... days after receipt in Stockholm of such an application made by either of the parties.

The award shall be issued on the basis of the present contract and legal regulations to be used in accordance with the principles of international law.

The award shall state the reasons for the decision, indicate the composition of the Arbitration Tribunal, the date and place of the decision and the allocation of the costs and expenses of the arbitration between the parties.

Both parties shall accept the award of the Arbitration Tribunal as final and binding upon them.

EXAMPLE OF A CLAUSE IN A CONTRACT BETWEEN A SOVIET ORGANIZATION AND A FOREIGN FIRM PROVIDING FOR ARBITRATION IN THE COUNTRY OF THE RESPONDENT PARTY

All disputes and differences which may arise between the parties in respect of or in connection with the present contract shall be referred for settlement to arbitration in the following manner:

1. If V/O "Sojuzexport" should be respondent in such dispute or difference, the matter shall be referred for settlement to the Foreign Trade Arbitration Commission of the U.S.S.R. Chamber of Commerce, Moscow, and shall be tried in conformity with the Rules of Procedure of this Commission.

2. If the firm should be respondent in such dispute or difference, the matter shall be referred for settlement to . . . . . .

. . . .
The arbitration award shall be final and binding upon both parties.

EXTRACT FROM THE RULES OF PROCEDURE OF THE FOREIGN TRADE ARBITRATION COMMISSION AT THE U.S.S.R. CHAMBER OF COMMERCE

(Approved by Decision of the Presidium of the U.S.S.R. Chamber of Commerce)

1. The Foreign Trade Arbitration Commission shall accept for arbitration disputes of every nature arising from foreign trade contracts and, in particular, disputes between foreign firms and Soviet trading organizations.

Such disputes shall include disputes arising from claims concerned with the purchase of goods abroad, the sale of goods abroad and agency contracts, as well as disputes concerned with the carriage, insurance, storage and despatch of such goods and other foreign trade operations.

Such disputes are accepted for arbitration upon a written declaration by the party concerned that the parties have agreed in writing to submit the dispute to arbitration by the Foreign Trade Arbitration Commission.

The agreement to submit the dispute for arbitration by the Foreign Trade Arbitration Commission may be contained in the contract from which the dispute arose, or it may take the form of a separate agreement concerning an existing dispute or one which may arise in future (special agreement, exchange of correspondence, clauses in other documents relating to the dispute in question).

2. The Points of Claim shall contain the following particulars:

    a) the names of the claimant and the respondent;
    b) the claimant's and the respondent's addresses;
    c) the claim made stating the facts on which the claim is based and indicating the evidence in support of the claim;
    d) the name of the member of the Foreign Trade Arbitration Commission whom the claimant appoints as his Arbitrator, or a statement to the effect that the appointment of the Arbitrator is left to the discretion of the President of the Foreign Trade Arbitration Commission.

3. The Points of Claim shall be accompanied by the originals or certified copies of the documents (the contract, correspondence between the parties, etc.) to which the claimant refers in support of his claims.

4. On filing Points of Claim with the Foreign Trade Arbitration Commission, the claimant shall make payment in advance on account of the fee to cover the expenses of the arbitration proceedings to the amount of 1 per cent. of the sum in dispute.

Such payment shall be credited to the current account of the U. S. S. R. Chamber of Commerce No. 1210047 in the Bank for Foreign Trade of the U. S. S. R. in Moscow or paid in cash direct to the U. S. S. R. Chamber of Commerce.

The receipt for such payment shall be filed with the Foreign Trade Arbitration Commission together with the Points of Claim.

5. The Points of Claim and all accompanying documents shall be filed with the Foreign Trade Arbitration Commission with copies for each respondent.

6. On receipt of the Points of Claim, the Foreign Trade Arbitration Commission shall forthwith inform the respondent that Points of Claim have been filed, and forward to him copies of the Points of Claim and of all accompanying documents.

Within fifteen days after receipt of such notice, the respondent shall inform the Foreign Trade Arbitration Commission which of the members of the Commission he chooses as his Arbitrator, or that he leaves the choice of Arbitrator to the discretion of the President of the Foreign Trade Arbitration Commission.

If the parties have agreed upon other time limits, the latter must be observed.

7. Where the respondent fails to choose an Arbitrator within the time specified in paragraph 6 of these Rules, the President of the Foreign Trade Arbitration Commission shall appoint an Arbitrator from among the members of the Commission.

8. The Arbitrators who have been either chosen or appointed shall be informed thereof by the Foreign Trade Arbitration Commission without delay and invited to choose an Umpire from among the members of the Commission within fifteen days following the receipt of such notice.

9. Where the Arbitrators fail to agree on an Umpire within the time specified in paragraph 8, the Umpire shall be appointed by the President of the Foreign Trade Arbitration Commission from among the members of the Commission.

10. By mutual consent of the parties, the settlement of the case may, in exceptional cases, be entrusted to a sole Arbitrator.

A sole Arbitrator is either chosen directly by the parties from among the members of the Foreign Trade Arbitration Commission, or, at the request of the parties, appointed by the President of the Foreign Trade Arbitration Commission from among the members of the Commission.

11. Where an Arbitrator is unable to take part in the hearing of a case, the Foreign Trade Arbitration Commission shall notify the party concerned thereof and request that another Arbitrator be chosen from among the members of the Foreign Trade Arbitration Commission within fifteen days.

If the party fails to choose an Arbitrator within this time, the Arbitrator shall be appointed by the President of the Foreign Trade Arbitration Commission from among the members of the Commission.

12. Where an Umpire is unable to take part in the hearing of a case, the Foreign Trade Arbitration Commission shall notify the Arbitrators thereof and suggest that another Umpire be chosen within fifteen days, the provisions of paragraph 9 of these Rules being applicable.

13. Upon the request of the claimant, the President of the Foreign Trade Arbitration Commission may deal with the security for the claim.

The amount and the form of the security shall be determined by the President of the Foreign Trade Arbitration Commission.

14. The day for the hearing of the case shall be fixed by the President of the Foreign Trade Arbitration Commission by agreement with the Umpire or with the sole Arbitrator.

. . . .

. . . .

. . . .

23

SOVIET FOREIGN TRADE ORGANIZATIONS AND THE NOMENCLATURE OF EXPORT AND IMPORT PRODUCTS

Purchase of goods from foreign companies by Soviet enterprises and organizations is made in an established manner through the ministries and other government agencies to which they are subordinate

Source: V/O Vneshtorgreklama, Ministry of Foreign Trade of the USSR, Moscow.

MACHINERY, EQUIPMENT AND VEHICLES

Metal-working equipment

Metal-cutting machine-tools
Stankoimport

Presses
Stankoimport, Metallurgimport,
Prommashimport

Hammers
Stankoimport

Other forging and pressing equipment
Stankoimport

Metal-working lines
Stankoimport, Metallurgimport

Equipment of enterprises of the
metal-working industry
Avtopromimport, Stankoimport,
Prommashimport, Machinoimport,
Techmashexport, Prommashexport

Power-generation and electrical equipment

Power-generation equipment
Energomachexport, Machinoexport,
Mashpriborintorg, Sudoimport,
Prommashexport

Electrical equipment
Energomachexport, Mashpriborintorg,
Stankoimport, Prommashimport,
Avtopromimport, Techmashexport,
Metallurgimport, Machinoimport

Electrodes
Sojuzpromexport

Electrical cables and wires
Raznoimport

Mining, metallurgical and oil equipment

Equipment for underground and
surface production of minerals
Machinoexport, Metallurgimport,
Tsvetmetpromexport, Prommashexport

Crushing, milling and dressing equipment
Metallurgimport, Machinoexport

Coking and gas industry equipment
Machinoimport, Tsvetmetpromexport

Metallurgical equipment
Metallurgimport, Machinoexport,
Tsvetmetpromexport

Oil refining industry equipment
Machinoimport, Techmashexport,
Tsvetmetpromexport

Drilling, production and exploration
machines and equipment
Machinoexport, Techsnabexport,
Machinoimport, Metallurgimport,
Mashpriborintorg

Other mining, metallurgical and oil
equipment
Metallurgimport, Machinoimport,
Prommashimport, Tsvetmetpromexport

Handling equipment

Cranes
Machinoexport, Machinoimport,
Metallurgimport, Sudoimport,
Sojuzvneshstrojimport

Winches
Machinoexport, Machinoimport,
Metallurgimport, Sudoimport

Hoisting machines
Machinoexport, Machinoimport,
Metallurgimport, Traktoroexport

Battery-driven trucks, motor-driven
trucks and other ground-type transport
Machinoexport, Machinoimport, Metallurgimport

Other handling equipment
Machinoexport, Machinoimport,
Sudoimport, Metallurgimport

Equipment for food and light industries

Food industry equipment
Techmashexport, Technopromimport,
Prommashexport

Refrigerating and air-conditioning equipment
Techmashexport, Techmashimport

Tobacco industry equipment
Technopromimport

Textile industry equipment
Techmashexport, Technopromimport,
Technoexport

Sewing industry equipment
Techmashexport, Technopromimport,
Technoexport

Leather, footwear and fur industries
equipment
Techmashexport, Technopromimport

Other light industry equipment
Technopromimport, Prommashimport

Equipment for chemical, pulp-and-paper, construction and other industries

Chemical industry equipment
Techmashimport, Techmashexport,
Prommashimport,
Technopromimport, Neftechimpromexport

Wood, pulp-and-paper and wood-working
industries equipment
Stankoimport, Prommashimport,
Techmashexport, Selkhozpromexport,
Neftechimpromexport

Wood-working machine-tools
Stankoimport, Prommashimport

Construction materials industry
equipment
Technopromimport, Machinoexport,
Machinoimport, Prommashimport,
Tsvetmetpromexport, Technostroyexport

Road and road-building machinery and equipment
Machinoexport, Machinoimport,
Sudoimport, Traktoroexport,
Zapchastexport

Pumping and compressing equipment
Machinoexport, Machinoimport,
Techmashexport, Sudoimport

Public utility, commercial and fire-
fighting equipment
Techmashimport, Techmashexport,
Prommashimport, Raznoexport,
Technopromimport, Sojuzkoopvneshtorg,
Raznoexport, Technopromimport,
Sojuzkoopvneshtorg

Polygraphic industry equipment
Technopromimport, Prommashimport,
Techmashexport

Communications equipment
Sudoimport, Aviaexport,
Mashpriborintorg, Electronorgtechnica,

Prommashexport, Techsnabexport

Equipment for other industries
Technopromimport, Techmashexport,
Prommashimport, Mashpriborintorg,
Engergomachexport, Novoexport,
Promsyrioimport, Tsvetmetpromexport,
Technoexport, Electronorgtechnica,
Machinoimport, Technostroyexport

**Buildings, communications, civil structures
and public utilities**
Industrial buildings and structures
Technoexport, Prommashexport,
Technostroyexport

Agricultural and forestry structures
Selkhozpromexport, Prommashimport

Dwelling houses and complexes
Technoexport, Technostroyexport

Facilities for research, educational cultural,
medicinal, commercial and public institutions
Technoexport, Prommashimport,
Technostroyexport

Public utilities, except those dealing
with water
Technoexport

Hydrotechnical and irrigational structures
Technoexport, Technopromexport

Pipelines
Tsvetmetpromexport, Technoexport

Other buildings, communications, civil
and public utilities
Technoexport, Prommashexport,
Technostroyexport

**Instruments, laboratory and medical equipment,
bearings, tools and abrasives**
Electrical and radio measuring equipment
Mashpriborintorg, Techsnabexport,
Vneshtechnika

Instruments for physical research, optical and
mechanical instruments and equipment and time
measuring instruments
Mashpriborintorg, Vneshtechnika,
Techsnabexport, Technointorg

Medical equipment and tools with the exception
of equipment of chemical and pharmaceutical
industries
Vneshtechnika, Machinoimport,
Techsnabexport, Medexport

Bearings
Stankoimport, Machinoexport

Tools
Stankoimport, Prommashimport

Diamonds, rubies, and other precious
technical stones
Almazjuvelirexport, Stankoimport,
Techsnabexport

Hard alloys
Stankoimport, Techsnabexport

Abrasives
Stankoimport

Process control instruments and laboratory
equipment
Stankoimport, Mashpriborintorg,
Techsnabexport, Metallurgimport,
Traktoroexport, Machinoexport,
Technoexport, Prommashexport

Mechanical values measuring instruments
Stankoimport, Mashpriborintorg,
Avtopromimport, Vneshtechnika

Tractors, agricultural machines and inventory

Tractors and garage equipment for them
Traktoroexport, Machinoexport,
Zapchastexport

Agricultural machines and equipment
Traktoroexport, Zapchastexport

Small agricultural equipment
Traktoroexport, Novoexport,
Sojuzkoopvneshtorg

Vehicles and auxiliary equipment thereto

Railway rolling stock and auxiliary equipment thereto
Energomachexport, Machinoimport

Trucks and garage equipment
Avtoexport, Avtopromimport

Ships, marine, vessel-lifting and diver
equipment; port equipment
Sudoimport, Technoexport

Aircraft
Aviaexport

Cars, motocycles and motor scooters
Avtoexport, Avtopromimport,
Zapchastexport, Vneshposyltorg

Other vehicles
Avtoexport, Machinoimport

FUELS, MINERALS AND METALS

Solid fuel
Sojuzpromexport, Exporties,
Novoexport

Crude oil
Sojuznefteexport

Petroleum products and synthetic liquid fuel
Sojuznefteexport, Sojuzchimexport,
Sojuzgazexport

Gas fuel, electric power, steam
and water
Sojuzgazexport, Energomachexport

Metal ores and their concentrates
Sojuzpromexport, Raznoimport,
Techsnabexport

Non-ore minerals, clays and soil
Sojuzpromexport, Strojmaterialintorg,
Raznoexport, Novoexport, Almazjuvelirexport

Ferrous metals
Promsyrioimport, Energomachexport,
Techsnabexport

Non-ferrous metals
Raznoimport, Promsyrioimport,
Techsnabexport

Precious metals and articles thereof to be
used for production purposes
Almazjuvelirexport

CHEMICAL PRODUCTS, FERTILIZERS AND RUBBER
Chemical products
Sojuzchimexport, Sojuzpromexport,
Sojuznefteexport

Dyes, lacquering, dying and tanning
materials
Sojuzchimexport, Sojuzkoopvneshtorg

Explosives and pyrotechnical articles
Sojuzchimexport

Cine- and photo-materials
Sojuzchimexport, Sojuzkoopvneshtorg

Fertilizer and preparations for
pest control

Rubber, rubber and rubber-asbestos articles
Avtoexport, Aviaexport,
Raznoimport, Strojmaterialintorg

Amorphous isotopes and chemicals
Techsnabexport

CONSTRUCTION MATERIALS AND PARTS

Construction materials
Strojmaterialintorg, Sojuzpromexport,
Raznoimport

Prefabricated houses, barracks
and construction parts
Exportles, Sojuzvneshstrojimport,
Strojmaterialintorg, Raznoimport

Metal storages, structures and tubings
Prommashimport, Promsyrioimport,
Sojuzvneshstrojimport, Engergomachexport

RAW MATERIALS AND PRODUCTS OF ITS PROCESSING

Timber material and pulp-and-paper articles
Exportles, Raznoexport, Novoexport,
Sojuzchimexport

Textile raw materials and semi-finished
products
Exportljon, Novoexport,
Sojuzkoopvneshtorg

Furs and fur raw materials (with the
exception of finished fur articles)
Sojuzpushnina, Sojuzkoopvneshtorg

Raw skins and hides and leather
Sojuzpushnina, Sojuzkoopvneshtorg

Seeds and planting materials
Exportkhleb

Essential oils, resins, medicinal and
medical raw materials
Sojuzchimexport, Medexport,
Sojuzkoopvneshtorg, Prodintorg

Technical greases and oils
Prodintorg, Sojuzchimexport

Concentrated and capacious forage
Exportkhleb, Novoexport,
Sojuzkoopvneshtorg,
Sojuzpushnina

Other raw materials
Sojuzchimexport, Promsyrioimport,
Exportkhleb, Sojuzpushnina, Sojuzkoopvneshtorg,
Strojmaterialintorg, Raznoexport, Exportljon,
Prodintorg

LIVE CATTLE

Live cattle
Prodintorg, Skotoimport

RAW MATERIALS FOR THE PRODUCTION OF FOOD

Grain (including groats)
Exportkhleb

Slaughter live cattle
Skotoimport, Prodintorg,
Sojuzkoopvneshtorg

Exportkhleb, Sojuzkoopvneshtorg,
Prodintorg, Sojuzplodoimport,
Raznoexport, Sojuzchimexport

FOODSTUFFS

Meat and dairy products, animal fat
and eggs
Prodintorg, Skotoimport,
Sojuzplodoimport

Fish and fish products
Prodintorg, Sojuzkoopvneshtorg,
Vneshposyltorg

Flour and leguminous plants
Exportkhleb, Sojuzplodoimport,
Vneshposyltorg

Vegetables, fruits and berries
Sojuzkoopvneshtorg, Sojuzplodoimport,
Vneshposyltorg

Sugar, vegetable oils and other food stuffs
Prodintorg, Sojuzkoopvneshtorg,
Sojuzplodoimport, Vneshposyltorg

Beverages and tobacco products
Sojuzplodoimport, Sojuzkoopvneshtorg,
Vneshposyltorg, Raznoexport

INDUSTRIAL CONSUMER GOODS

Cotton, wool and other textiles (except
technical textiles)
Exportljon, Sojuzkoopvneshtorg,
Vneshposyltorg, Novoexport,
Medexport

Clothes and linen
Exportljon, Sojuzpushnina,
Sojuzkoopvneshtorg,
Vneshposyltorg, Novoexport,
Raznoexport

Haberdashery
Raznoexport, Novoexport,
Sojuzkoopvneshtorg, Vneshposyltorg,
Sojuzpushnina, Exportljon

Leather, rubber and other footwear
Raznoexport, Vneshposyltorg,
Sojuzkoopvneshtorg

Tableware and table covers
Raznoexport, Sojuzkoopvneshtorg

Furniture
Exportles, Sojuzkoopvneshtorg

Medicines, articles of sanitation
and hygiene; perfumery, cosmetics
and vitamins
Medexport, Sojuzchimexport,
Sojuzkoopvneshtorg, Vneshposyltorg,
Prodintorg

Cultural and entertainment goods
Raznoexport, Novoexport, Mezhdunarodnaya
Kniga, Sovexportfilm, Sojuzkoopvneshtorg,
Vneshposyltorg, Almazjuvelirexport,
Raznoimport, Exportles, Mashpriborintorg,
Zapchastexport, Techmashimport,
Avtoexport, Technointorg

Industrial consumer goods excluded from
above groups
Raznoexport, Electronorgtechnica,
Novoexport, Exportles, Strojmaterialintorg,
Almazjuvelirexport, Sojuzkoopvneshtorg

24

BUSINESS CONVERSATIONS

CONVERSATION

A. — You've probably received the telegram I sent you from Paris on Tuesday, haven't you?

B. — Yes, we have. We were expecting you the day before yesterday.

A. — I'm sorry, I was detained in Paris on business.

B. — How is business in general?

A. — I must say that we aren't quite satisfied with our present sales. We used to get regular large orders from a number of the largest hotels and restaurants in England but lately we have been doing less business with them.

B. — I'm surprised to hear it. How do you account for this decline in the amount of your orders? We don't feel here at all that the demand for caviar is weaker than before. On the contrary, we are getting now more enquiries for caviar than ever.

A. — I wouldn't say that there is a big decrease in the volume of our business, but many hotels are inclined to use, instead of caviar, cheaper stuffs like lobsters or oysters, for instance. I hope you are not going to raise your prices this year.

B. — As a matter of fact, our prices are now about 10 per cent higher than last year.

A. — What are you prices now? We've written to you that we need altogether about 20 tons of caviar.

B. — Our prices today are ... shillings for beluga caviar, ...

shillings for osetrova and ... shillings for pressed per pound f. a. s. Leningrad. The terms of payment would be the same as in our old contract.

A. — Can't you reduce your increase from 10 per cent to 5 per cent?

B. — I'm sorry, it's impossible.

A. — I think I'll have to cable my Board of Directors and ask them if they agree to your present prices. I'll call here again as soon as I get their answer.

B. — All right. But I must tell you that we can hold these prices open for your acceptance till the 3rd February only.

A. — I'll send the cable at once. Good-bye.

CONVERSATION

A. — We've carefully examined the specifications and drawings you sent us with your tender for a steam turbine set. Frankly speaking, we are rather disappointed with the design worked out by you.

B. — I'm sorry to hear it. I'd like to know what your objections are.

A. — Here is a copy of our experts' detailed report. Our experts point out in particular that the efficiency of the turbine is low as compared with that of modern turbines.

B. — I'll acquaint myself with your experts' observations and then call on you again. Couldn't I get another copy of the report, as I'd like to send it to London?

A. — Here is a second copy. When writing to your company, please mention also that, apart from technical objections, we consider your price to be very high.

B. — I'll do so. Good-bye.

A. — Good-bye.

CONVERSATION

A. — I've called on you to ask whether you could supply us with two portable compressor stations which we need for supplying various pneumatic tools with compressed air.

B. — What type of compressor do you need? You've got our catalogue of compressors, haven't you?

A. — I have it with me and I think that Model КСЭ-5 would suit our purpose. Are many Soviet industrial organizations using this model and are they satisfied with it?

B. — This model is used by very many Soviet plants. We've also delivered quite a number of these compressors to different countries in Europe and Asia and I must say that all our customers are very much satisfied with their performance.

A. — What type of electric motor do you deliver with the compressor?

B. — The compressor is usually delivered with a slipring A. C. motor, 3 phase, 400/440 volts. Will the voltage suit you?

A. — Yes, it will do. What is the price of the compressor?

B. — The total price including the electric motor and a standard set of accessories and spares is ... c. i. f. Bombay. Packing will be charged extra. The price doesn't include erection and technical service.

A. — Do you guarantee the quality of the material and normal operation of the compressor?

B. — We guarantee that the compressor and the motor are manufactured of high-quality material and the workmanship is very good. Should the compressor prove defective within 16 months of the date of shipment, we undertake to repair or replace any defective part free of charge. However, we do not accept any responsibility for damage which is due to improper storage, careless handling and maintenance of the machine and for damage during transit.

A. — When can you ship the compressors?

B. — The compressors can be dispatched to Odessa within 12 weeks of the date of our confirmation of the order and then shipped by the first steamer bound for India.

CONVERSATION

A. — We've got the samples of paraffin wax sent by you by parcel post.

B. — I hope you are satisfied with the quality of the samples, aren't you?

A. — The quality is all right. What price can you quote us for, say, 300 tons of Grade A?

B. — Our price today is forty-five pounds ten shillings per long ton c. i. f. London.

A. — When could you ship the goods?

B. — We could ship the goods from Leningrad within three weeks upon receipt of your order. May I give you a copy of our General Conditions? You'll find in it our usual terms of payment and other conditions.

A. — Thank you. I'm going to cable your price and terms to my company and call on you again as soon as I get the answer.

B. — All right, but please bear in mind that the price is without engagement on our part and subject to the goods being unsold.

CONVERSATION

A. — Can you supply us with 1,000 tons of manganese ore containing minimum 85 per cent of peroxide of manganese?

B. — Yes, we can. What time of shipment do you need?

A. — The ore must be shipped in the first half of March at the latest.

B. — We could ship the ore in March, that is not later than the 31st March.

A. — What is your price?

B. — Our price is thirty-six pounds twelve shillings and six-pence per English ton c. i. f. London. The ore would be shipped in bulk, as usual.

A. — And what about the moisture?

B. — We'll deduct three per cent from the weight as final compensation for moisture. That means that you'll have to pay for 97% of the weight of the ore only.

A. — Who will determine the contents of peroxide of manganese in the ore?

B. — Sampling and analysis are usually carried out by our laboratory at Poti. The results of the analysis are to be binding upon both the sellers and the buyers.

A. — What are your terms of payment?

B. — Our terms are in cash against shipping documents in London within 3 days after presentation of the documents. As we haven't had any dealings with your company before, you would have to supply us with a bank guarantee as a security of the fulfilment of the contract.

CONVERSATION

A. — I suppose you've received our quotation for some machinery for an automobile plant, haven't you?

B. — Yes, we have. We are now comparing your price and terms with offers received from other manufactures. But I must tell you at once, Mr. A., that we can't agree to some points in your offer.

A. — Which terms do you mean?

B. — First of all, we can't agree to a sliding price.

A. — I assure you, Mr. B., that very many British firms insist on sliding prices when the time of delivery is longer than 12 months.

B. — But you know, of course, that most continental firms are quoting now fixed prices. We can't agree either to pay 30 per cent of the price in advance. We are prepared to pay 10 per cent of the amount of the order in advance, 85 per cent of each part delivery within 90 days after the dispatch to us of the shipping documents and the remaining 5 per cent after the expiration of the guarantee period.

CONVERSATION AT THE OFFICE

Secretary. — The U. S. S. R. Chamber of Commerce has sent us this letter from a London company — Brown & Co., Ltd. They are interested in Caviar.

Manager (*reading the letter*). — Are they in the Trade Directory?

Secretary. — Yes, they are. There are only three lines about them in the Directory, as Brown & Co., Ltd., are a private company.

Manager. — What's their share capital?

Secretary. — It's 20,000 pounds, fully paid. What shall I write to them?

Manager. — Write to them we can't offer any caviar now, but at the beginning of February we are going to start negotiations with our customers for the sale of caviar of the new catch. Ask them to let us know what quantities and what time of shipment they need. Send also an enquiry to the London Information Bureau about their financial position.

Secretary. — Very good. I'll write the letters at once.

CONVERSATION BETWEEN THE MANAGER OF A DEPARTMENT OF SOJUZIMPORT AND A REPRESENTATIVE OF A FOREIGN MACHINE-BUILDING COMPANY

R. — I've brought a detailed quotation for a precision boring machine you need. May I hand you the offer? (*The representative hands over the documents.*)

M. — Thank you. With your permission, I'll look it through in your presence. (*The Manager looks through the offer.*) — I see that the machine is designed for finishing operations only, isn't it?

R. — Quite right. Before being mounted on our machines, the parts must undergo roughing and semi-finishing operations. We understand from your enquiry that you intend to perform only finishing operations on these machines.

M. — That's right. Now, about the fixtures. It is very important that the location of the centre hole in relation to the top of the part should be as close as possible to the tolerance.

R. — Our fixtures fully meet your requirements. Besides, by means of our hydraulically operated fixture the parts are easily mounted and fixed.

M. — What is the output of the machine?

R. — At 80% efficiency the estimated production is 24 pieces per hour which is even a little higher than the output specified in your enquiry.

M. — We shall, of course, require your written guarantee that the production of the machine will not be below the figure specified by us.

R. — We are prepared to give such a guarantee as we have already delivered many machines of a similar type and their performance is highly satisfactory in all respects.

M. — I see that the machine is of much larger dimensions than those our clients have specified. We'll have to get in touch with them and find out whether this is acceptable to them. We must also have their confirmation of some other technical data stated in your offer.

R. — May I ask you how many machines you intend to buy?

M. — It depends on the price and the terms of payment and delivery.

R. — As to the time of delivery, we have stated in our offer that we could deliver the first two machines within 6 months and two machines every month after that.

M. — Couldn't you speed up the delivery?

R. — I'm afraid it is very difficult as we depend on our suppliers of electrical equipment, and they cannot deliver earlier. What time of delivery would suit you, may I ask?

M. — We require the first four machines in four months' time and then two machines monthly.

R. — I'm sorry, but I cannot confirm these terms now. I'll have to cable my company and give you an answer in a day or two. By that time I hope to get a reply to my cable.

M. — All right. Now about the price. I am surprised to see that it is higher than in our last order.

R. — The total price of the machine and the fixtures is, indeed, a little higher, but this is because the fixtures have been perfected and are practically of a new design. The price of the machine without the fixtures is the same as before.

M. — Would you mind itemizing the price? I'd like to see how the total price is made up.

R. — I could do it straight away.

M. — If you please.

R. — Now you have a separate price for the machine and here are the prices for the fixtures and tools for each item separately.

M. — The prices for the fixtures and tools are too high, even if the technical improvements are considered. Nor can we agree to the price of the machine considering that our last order was for one machine only and now we intend to place an order for several machines.

R. — We have taken this into consideration as we have not increased the old price in spite of the rise in cost of materials.

M. — I'm surprised that a slight rise in the cost of materials should prevent you from making an allowance, considering the size of the order. We've got offers from competitive firms and there is no mention in them of any rise in prices of materials.

R. — I'll look into the matter and see what I can do. I am afraid, however, that we shan't be able to make a considerable deduction from the price, as all the prices and discounts were very carefully calculated and checked by our Sales Department.

M. — You will realize, of course, that however much we should like to continue our business relations with your company, the order will be placed with the firm which will offer the most favourable prices and terms.

R. — I'll let you know tomorrow what deduction from the price we could make.

M. — All right. I've got some questions about the terms of payment, but we could discuss them tomorrow, as I'd like the Manager of our Financial Department to take part in the discussion, and he is engaged at the moment.

TELEPHONE CONVERSATION

A. B. Nikitin. — Is that Brown & Co., Limited? I want Mr. White, please.

Telephone operator. — Just hold on a minute, please. His number is engaged at the moment. ... Are you there? I'm putting you through now.

Mr. White. — Mr. White speaking. Who is calling?

A. B. Nikitin. — Good afternoon, Mr. White. This is Mr. Nikitin of Sojuzimport, Moscow, speaking. We've just got copies of the shipping documents for the goods shipped by s. s. "Clyde" against Contract No. 1225.

Mr. White. — Is anything wrong with the documents?

A. B. Nikitin. — You see, you haven't sent us a copy of the invoice and we can't therefore instruct the Bank to open a Letter of Credit.

Mr. White. — Haven't we? Please hold the line for a minute, I'll speak to the clerk who is dealing with this contract. ... Are you there, Mr. Nikitin?

A. B. Nikitin. — Yes, I'm listening, Mr. White.

Mr. White. — I'm so sorry, Mr. Nikitin. The copy of the invoice was indeed left behind. We'll send it by air-mail straight away. I needn't tell you how sorry I am for the trouble we've caused you.

A. B. Nikitin. — It'll be all right, Mr. White, if we get the invoice tomorrow. Good-bye.

Mr. White. — Good-bye.

TELEPHONE CONVERSATION

Mr. Smith. — Is that the Soviet Trade Delegation?

Operator. — Yes, it is.

Mr. Smith. — Put me through to Mr. Petrov's office, please.

Secretary. — Mr. Petrov's secretary speaking.

Mr. Smith. — My name is Mr. Smith. I'd like to speak to Mr. Petrov.

Secretary. — I am sorry, but Mr. Petrov isn't available at the moment. Would you like to leave a message for him?

Mr. Smith. — I have an appointment with Mr. Petrov for 2 o'clock this afternoon, but I am sorry I can't come today. I must go to Paris on business and I'll be back only on Friday morning. Can Mr. Petrov see me at two o'clock on Friday afternoon instead of today?

Secretary. — As far as I know, Mr. Petrov hasn't got any engagement for Friday afternoon, but I must speak to him before I can give you a definite answer. Will you leave your telephone number with me?

Mr. Smith. — Yes, certainly, I'll leave you the telephone number on which you can contact my secretary. It's London Wall 2230 (double two three oh), extension 21 (two one).

Secretary. — I beg your pardon. Will you spell the exchange, please?

Mr. Smith. — I'll spell the first three letters that you must dial: L for London, o for orange, n for nobody.

Secretary. — Thank you very much, Mr. Smith. Just to make sure I'd like to repeat the number. It's Lon 2230 extension 21. I'll contact your secretary when I've spoken to Mr. Petrov.

Mr. Smith. — Thank you. Good-bye.

Secretary. — Good-bye, Mr. Smith.

TELEPHONE CONVERSATION

Mr. Smith. — Is that Sojuzexport? I'd like to speak to Mr. Petrov, please.

Secretary. — Just hold the line a minute ...

A. B. Petrov. — Mr. Petrov speaking.

Mr. Smith. — Good afternoon, Mr. Petrov. This is Mr. Smith of Brown & Co, Limited, speaking. We've got your samples of paraffin wax and I think that Grade A would be suitable for our needs. Your price, however, seems to me rather high. Can't you reduce it? We've got competitive offers at lower prices.

A. B. Petrov. — It depends on the quantity you are going to order. If you should increase the quantity to 150 tons at least, we could allow you a discount of 5 per cent. In that case the price would work out at £43/4/6 per long ton.

Mr. Smith. — All right. I agree to take 150 tons. When could you ship this lot?

A. B. Petrov. — During the first half of August.

Mr. Smith. — That is rather late. Couldn't you ship it at the end of July?

A. B. Petrov. — I'm afraid there won't be a boat available for London at that time, but we'll do our best to ship this lot as early as possible.

Mr. Smith. — Thank you, Mr. Petrov. When can we expect to get your contract for the 150 tons of paraffin wax?

A. B. Petrov. — We're going to send it by air-mail tomorrow.

Mr. Smith. — Thank you. Good-bye.

A. B. Petrov. — Good-bye.

TELEPHONE CONVERSATION

Mr. Brown. — Is that Sojuzexport? Put me through to Mr. Petrov, please.

Secretary. — His number is engaged at the moment. Hold on a minute, please ... Are you there? I'm putting you through now.

A. B. Petrov. — Mr. Petrov speaking.

Mr. Brown. — Good morning, Mr. Petrov. This is Mr. Brown of Smith & Company, Limited, speaking. Can you tell me whether you've already chartered a steamer for the transportation of ore against Contract No. 25?

A. B. Petrov. — Yes, we have. The name of the vessel is "Pirogov".

Mr. Brown. — I can't hear you. How do you spell the name of the steamer?

A. B. Petrov. — P for Peter, I for Isaac, R for Robert, O for orange, G for George, O for orange and V for Valentine — Pi-ro-gov.

Mr. Brown. — Will you, please, spell it again?

A. B. Petrov. — P for Peter, I for Isaac, R for Robert, O for orange, G for George, O for orange, V for Valentine.

Mr. Brown. — Thank you. I've got it now: Pi-ro-gov. Please send us a copy of the Charter-Party for this boat.

A. B. Petrov. — We sent it to you yesterday.

Mr. Brown. — Thank you, Mr. Petrov. That's all. Good-bye.

A. B. Petrov. — Good-bye.

TELEPHONE CONVERSATION

A. — Is that Brown & Co.?

B. — You've got the wrong number. This is Central 6708 (six-seven-oh-eight)

A. — So sorry ... Is that Brown & Co.?

C. — Yes, it is.

A. — I want Mr. Soames, please.

C. — I beg your pardon?

A. — Mr. Soames.

C. — Sorry, I didn't quite catch the name. How do you spell it?

A. — Soames: S for Sam , O for orange, A for Andrew, M for Mary, E for Edward and S for Sam — Soames.

C. — Oh, Soames. I'm sorry, Mr. Soames is away from the office at the moment. Who is calling?

A. — This is Mr. A. from the Soviet Trade Delegation. When will Mr. Soames be back?

C. — He'll be back at three o'clock. Will you leave a message?

A. — No, thanks. I'll ring up again at half past three. Good-bye.

TELEPHONE CONVERSATION BETWEEN A GRAIN BROKER OF V/O "SOJUZEXPORT" AND THE MANAGER OF THE GRAIN DEPARTMENT OF V O "SOJUZEXPORT"

I

Broker. — Hello! Is that Sojuzexport? This is Mr. Simpson speaking. Is Mr. Ivanov there?

Manager. — Mr. Ivanov speaking.

Broker. — We have an enquiry for about 5,000 tons of wheat on sample 411 but it is impossible to obtain your price limit.

Manager. — What figure can you get?

Broker. — I think not more than 32 pounds although we are doing our best.

Manager. — This parcel is of special quality. Don't sell this wheat below 33 pounds, please.

Broker. — But this means ten shillings above the price of the last parcel.

Manager. — The difference is quite reasonable considering the high quality of the wheat.

Broker. — There's another difficulty. Buyers want December shipment instead of January.

Manager. — Offer them, please, 15th December — 15th January. Should they insist on December shipment, call us up again and we'll see in the meantime whether we can arrange tonnage. And what about barley?

Broker. — There's little demand just now, as there are large stocks of maize in Liverpool. Besides, large shipments of maize are expected from the States.

Manager. — But you've heard of our sales of barley in Rotterdam and Antwerp, haven't you?

Broker. — Yes, I have, but the situation is different here. I'm expecting a bid from a large manufacturer of feeding stuffs. May I agree to January shipment?

Manager. — Yes, you may.

Broker. — All right. I'll call you up again to-morrow. Good-bye.

Manager. — Good-bye.

II

Manager. — Hello! Are you Simpson and Mills? Put me through to Mr. Simpson, please.

Broker. — Mr. Simpson speaking.

Manager. — This is Mr. Ivanov of Sojuzexport. We have some trouble with the s. s. "Fairfield" chartered against contract 65 to load the first cargo of wheat for Frank & Sons, Limited.

Broker. — What is the matter with the boat?

Manager. — We've just had a telegram from the Owners that the "Fairfield" has been badly damaged in a collision on her way to Novorossiisk and she has been towed to Genoa for repairs.

Broker. — Is the damage serious?

Manager. — Evidently it is, as they state she won't be able to arrive at the port of loading before December 15th.

Broker. — What are you going to do about it? Haven't you got another boat which could load before the 15th December?

Manager. — Unfortunately, is it practically impossible to secure another boat of the same size. We could arrange shipment by s. s. "Binta", which is a larger vessel of 6,500 tons, 10 per cent, although it would mean a considerable change in our loading program. Will you get in touch with the Buyers and ask them to accept against contract No. 65 a cargo of 6,500 tons, 10 per cent, instead of 6,000 tons, 10 per cent?

Broker. — I'll get in touch with them at once and try to settle the matter.

III (next day)

Broker. — I've had a talk with the General Manager of Frank & Sons, Ltd., about the cargo of wheat against Contract No. 65.

Manager. — What does he say?

Broker. — I've persuaded him to accept 6,500 tons, ten per cent, although he says that it would mean extra storage expenses for them, as they don't need the additional quantity till February. However, he agrees to accept the cargo on condition that it is not shipped before the 12th December.

Manager. — It's all right, as the vessel is not due to arrive at the port of loading before the 9th December. Thank you very much, Mr. Simpson. Good-bye.

TELEPHONE CONVERSATIONS BETWEEN A DEPARTMENT MANAGER OF V/O "SOVFRACHT" AND FOREIGN BROKERS ABROAD

I

Broker. — Good morning, Mr. Petrov. Any news today?

Manager. — So far nothing important, but I may get, later on in the day, an order for a general cargo from London to Leningrad — about 5,000 tons. I'm told that the position required would be 20—30 January.

Broker. — There are very few steamers of such a size and position in the market and it will, therefore, be very difficult to cover this order. I might arrange a steamer of about 6,000 tons ready to load about 25th January.

Manager. — I don't think it will be possible to arrange such a size, but I'll have a word with the Shippers. Meantime, please do your best to find a suitable steamer. What's the general news?

Broker. — There are some f. o. b. orders quoting in the market at a low rate but Owners aren't interested unless tempting rates are offered and my opinion is that owing to the scarcity of tonnage on the market, Shippers will have to pay higher rates.

Manager. — Thanks, Mr. Smith. As soon as I get the order, I shall telegraph immediately.

II

Broker. — Good evening, Mr. Petrov. My reason for calling you up is to tell you that I have found a boat suitable for your cargo. It is the s. s. "Albert", 5,000 tons ready about 5th February. The rate is thirty-five and six. I have the steamer firm only until 3 o'clock so you must make a quick decision.

Manager. — The steamer is rather late for our cargo, Mr. Smith, but I'll get the Charterers on the other 'phone and hear what they will say. What's the actual draft of the steamer fully loaded?

Broker. — We reckon she will draw not more than 27'6" (twenty-seven feet and six inches) in fresh water.

Manager. — I've got the Charterers on the other line, Mr. Smith, and they agree to accept your steamer provided the rate of freight is reduced to thirty-three and six.

Broker. — That's rather on the low side. Can't you raise this figure to thirty-four and six?

Manager. — Sorry, it's the most they can offer.

Broker. — O. K. then, the steamer's confirmed at thirty-three and six and we'll write out the Charter-Party. Good-bye.

III

Manager. — Good morning, Mr. White. Would you be good enough to get the Owners of the s. s. "Maria" on the 'phone and find out when the steamer will complete loading.

Broker. — They have just 'phoned, Mr. Petrov. They say that the steamer has only 3,000 tons on board.

Manager. — What are the prospects?

Broker. — The point is, a holiday interferes but we calculate the steamer will complete loading about 15th February. With overtime, we might complete loading about the 12th.

Manager. — Could you find out how much overtime we shall have to pay to stevedores and crew to enable steamer to leave the loading port not later than 12th February?

Broker. — If the weather is favourable, we might guarantee to finish loading on the 12th but the expenses will amount to about $ 120.

Manager. — O. K. We authorise you to arrange overtime with the stevedores but bear in mind that the expenses are not to exceed $ 120.

Broker. — I'll do my best and will keep you advised as to how matters go. — Good-bye.

IV

Broker. — Good afternoon, Mr. Petrov.

I've just sent you a telegram to the effect that the s. s. "Maria" sailed on 11th February, and the extra cost is $ 106.

Manager. — Thank you very much. Meantime, Charterers have asked for an option to discharge the steamer at two ports, Odessa and Novorossiisk.

Broker. — I've got the Owners on the other line and they say they might agree to send the steamer to two ports of discharge provided Charterers guarantee a quick discharge.

Manager. — You may be sure that we shall do everything to discharge as quickly as possible.

Broker. — In that case Owners agree and the extra charge will be 2s per ton on the entire quantity, as usual.

Manager. — Very well, Mr. Smith. I confirm this option. Good-bye.

V

Manager. — Good morning, Mr. Brown. Did you get our telegram regarding the s. s. "Clyde"?

Broker. — Yes, I got your telegram this morning and I have already had a talk with the Owners. Unfortunately Owners cannot accept all conditions in your telegram. They accept your date of loading, they also agree to cut the size of the steamer to 6,000 tons, 10%, but they insist on thirty-six and six. I fear that your offer at thirty-four and six will be of no interest to Owners.

Manager. — In my opinion, the Owners' demand is too high.

The market position today is rather weaker in comparison with yesterday. As a matter of fact, we have today several proposals at the rate of thirty-five and six and there is no doubt that if we make a firm counter-offer we'll be able to get the boat at thirty-four and six.

Broker. — I quite agree with you that the market position is today a little bit weaker, but the Owners say that they have to-day another offer from the River Plate at such a rate that makes them reluctant to accept your offer. Anyhow will you be so kind as to extend your offer until 5 p. m. today, and will you give us a discretion up to six pence. We'll then try to push the business through.

Manager. — I am very sorry, we cannot improve our terms. The best we can do is to renew our authority until 5 p. m. but at the rate not over thirty-four and six. If you do not confirm the boat by 5 p. m., in all likelihood the business will be taken off by your competitors.

Broker. — All right, I shall do my best to induce the Owners to accept your offer. Good-bye.

Manager. — Good-bye.

BIBLIOGRAPHY

BOOKS

American Management Association. *East-West Trade: An Analysis of Trade between Western Nations and the Soviet Bloc*. New York: American Management Association, 1964.

Cherviakov, P. A. *Organizatsiia i tekhnika vneshnei torgovli SSR (Organization and Techniques of the Foreign Trade of the USSR)*. Moscow: I.M.O., 1962.

Committee for Economic Development. *A New Trade Policy toward Communist Countries*. New York: Committee for Economic Development, 1972.

Conygham, William J. *Industrial Management in the Soviet Union: The Role of the CPSU in Industrial Decision Making, 1917-1970*. Stanford, Calif.: Stanford University Press, 1973.

Feonova, L. A., et al. *Organizatsiia i teknika vneshnei torgovli SSSR (Organization and Technique of Soviet Foreign Trade)*. Moscow: I.M.O., 1974.

Giffin, James H. *Legal and Practical Aspects of Trade with the Soviet Union*. 2d ed. New York: Praeger, 1975.

Goldman, Marshall I. *Detente and Dollars: Doing Business with the Soviets*. New York: Basic Books, 1975.

Greer, Thomas. *Marketing in the Soviet Union*. New York: Praeger, 1973.

Hardt, John P., and M. Hoffenberg. *Mathematics and Computers in Soviet Economic Planning*. New Haven: Yale University Press, 1967.

Kennan, George F. *On Dealing with the Communist World*. New York: Harper & Row, 1964.

Kosnik, Joseph. *Natural Gas Imports from the Soviet Union*. London: Praeger, 1975.

Marer, Paul, ed. *Eximbank and East-West Trade*. Bloomington, Ind.: International Development Research Center, 1975.

Margold, Stella K. *Let's Do Business with Russia*. New York: Harper and Brothers, 1948.

Pisar, Samuel. *Coexistence and Commerce*. New York: McGraw-Hill, 1970.

Pozdniakov, V. S. *Gosudarstvennaia monopoliia vnesbnei torgovli v SSSR (The State Monopoly of Foreign Trade in the USSR)*. Moscow: Mezhdunarodnye otnosheniia, 1969.

———. *Sovetskoye gosudarstvo i vnesbniaia torgovliya—pravovya voprosy (The Soviet State and Foreign Trade—Legal Questions)*. Moscow: Mezhdunarodnye otnosheniia, 1976.

Quigley, John B. *The Soviet Foreign Trade Monopoly*. Columbus: Ohio State University Press, 1974.

Rozenberg, M. G. *Pravovoe regulirovanie otnoshenii mezhdu vsesouznymi vneshnetorgovymi ob' edineniiami i sovetskimi organizatsiiami—zakazcbikami importnykh tovarov*. Moscow: I.M.O., 1966.

Smith, Glen Alden. *Soviet Foreign Trade*. New York: Praeger, 1973.

Starr, Robert, ed. *Business Transaction with the USSR*. New York: American Bar Association, 1975.

Stowell, Christopher E. *Soviet Industrial Import Priorities*. New York: Praeger, 1975.

USSR Central Statistical Directorate. *Narodnoye Khozyaistvo SSSR v. 1972 G (National Economy of the USSR in 1972)*. Moscow: Statiska, 1973.

USSR Ministry of Foreign Trade. *Vneshnyaya Torgovliya (Foreign Trade)*. Soviet yearbooks, 1960 through 1973. Moscow: Mezhdunarodnye otnosheniia, 1960 through 1973.

Vaganov, B. S., ed. *Organizatsiia i tekhnika vnesbnei torgovli SSR i drugikh sotsialisticheskilcb stran (Organization and Techniques of the Foreign Trades of the USSR and Other Socialist Countries)*. Moscow: I.M.O., 1973.

Zentner, Peter. *East-West Trade: A Practical Guide to Selling in Eastern Europe*. London: Parrish, 1967.

Zwass, Adam. *Monetary Cooperation Between East and West*. White Plains, N.Y.: International Arts and Sciences Press, 1975.

NEWSPAPERS AND PERIODICALS

"Armand Hammer: On Trade with Russia." *Business Week*, July 13, 1974.

Armitage, John A. "The Political Climate and U.S.-Soviet Trade." *Columbia Journal of World Business*, Winter 1973.

"Arthur Andersen Office Due in Moscow." *New York Times*, March 19, 1974.

"Bendix Breaks Ground in Trade with Russia." *Business Week*, January 31, 1977.

Berman, Harold J., and George L. Bustin. "The Soviet System of Foreign Trade." *Law and Policy in International Business* 7 (Fall 1975).

Brainard, Lawrence J. "Financing Eastern Europe's Trade Gap: The Environmental Connection." *Euromoney*, January 1976.

———. "The Outlook for East-West Trade Credit." *Euromoney*, July 1975.

"Charter of the All-Union Export-Import FTO." *Vneshniaia torgovlia (Foreign Trade)*, USSR, Ministry of Foreign Trade, no. 8 (1966).

DeBorchgrave, Arnaud. "Russia's Trade Coup." *Newsweek*, July 26, 1976.

Fitzpatrick, Peter B. "Soviet-American Trade, 1972-1974: A Summary." *Virginia Journal of International Law* 15 (Fall 1974):67.

Giffen, James Henry. "Developing a Marketing Program for the USSR." *Columbia Journal of World Business* 8 (Winter 1973).

Goldman, Marshall I. "Who Profits More from U.S.-Soviet Trade?" *Harvard Business Review* 51 (November-December 1973).

Goldman, Marshall I., and Alice Connor. "Businessmen Appraise East-West Trade." *Harvard Business Review* 44 (January-February 1966).

Hambleton, George B. E. "Company Presence in the USSR." *Columbia Journal of World Business* 8 (Winter 1973).

Heath, A. J. "Sale of Industrial Goods to the U.S.S.R.: An Analysis of Standard Russian Forms of Agreement." *Harvard International Law Journal* 17 (1976).

Hoya, Thomas W., and Daniel D. Stein. "Drafting Contracts in U.S.-Soviet Trade." *Law and Policy in International Business* 7 (1975).

"Interview with Armand Hammer." *Business Week*, July 13, 1974.

Kiser, John W., III. "Technology Is Not a One-Way Street." *Foreign Policy* 23 (Summer 1976).

Kraft, Joseph. "Business with Russia." *The Washington Post*, November 16, 1971.

Laptev, Vladimir V. "The Legal Status of Soviet Foreign Trade Organizations." *Denver Journal of International Law and Policy* 5 (1975):284.

Laquer, Walter. "Is Russian-American Trade Overrated?" *New York Times*, February 2, 1975.

McGarry, William A. "Why I Am Helping Russian Industry—Interview with Henry Ford." *Nation's Business*, 1930.

Meyer, Herbert. "What's It Like to Do Business with the Russians." *Fortune*, May 1972.

Nitze, Paul. "How the Soviets Negotiate." *Wall Street Journal*, January 24, 1975.

"Occidental Signs Deal with Soviets." *New York Times*, June 29, 1974.

Oliver, John B., and Elliott J. Weiss. "Is Selling Technology to the Soviets Dangerous?" *Harvard Business Review* 53 (January-February 1975).

Osnos, Peter. "Doing Big Business with Moscow." *The Washington Post*, November 4, 1974.

Pearson, John. "The Big Breakthrough in East-West Trade." *Business Week*, June 19, 1971.

Pisar, Samuel. "How We Will Do Business with Russia: Interview with an Authority on East-West Trade." *U.S. News and World Report*, July 31, 1972.

Reston, James B. "Negotiating with the Russians." *Harper's Magazine*, August 1947.

"The Rules Ease on Trade with Russia." *Business Week*, June 12, 1971.

"Russians Are Stepping Up Exports of Tractors to United States." *New York Times*, May 19, 1975.

Sauer, Walter C. "Eximbank Credits Back East-West Trade." *Columbia Journal of World Business* 8 (Winter 1973).

"The Scent of Honey: A Survey of East-West Trade." *The Economist*, January 6, 1973.

Schukin, George S. "The Soviet Position on Trade with the United States." *Columbia Journal of World Business* 8 (Winter 1973):48-50.

Smith, Paula. "The Answer Man in Soviet Trade." *Dun's Review*, October 1975.

"Soviet Has Trade Surplus with West, C.I.A. Reports." *New York Times*, April 8, 1975.

"Soviets' Trade Pragmatic." *The Washington Post*, March 2, 1977.

"Soviet Truck Project Spurs United States Business." *New York Times*, March 5, 1974.

"Soviet Union: A Cash Pinch Slows Trade with the U.S." *Business Week*, December 1, 1975.

"Soviet Woos Gulf Oil in Drilling Deal." *New York Times*, February 22, 1975.

"Sperry Rand Mixes a Lot of Hard Work and Some Vodka to Land Big Soviet Job." *Wall Street Journal*, August 18, 1975.

"Sperry Rand, Soviet Union Sign Cooperative Technology Accord." *Computer News*, May 27, 1974.

"The Style and Tactics of Moscow's Traders." *Business Week*, October 21, 1972.

Ulman, Neil. "Russia Finds Building of Biggest Truck Plant Can Be a Big Headache." *Wall Street Journal*, June 23, 1976.

"United States Companies Sign Soviet Gas Pact." *New York Times*, November 23, 1974.

"United States Group Given Soviet Contract." *New York Times*, April 20, 1974.

Vernon, Raymond. "Apparatchiks and Entrepreneurs: United States—Soviet Economic Relations." *Foreign Affairs* 2 (January 1974).

"Why Armco Won a Russian Contract." *Business Week*, August 9, 1976.

Yergin, Daniel. "Politics and Soviet American Trade: The Three Questions." *Foreign Affairs* 55, no. 3 (April 1977).

"You Can Do Business in Russia." *U.S. News and World Report*, July 7, 1975.

Zakharov, S., and V. Sulyagin. "Sistema ASOP-Vneshtorg: Tseli, zadachi, struktura." *Planovoe Khozyaistva*, no. 12 (December 1974).

PUBLIC DOCUMENTS

United Nations. *Guide for Use in Drawing Up Contracts Relating to the International Transfer of Know-How in the Engineering Industry*. New York: United Nations Publication, 1970.

_____. *Guide on Drawing Up Contracts for Large Industrial Works*. New York: United Nations Publication, 1973.

U.S. Congress. House. Committee on Foreign Affairs. *Basic Documents on East-West Trade*. 90th Cong. 2d sess. Washington, D.C.: Government Printing Office, 1968.

_____. "U.S.-Soviet Commercial Relations: The Interplay of Economics, Technology, and Transfer, and Diplomacy" by John P. Hardt and George D. Holliday. Case Study for Subcommittee on *National Security Policy and Scientific Developments*. 93rd Cong., Washington, D.C.: Government Printing Office, June 10, 1973.

U.S. Congress. House. Subcommittee on International Trade, Banking and Currency Committee. "Technology Transfer in Expanded Commercial Relations between the U.S. and USSR" by Robert W. Campbell. *International Economic Policy*. Hearings. Washington, D.C.: Government Printing Office, April 24, 1974.

U.S. Congress. House. Subcommittee on International Trade and Commerce. *Export Licensing of Advanced Technology: A Review*. Hearings. March 11, 15, 24, and 30, 1976. Washington, D.C.: Government Printing Office, 1976.

U.S. Congress. Joint Economic Committee. "Soviet Efforts to Increase Exports of Manufactured Products to the West" by Paul Ericson. *New Directions in the Soviet Economy*. Washington, D.C.: Government Printing Office, October 1976.

_____. "Soviet Foreign Trade Planning" by Lawrence J. Brainard. *Soviet Economy in a New Perspective*. Washington, D.C.: Government Printing Office, October, 1976.

U.S. Congress. Senate. Committee on Government Operations. "The Technique for Dealing with Russia" by George F. Kennan. *The Soviet Approach to Negotiation*. Washington, D.C.: Government Printing Office, 1969.

U.S. Department of Commerce. "Foreign Trade Organizations in the USSR. Product Index and Directory." Washington, D.C., 1974.

_____. "The Legal Status of Soviet Foreign Trade Organizations" by V. S. Posdniakov. *American Soviet Trade*. A Joint Seminar on the Organizational and Legal Aspects. Washington, D.C.: Government Printing Office, September 1976.

_____. *Proceedings of the East-West Technological Trade Symposium*. Springfield, Va.: National Technical Information Service, March 1976.

_____. *Selected USSR and Eastern European Economic Data*. Washington, D.C.: Government Printing Office, June 1973.

_____. "Soviet Organizations Involved in Industrial Cooperation Projects" by V. S. Koshentayevskiy. *American Soviet Trade*. A Joint Seminar on the Organization and Legal Aspects. Washington, D.C.: Government Printing Office, September 1976.

_____. "The System Regulating Exports and Imports in the USSR" by V. G. Smirov. *American Soviet Trade*. A Joint Seminar on the Organizational and Legal Aspects. Washington, D.C.: Government Printing Office, September 1976.

_____. *Trading with the USSR: Overseas Business Reports*. OBR 74-01. Washington, D.C.: Government Printing Office, January 1974.

_____. *U.S.-Soviet Commercial Agreements, 1972*. A letter by Peter G. Peterson, Secretary of Commerce, to N. S. Patolichev, Soviet Minister of Foreign Trade. Washington, D.C.: U.S. Department of Commerce, January 1973.

_____. *U.S.-Soviet Commercial Agreements, 1972: Texts, Summaries, and Supporting Papers*. Washington, D.C.: Government Printing Office, 1973.

_____. *U.S.-Soviet Commercial Negotiations in a New Era* by Peter G. Peterson,

Secretary of Commerce. Washington, D.C.: Government Printing Office, August 1972.

———. *U.S.-USSR Cooperative Agreements: Report*. Washington, D.C.: Government Printing Office, 1972.

———. *U.S./USSR Licensing Prospects, 1973*. Washington, D.C.: Government Printing Office, 1973.

U.S. Department of Defense. Office of Director of Defense Research and Engineering. *An Analysis of Export Control of U.S. Technology*. Washington, D.C.: Office of the Director of Defense Research and Engineering, February 4, 1976.

U.S. Library of Congress. *KAMAZ: U.S. Techology Transfer to the Soviet Union* by Scott Finer, Howard Gobstein, and George Holliday. Washington, D.C.: Library of Congress, 1975.

INDEX

About the Author

MISHA G. KNIGHT, raised and educated in the Soviet Union, is a former staff member of the USSR Ministry of Foreign Trade. He is president of Inter-Global Associates, a New York-based consultancy firm which directs export-import operations and provides consulting services to American, Canadian, and European businesses in Soviet and East European markets, and founder of the U.S.–USSR Roundtable, an organization which conducts seminars and conferences on Soviet-American trade and economic relations. His articles have appeared in such publications as *Countertrade and Barter*, *Global Trade Executive*, and *Industry Week*.